STO

ACPL ITEM
DISCARDED

12.95

S0-BWX-577

6.21.77

REVOLUTIONARIES
IN MODERN BRITAIN

Revolutionaries
in Modern Britain
PETER SHIPLEY

THE BODLEY HEAD
LONDON SYDNEY
TORONTO

© Peter Shipley 1976
ISBN 0 370 11311 X
Printed in Great Britain for
The Bodley Head Ltd
9 Bow Street, London WC2E 7AL
by Unwin Brothers Limited, Woking
Set in Monotype Plantin
First published in 1976

CONTENTS

1967009

PREFACE

My aim in this book is to trace the development of the movements, organisations and groups that actively seek revolutionary changes in British society, covering a period roughly from 1956 to the present day, and to describe and explain their beliefs, aims, structure, sources of support, activities and motivation.

The revolutionary tradition is deeply embedded in European history and is very much a part of contemporary world affairs. To write about its theory or practice requires therefore little justification; what may need some initial explanation however is the study of a revolution that has not yet happened, in a country that for the greater part of three hundred years has prided itself on the absence of revolution as a means of settling its affairs.

In Britain as in much of the western world protest and unrest characterise the modern age. The complex picture of social and political tensions contains many confused elements, jostling with each other for prominence. Among these, the idea of revolution as the ultimate solution to a whole range of diffuse problems has become an important influence on the expression of discontent and the direction of radical activity. For a variety of disaffected individuals and groups, its pursuit offers an ideal and a purpose, and in itself has become a way of life.

By revolution I do not mean the effects of those scientific and industrial changes spread over many decades, but fundamental yet sudden transformations in the way society is organised and run. In the context of modern Britain, revolution would involve the abolition (either by force or peaceful means) of the existing institutions of government, the dismantling of an economic system based on private enterprise and wealth, the re-ordering of society in the interests of particular social groups (usually the 'working class') to the exclusion of all others, and the creation of a new purpose for the individual as well as a new direction for society, all under the guidance of a doctrine or a regime that would permit no alternative or 'counter-revolutionary' tendencies.

One indication of the gathering momentum of this revolutionary impulse has been the proliferation of organisations that attempt to channel it into concerted effort. To study this movement I have drawn on the revolutionaries' own writings—their newspapers, magazines,

7

books, pamphlets and leaflets. My reasons for approaching the subject in this· way are, firstly, that it seemed basically worthwhile as a means towards understanding the character of the revolutionary movement, given the immense importance its members attach to the written word; almost without exception modern revolutionaries consider the publication of some kind of journal as an essential part of their work, and despite the deadening effects of some of their dogma, these writings reveal a great deal about the nature of their movement. Secondly, relatively few attempts appear to have been made to study the revolutionaries in this way, except those works concerning the British Communist Party; and thirdly, it seemed that there was a vast amount of material with which the general reader might usefully be acquainted, although I can hardly claim to have exhausted the available sources.

The troubles of Ireland were, I decided, a separate story, with too many dimensions outside the scope of this book, and I have therefore confined my study to events on the mainland, except to note the relationships between some Irish and British revolutionaries and to observe the effects of the Irish conflict (with its overspill on to the rest of Britain in the form of terrorist attacks) on the attitude and expectations of British revolutionary groups.

This book is primarily about the application of ideas through organised activity rather than about the philosophical or theoretical content of the ideas themselves, the discussion of which belongs to another place. But for those for whom organised revolutionary activity means clear-cut conspiracies, preferably controlled by Foreign Agents, there may be some surprises in store.

As in so many aspects of contemporary history, there are here as many avenues shrouded in the fogs of political controversy, impenetrable even to the most curious traveller, as there are those whose winding courses show no signs of reaching a destination. In such studies as these it is also notoriously difficult to strike a balanced, detached view, but I have attempted in the main not to interpose my own views between the subject and the reader, in so far as the act of interpretation makes it at all possible.

No one but myself is responsible in any way for the choice of subject matter, the research and the argument of this book. I would however like to thank the following: the Librarian of the London School of Economics for allowing me to consult the material in his care; the Director of the Institute for the Study of Conflict for allowing me to use the facilities of his library, and for the co-operation of his staff; Kenneth Garland, for so ably undertaking the compilation of the Index; Robert Lyons and Ken Douglas, for reading and commenting on various drafts; Ian Greig, for the discussions we have had on this topic during many years' friendship, and to those various friends and individuals, including Peter Hamilton, who have taken the trouble to discuss particular aspects, as seen from both sides of the barricades. Above all I must thank my wife, Fiona, for typing the manuscript and for the love and patience that made the book possible.

Peter Shipley

Caterham, Surrey
November 1975

I

The Awakening
of the Revolutionaries

In the capital cities of the world, few sights have become more familiar in recent times than the street demonstration. At least, in those countries where the right of free assembly exists, the banner-waving, slogan-chanting columns of marchers are an accepted if emotive feature of political life. According to police figures, 1,321 demonstrations took place in London during the three years from the beginning of 1972 to the end of 1974, and only 54 of them gave rise to any violent incidents.[1]

In Britain the demonstration stands for the most part in a mainly peaceable tradition of protest and dissent, as an integral part of democracy, available to all as a means of drawing the attention of government, press and public to a topic of current concern, no matter how transient or sectional it may be. But most demonstrations are forgotten soon after the marchers turn out of Whitehall or as the last echo dies away in Trafalgar Square or at Hyde Park Corner; through such frequent use, this infectious exercise has become ritual ceremony in which the assertion of democratic rights is largely symbolic.

Exceptionally, some causes do bring on to the streets large numbers of people, drawing to the surface a depth and strength of feeling on a fundamental issue of the day. The protests at the beginning of the 1960s to 'ban-the-bomb' or those a decade later against the introduction of legislation to govern industrial relations, each in its own way, evidenced significant currents of opinion, while others, such as the confrontations around the American Embassy in Grosvenor Square in 1968 on the issue of the Vietnam war, are remembered for the tumult they occasioned.

The customary format of the demonstration encompasses infinite variety in the specific subjects raised, the identities of the participants, their beliefs, the interests they represent and their purpose in demonstrating. In those exceptional instances the demonstration has reached

[1] Notes—p. 227 *et seq.*

10

its peak of development as a vehicle for the expression of various shades of radical and socialist opinion. And among the most energetic demonstrators of all have been the members and sympathisers of organisations such as the International Socialists (IS) and the International Marxist Group (IMG).

Since they first adopted the practice during the student and Vietnam war movements during the second half of the 1960s the demonstration has become a hallmark of their political style. Sometimes virtually alone and sometimes in the company of representatives of a much wider spectrum of opinion, they have employed it to voice their disapproval of the actions of successive British governments and the armed forces in Northern Ireland, to oppose those governments' economic policies, to protest against racialism and immigration laws, to try to prevent the National Front from meeting in public, to press for the release of the imprisoned building workers known as the 'Shrewsbury Pickets', to support women's liberation, to register their opposition to right-wing dictatorships that have existed at various times in Portugal, Greece and Chile, and to express their solidarity with fellow revolutionaries across the world in their struggles against the evil trinity of imperialism, capitalism and fascism.

In the case of groups such as the International Socialists or International Marxists, the demonstration is not therefore a display of rights presently enjoyed, but is intended to suggest that the present system of democracy denies in substance most essential rights to the majority of the population. Their marches convey their own symbolic meaning: the immediate issue raised is held to represent a wide range of other alleged ills, for which a 'ruling class', its institutions and its philosophies are held responsible. The demonstration is a gesture of defiance against an allegedly corrupt, unjust old order that gives particular expression to a general dissatisfaction with the entire structure and purpose of society. In this context, the redress of specific grievances—a goal rarely achieved—is wholly subordinate to a larger purpose.

The demonstration occupies a central place in their political campaign on single issues; each campaign is held together by its co-ordinating committee, expends its energies on countless rallies and meetings, and is sustained by a welter of frantic propaganda, overflowing with profound appeals to the masses and an esoteric mythology well stocked with heroes and demons. And as one observer noted in 1968, a year of demonstrations and abortive revolts, ultimately 'the truth is that mass demonstrations are rehearsals for revolution: not strategic or even tactical ones but rehearsals of revolutionary awareness.'[2]

Some exponents of the technique would agree that through the careful selection of symbolic issues revolutionaries can hope to mobilise a large amount of support, the display of which they can turn to their advantage and win converts to their cause. Demonstrations can also expose the authorities, in weakness or repression, and so undermine public confidence in their ability fairly and effectively to maintain order. As an elementary form of direct action militant demonstrations are a part of the constant war of propaganda, agitation and organisation to challenge existing authority and point the way to the mass movement which lays down the basis and the style of the revolutionary regime.

But many other prospective revolutionaries reject this point of view. For them the demonstration does not open up the road to revolution; that is to be reached by other routes. Instead they see the movement as a whole becoming equated with the failure of the 'demo'-oriented activists to build an unstoppable mass force: it is all mere fun and fashion, a passing gesture which rambles or feverishly scampers to no particular destination causing at most a minor nuisance en route, but probably dismissed as an inconsequential if voluble curiosity of misguided idealism.

The results of this can be to drive the revolutionaries into isolation, preoccupied with doctrinal disputes or falling into violent acts of frustrated fanaticism. Above all the revolutionaries who doubt the value of demonstrations regard them as essentially tools of the present system which provides society with a safety-valve for the harmless release of rebellious spirits.

The dual identity of the demonstration—as both liberal democracy in action and the prelude to socialist revolution—highlights the paradox of those who seek the latter out of the former. It serves also to illustrate the energy and impatience of the modern revolutionary and suggests some of the doubts and divisions in his movement. More importantly it raises the question of how revolution would be achieved in a parliamentary welfare state, in what circumstances it would occur, what it would mean, and indeed why it should be so intensely sought after at all: 'Revolutions take place', wrote a British professor of politics, 'when governments break down, not just by purposeful and heroic struggles from below.'[3] In other words the occurrence of a great upheaval in which institutions are overthrown, the social structure torn apart and the whole purpose of a society—philosophical, economic and political—directed towards new ends, depends on factors that are beyond the direct control of a few dedicated activists, although they can contribute some decisive strokes of assistance to the process at critical moments.

Much of the theoretical literature on the nature of revolution emphasises four groups of extensive, historical factors which combine to produce drastic changes in the way society is ordered and run, surpassing mere palace coups. Firstly, there is a political aspect of an incompetent and weak leadership which unites all its opponents against it and by the unintended consequences of its own actions precipitates its own downfall. Secondly are economic considerations of crisis and chronic instability, or of rivalries and relative senses of deprivation between groups whose respective aspirations of rising or stable wealth outmatch static or falling capabilities. Thirdly are the social conditions created by rapid change and mobility which will have weakened the fabric of the old order, and finally are intellectual factors of conflicting values and philosophies, particularly between the beliefs maintained by a ruling elite, and those propounded by an alienated intelligentsia.

The convergence of these crises over a period of several decades may provide the pre-conditions for revolution, which await ignition by a *cause celèbre* or a sudden cataclysmic crisis that sets the flame alight. When the simmering pot of troubles has finally boiled over revolution acquires a momentum of its own: as power is transferred from one social group to another and rival factions struggle for domination, those who begin the revolution rarely stay in control to complete the process, as the experience of 17th century England, then France, and Russia in 1917 have all amply demonstrated.

In contemporary Britain, however, is a 'revolutionary situation' emerging that would set these events in train? Many of the changes that have taken place since the end of the Second World War were intended to, and at first did, lessen social conflict and tension: the creation of a welfare state; rapid scientific and technological advance; the general affluence of a consumer society; a broad measure of agreement between the major political parties on many central issues; greater social mobility and the breaking down of many old taboos associated with the ideals and assumptions of the departed imperial Britain, all in their own ways raised hopes for conditions of prosperity and harmony. Yet, although they eradicated many of the worst evils of large-scale unemployment and instability that beset the inter-war years, they have engendered new discontents and have given way to a sense of crisis rather than well-being.

Crisis has become one of the most overworked words of modern British politics and journalism. It is most frequently invoked to describe the economic problems that have prevailed with varying degrees of intensity over a generation—Britain's lack of growth and international competitiveness, the deficit in the balance of payments, the rising rate of inflation and the discordant state of industrial relations. Against this background of relative failure—compared with the records of many other western industrial countries—the efficiency and assumptions of government have frequently been called into question.

Numerous political innovations have been launched, administrative machinery tinkered with, structural reforms suggested and shelved, but the outcome of so many improvements has been deterioration, and many of the supposed benefits of a progressive welfare state appear instead as onerous burdens. And beneath the rusting, groaning economic structure is a deeper crisis, of national purpose and identity, which stems from the decline of Britain as an imperial power and its failure to 'find a role', coupled with a decline in the forms of organised religion that had provided in the 19th century a moral framework to justify the actions, purposes and structure of a supremely powerful imperial and commercial nation.

The elements of crisis are real and at hand, creating the tensions, discontents, and social conflicts out of which revolutionary sentiments have begun to grow. But do they in their depth or intensity appear to fulfil the definition of pre-revolutionary conditions that indicate the prospect of an imminent total transformation of society? Economic crises have become a national way of life, there has yet been no mass political disaffection that would hand millions of citizens into the eager embrace of ambitious revolutionaries, and many far-reaching changes in the social structure and in behaviour have been absorbed with relative smoothness into a pattern of continuity. Above all the classic Marxist notions of a 'social question' of grinding poverty and misery simply do not apply. Perhaps the gradual emergence of a category of disenchanted, mainly middle-class intellectuals could be offered to indicate the presence of a pre-condition for revolution in modern Britain, or the disaffection of the educated young, or the assertiveness of organised labour.

All of these problems could be regarded as part of a historic continuum, an unending process of change and evolution that is at times painful and hesitant rather than as the constituents of a potent mixture which threatens to engulf society and tear it apart. The line between latent and explosive crisis is however a narrow one, and given the ingredients it may be crossed under the force of prejudice, myth or belief that wishes to impel society towards an upheaval. In such matters it is what men believe or want to believe that so often moves them to action. What may be acceptable in Britain to the passive majority has in this way become repellent to an active minority, who believe that it is a thoroughly unjust society where crisis and conflict do assume menacing proportions.

'In Britain today millions of working people face the future with great concern. Organised workers see their living standard and trade unions under attack . . . Black people are discriminated against and

14

increasingly assaulted by thugs inspired by racist politicians and right wing groups. Demonstrators are beaten and jailed. Pickets are arrested and jailed. Young people and black workers are constantly harassed and more and more basic democratic rights are ignored, restricted and abolished . . . the basic human needs of housing, transportation, medical care, education and an improved quality of life are all less and less obtainable and yet all of this—unemployment, rising prices, anti-trade union laws, poverty, racialism, discrimination against women, state violence, and a mass of other inequalities and problems—is occurring in the richest society ever known in Britain.'[4]

The writer is conscious of the irony in his argument that economic and social crisis have emerged not as a result of capitalism's failure but from its very success. It appears equally paradoxical that the answer to the problems of a parliamentary democracy is the revolutionary overthrow of the system. But for the ideologue, the evidence of this crisis justifies his predetermined position: that a social system based on the private ownership of wealth, in which parliament and government protect only the interests of the capital-owning minority, is inherently oppressive and incapable of reform. It must be made to give way to a socialist order the creation of which would entail the abolition of the traditional institutions of government, the monarchy, parliament, legal system, police, armed forces and civil service, to be replaced, where appropriate, by the trusted instruments of the new regime; the dismantling of the economic system from multi-national corporations downwards; the restructuring of society in the interests of the 'working class' or the 'masses'; the reappraisal of the basic purposes of social institutions such as educational system and welfare services, to meet the needs of the individual; and the reorientation of Britain's relations with the rest of the world.

During the last two decades in Britain the small numbers of committed revolutionaries have attempted to convince the working classes and sundry other social groups of the correctness of this cause, enlarging and generalising their particular problems and experience into a total critique of existing society. The young and the intellectual, whose desire to overturn whatever system may prevail is hardly novel, have not merely rejected capitalism for its alleged injustice, but also the moral values of successful capitalism, for its materialism and selfishness. The intellectual young have provided so many of the most dedicated revolutionary activists and propagandists, while the 'masses' have appeared relatively apathetic. In their place immigrant and black liberation groups, claimants', women's liberation and 'gay lib' have, with varying degrees of success, been incorporated into the changing social structure of revolution as oppressed minorities, whose suffering cannot be alleviated in the present social systems. 'Women in capitalist society are victims of sexual oppression'—the argument runs, in its most extreme form—'which is exploited by the ruling class in the same way as racism.'[5] And for homosexuals 'gay liberation does not just mean reforms. It means a revolutionary change in a whole society ... we can use our righteous anger to uproot the present oppressive system with its decaying and constricting ideology, and together with other oppressed groups can start to form a new order, and a liberated life-style ... '[6]

The sub-cultures of minorities and youth have been extensively drawn upon and interwoven into a grand design that purports to unite disparate elements against common enemies. Together, they counterpose values of socialism and egalitarianism against those of acquisitive, competitive materialism, oppose the overweening power exercised by giant centralised bureaucracies, industrial corporations and party political machines over the individual; protest against the failure of those institutions to meet the needs of ordinary people; reject the shoddy culture of mass commercialism, and recoil in horror at continued poverty, not merely in Britain but in much of the rest of the world. The translation of these discontents into an active political movement is itself a sure symptom of an ailing society, whose complaints can only be exacerbated by attacks mounted by the disaffected; this in turn leads to greater problems and more alienated elements, on a descending spiral that twists itself into the explosive conjunction of crisis and revolutionism in which the contributory factors and the struggles from below come together.

Yet between the miscellaneous alienated groups, each with its own reasons for discontent, and the committed revolutionaries who would lead them to socialism, there is little unity of purpose. Only in their opposition to the present order do they agree; in detail their vision is remote and ill-defined.

The division of motive, belief and purpose among those attracted to the revolutionary ideal, as well as their overall numerical growth, are reflected in the structure and composition of their emergent movement. In 1956 the British Communist Party had 33,000 members; on its left were less than a thousand other people in half a dozen organisations from the Independent Labour Party to the anarchist Freedom Press Group. By 1975, 28,000 Communists found themselves outflanked by a host of organisations which regarded them as distinctly archaic remnants of an 'Old Left'. There were 14,000 Trotskyists (or quasi-Trotskyists) in nine groups; approximately 1,500 supporters of eight pro-Chinese bodies; a similar number of anarchists in six national groups and at least a half dozen other organisations with branches across the country.

In addition were an indeterminable number of activists in innumerable smaller groups, pursuing the interests of particular sections of the community, engaged in local activities, or in research bodies, newspapers, magazines, publishing houses, single-issue campaigns, or working with overseas groups in exile, all with the common general aim of the social and political transformation of society. The revolutionary movement is therefore a diverse and complex phenomenon, which contains a wide variety of ideas and interests, with activities ranging over many areas and assuming many different forms. The problems that confront them are likewise extensive, as they strive to increase their influence and communicate with the working class in whose name they act.

The usefulness of the present political system—whether it is worthwhile joining an existing party or a pressure group of more modest aims—is a topic endlessly debated by revolutionaries when working out their strategy. If there is no hope for progress through established channels of political activity what are the alternatives? Should revolutionaries concentrate on building up support on single-issue campaigns or try wider appeals? Should they discard the present system entirely and create their own party organisation and trade union bodies, to prepare for open conflict with authority? Should the political and industrial concepts of struggle themselves be abandoned in favour of community centred action, on housing, rents, schools, and amenities, building from the 'grass-roots' upwards? Or should original concepts of alternative structures be developed to evolve the nucleus of the new order in the shell of the old? Is violence inevitable, and in what manner should revolutionaries respond to state violence? What forms of direct action should be used?

In answer to such questions the Marxists stress the need to develop a sound theoretical foundation and neo-Bolshevik groups emphasise correct and strong leadership to guide the proletariat to the seizure of power. Others reject the concept of revolution as a specific act of this sort, preferring to regard it as a gradually unfolding process, while some anarchists and libertarians decry all notions of theory and leadership, and attempt to discover the promised land through experiment and personal experience, with a view to a post-industrial society of small crafts and a decentralised regime where decision making is shared by all. Most revolutionaries are guided in these matters by the examples of revolutions elsewhere in the world and by historical traditions. Marxism and anarchism with all their variations provide the mainstreams of revolutionary thought, while the regimes of present-day Yugoslavia, Cuba, North Vietnam and China are most frequently invoked as models for a future British socialist state that would avoid the ruthless dictatorship and rigid centralisation of the Soviet Union.

In addition there is a domestic radical tradition which goes back to the Peasants' Revolt of 1381, the Civil War of the 17th century, the tumult of the Industrial Revolution and Napoleonic war periods, the Chartists of Victorian England, and the evolution of the labour movement and the great industrial unrest from the end of the 19th century to the general strike of 1926. The modern revolutionaries consider themselves the inheritors and resurrectors of this long-buried tradition. The revival of revolutionary activity has not however occurred overnight, nor have all the component parts of the contemporary movement come together suddenly or at once. In two decades of development, hesitant and uncertain at first, but with greater intensity during the second half of the period, the revolutionary movement has passed through a succession of distinctive phases.

The first stirrings of reawakened activity on the radical left came in 1956, after ten years of conformity and quiescence, during which ideology in the pragmatic sophisticated west, was pronounced dead. It was the era of the Cold War, the universities were hotbeds of apathy, the trade unions dominated by anti-communist leadership, and direct action and dissent had been smothered by consensus politics. The year ended with the British and French débâcle at Suez, the Soviet Union's ruthless suppression of the Hungarian revolt, and Mr Khruschev's denunciations of some of the errors of Stalinism. Political debate was reopened and a new mood was stirring, whose tenor was symbolised by the 'Angry Young Men' of the theatre.

During the next two years one Communist in three resigned from the party, some to join the Labour Party and others to leave politics altogether in a state of disenchantment. Some former Communists became involved in the movement known as the 'New Left'. Two academics, E. P. Thompson and John Saville, founded the *New Reasoner* to cater for erstwhile Communists engaged in discussion of possible alternatives. At the same time at Oxford, the *Universities and Left Review* appeared, representing the views of a younger group that had not been associated with the Communist Party. By 1960 they had converged on to much the same territory and amalgamated to become the *New Left Review*.

The movement of which these magazines were a part was at first an intellectual one with no definite organisational forms. It sought the updating of socialist theory to describe the kind of society that was emerging in Britain and in the words of the *Universities and Left Review* tried to make 'some principled critique of the quality of life and to take a perspective for the socialist and humanist transformation of our society'.[7] It was resolutely opposed to Stalinism and its excesses, and substituted for traditional Marxist notions of the oppression of the masses, which in a physical sense no longer applied in the west, the concept of alienation; this was rediscovered in the early writings of Marx and some previously obscure Marxian theoreticians, and stressed capitalism's denial of the full expression of the individual's character and the estrangement between the worker and his work under that system. In addition, the New Left placed much emphasis on the role of culture, literature and communication in society. On this, writers such as Raymond Williams and Richard Hoggart lent considerable intellectual weight to the debate, which by 1960 also extended to between thirty and forty Left Clubs throughout the country.

In its first edition the *New Left Review* left no doubt as to the magnitude of the problems facing socialists: they covered theory, communication and organisation. 'The distinct wariness between intellectuals and industrial workers *must* be broken down. It is one of the most dangerous aspects of the present plight of the socialist move- ment . . . we need not only discussion groups but centres of socialist work and activity, rallying points of disturbance and discontent within the local community, the nerve centres of a genuinely popular and informed socialist movement.'[8] And at this very time some new forms of organisation were emerging.

Foremost among these was the Campaign for Nuclear Disarmament, founded in January 1958 to press for the unilateral renunciation of nuclear weaponry by Britain. It brought together many traditions— Christian, pacifist, liberal, the Labour left, anarchists, Trotskyists, and from 1960 the Communist Party, as well as many unattached young idealists and middle-class intellectuals. It assumed the fervour of a crusade, commanding wide support, and with a sense of moral superiority and purpose that transcended the bounds of conventional politics. Its euphoria was however short-lived.

By the early 1960s the inherent divisions of opinion and purpose among its supporters destroyed the Campaign as a popular movement. On one side were those who wished to use it as an instrument to put pressure on the Labour Party and who after 1961, when the party had reversed its support of unilateralism, saw their cause crumble away; on another side were those for whom the issue was not primarily a political one but essentially moral, in the uncompromising evil of nuclear weaponry; then there were those militant elements who believed in direct action tactics and organised themselves in October 1960 into the Committee of 100 led by the philosopher Bertrand

Russell; and finally were the Marxist groups who saw the bomb as a symbol of capitalist sinfulness and oppression and wished to involve workers in strike action to stop its production and distribution.

From the end of 1961 onwards, as the militant sections became more prominent and the moderates' hopes of winning the day by conventional pressure politics faded, the eminent sympathisers dropped away together with the mass support for the annual Aldermaston marches. By 1964 the campaign was reduced to a pale shadow of a movement from which so much had been hoped only a few years before.

Besides the CND and the intellectual New Left, Marxist socialists had much else to occupy their attention. The Socialist Labour League was formed in 1959, drawing trade unionists, Labour Party members and former Communists behind what soon revealed itself as a hard-line Trotskyist leadership; not for the last time some old and half-forgotten lefts emerged from under the veneer of a 'New' Left. The search for new forms of organisation was epitomised by Lawrence Daly (later well known as a leader of the National Union of Mineworkers) in the Fife Socialist League, set up after his departure from the Communist Party, and which aimed 'to conduct analytical educational and propaganda work, free from the restrictions imposed by Labour and Communist machines'.[9] At its most ambitious the desire for this kind of political independence was expressed by Eric Heffer, then the National Secretary of the tiny Socialist Workers Federation:

> 'A revolutionary party is required, not because some comrade thinks it a good idea but because it is an absolute necessity if we are ever to achieve a socialist Britain. Neither the Labour Party nor Communist Party can guide the workers in their struggle for socialism. Therefore as Marxists we must begin anew. To enter the Labour Party is in fact to look for a short cut, assuming that those entering the Labour Party retain their socialist beliefs.'[10]

Shortly after the turn of the decade the rapid decline of CND, the failure of the intellectuals to communicate their ideas to a wider audience, and the failure of new, independent organisations to emerge (with the exception of the highly sectarian SLL), the Marxists were forced to revise their strategy. Many did enter the fold of the Labour Party which was in a demoralised state after the battles of Left against Right and the general election débâcle of 1959. Heffer himself succumbed to the temptation and has been a Labour Member of Parliament since 1964. The Young Socialists, formed in 1960 to remedy a gap in the party's recruitment, became a prime target and within four years was dominated by a group closely associated with the SLL, while supporters of the Socialist Review Group (who had in 1960 launched a journal called *International Socialism* by which the organisation has since become known) were also an active pressure group within its ranks. After the death of Hugh Gaitskell, some sections of the left saw greater opportunity for advancement and as the thirteen years of Conservative rule staggered to their tired, stale conclusion, the socialists prepared for their kind of Labour government. Magazines and newspapers such as *The Voice of the Unions* (1963) and *The Week and Militant* (1964) took up this task.

There was still much discussion between those inside and outside the Labour Party, and themes such as workers' control, colonial revolution and anti-racialism were raised during the first half of the decade, but there was no popular movement of discontent to which they could be attached. The anarchists stood out as the one example of progress in a period of little visible advance. Their concepts had gained an unexpected boost in the militant direct action techniques of the Committee of 100 so that by 1964 an Anarchist Federation of Britain, the first such national co-ordinating body for eighteen years, began a revival of the movement that lasted for the rest of the decade.

During the second half of the 1960s the revolutionary movement was transformed. The upsurge in activity was prompted initially by disillusionment among radicals and socialists of various shades with the performance of the Labour government. By 1966 it was evident that its intention was not to reshape society but to improve the efficiency of capitalism while carrying out some marginal social reforms. Discontent was aroused by the various attempts to control or freeze wages, beginning with the prices and incomes policy of 1965, the government's unwavering support for American policy in Vietnam, the failure to end the *de facto* independence of Rhodesia, and towards the end of Labour's tenure of office, the proposals for industrial relations contained in *In Place of Strife*, intended to overcome the increasing number of strikes, official and unofficial.

Groups such as the Liaison Committee for the Defence of Trade Unions (1966), the All Trade Union Alliance (1968) and the Institute for Workers' Control (1968) each expressed rank and file disaffection in the Labour movement, but the principal catalyst upon the revolutionary left during these years was the 'student movement' one of the most widely diffused and widely written about phenomena of the post-war period.[11] Many of the sit-ins, demonstrations and rallies that became a regular feature of university or college life during the later years of the 1960s were occasioned as much by local issues—student representation on governing bodies, examination reform, library facilities or dissatisfaction with course content—as by the grand moral ones. The rapidly expanded student population became suddenly conscious of its identity and potential influence, and its voice of inchoate protest was paralleled in a generalised way across the industrialised world, drawing the British student radicals into a fever of romantic, international idealism.

They witnessed the experiences of the American Students for a Democratic Society, the German Extra-Parliamentary opposition, the Japanese 'Zengakuren' and the French Revolution manqué of 1968. They identified with Ho Chi Minh and Ché Guevara, leaders of the guerrilla war against the universal enemy of 'capitalist-imperialism'. And the Vietnam war crystallised the diffused strands into a vicarious revolutionism expressed in a new 'New Left' through a mixture of Trotskyism, Maoism, Anarchism and Situationism. In two years the transition from a Radical Students Alliance in 1966 to a Revolutionary Socialist Students Federation in 1968 symbolised the change in emphasis.

However, the domestic political aspirations of the student revolutionaries failed completely. The 'Red Base' theory, which advanced the students as a new revolutionary vanguard in the west, firstly by their organising the universities into 'soviet' camps and then to convert the workers in the world outside, never got off the ground. Within a year of its foundation in the wake of the Paris revolt, the RSSF had collapsed under the weight of doctrinal arguments between rival factions, and by the autumn of 1970 the *Black Dwarf*, unofficial spokesman of the British Extra-Parliamentary opposition since May 1968, had followed the same fate. By 1970 Vietnam had lost its appeal as a mobilising issue, and the mood, the nervous energy, the novelty value and the desire to outrage conventional opinion, which fuelled the movement, had evaporated. The revolutionaries had themselves contributed to the demise of the distinctly 'student' movement: their ideological assumptions were false, their squabbles destructive and from 1970 onward they turned their energies elsewhere.

The precise issues and events of the second half of the 1960s are forgotten, but they did serve to transform the character of the revolutionary left. A steady stream of recruits had been discovered (although it had not become a torrent), some notions about the nature of change in the west had been overturned, while the wildest forecast of an irreversible surge of revolt did not materialise; new forms of internationalism and direct action suggested possible future lines of development and a host of organisations emerged ready to apply them in new arenas: the IS and IMG left the Labour Party to fasten on to the student dissent, a plethora of pro-Chinese groups appeared, together with several anarchist ones.

In retrospect the student movement of the 1960s can be seen as a part of a wider youth-centred culture that was taking shape at that time. Gradually the political aspects of militant activism and the cultural ones initially focused on pop and fashion have come closer together to evolve new concepts of social and political change. After 1968 many non-Marxist radical students, including the Young Liberals, tired of set-piece demonstrations and the increasingly intransigent dogma of the sects represented in the RSSF. Nor did they hold much hope for success from industrially based agitation. Instead they turned to local and minority politics, with the community as the basic unit for action. Squatting, communes and the regional 'underground press', as alternatives to industrialised, urban existence, began to take shape at the end of the 1960s followed by claimants', women's, and 'gay' liberation at the beginning of the 1970s.[12] They have become the basic ingredients of libertarianism, a fragmented, nebulous movement which engages a reformist liberal element to those who would accept the label of anarchist and represents the activist wing of the Alternative Society, the various, confused attempts of mainly young people to devise new styles and philosophies of life.

During the first half of the present decade many revolutionaries, however, have adjusted their attitudes to meet the effects of increasing economic crisis. While the diversified local activities of libertarianism engaged some student radicals, nationally the students' union has turned away from protest on remote issues to more mundane concerns of grants, accommodation and jobs, aided by the growing influence of the Communist Party—so scornfully dismissed by the rebels of 1968. Trotskyist groups in particular rejected the student vanguard theories in favour of mass picketing, factory occupation, general strikes and workers' militia as the ingredients of revolution.

All the revolutionaries characterise the seventies as an era of attack by government and employers on the workers' standards in a time of capitalist crisis. The ceaseless battles between the trade unions and the Conservative government have left indelible marks on British society and offered revolutionaries glimpses of a system approaching collapse. The causes and the style of the Shrewsbury Pickets, the Pentonville Five (dockers gaoled in 1972 for contempt of the Industrial Relations Court), the emergence of workers' co-operatives, and above all, the miners' strikes of 1972 and 1974 have commended themselves to the revolutionaries who have expended much energy in trying to convert what they see as an unconscious revolutionism into a positive political movement. The most significant contribution to these events by revolutionaries have come from the Marxist trade union leaders and their apologists associated with Communist or Labour parties rather than from the vocal but smaller independent organisations.

They have been able to combine their political aim with the economic militancy of the rank and file to produce a potent combination which has re-opened the possibility of using the mainstream of the Labour movement as an agent of revolution.

Related to the economic aspects of the capitalist offensive, the revolutionaries consider there has been a similar attack on civil liberties. The Angry Brigade trials, the alleged harassment of immigrants and youth by police, the prosecution of the magazine *Oz*, and the consequences of the continuing conflict in Ireland have drawn as much vitriol as the capitalist infrastructure itself and have highlighted the roles of the army, police and the legal system in bolstering the present system in a time of crisis. Since the civil rights phase of 1968–69 the far left has solidly backed the republican cause in Northern Ireland, and the successive collapses of authority there have reinforced its view that Ireland is Britain's Achilles heel that would be won over first before revolution on the mainland. Events there, and elsewhere, have however forced the British revolutionaries to face the problem of terrorism, with some surprising results.

During this most recent period the points of tension in society have increased and sharpened. The revolutionaries have eagerly responded by diversifying their own efforts so that by the 1970s three distinct approaches to revolution were evident—one in the traditional organisations of the Labour movement, another in small independent mainly Marxist organisations, and a third in the amorphous libertarian movement. Their combined influence and following is greater than at any other time in the post-war period. The revolutionaries' analysis of crisis however predates the effects of the huge increases in fuel costs from the end of 1973, the rapidly rising rate of inflation in the following two years and the growing numbers of unemployed: these events merely sharpened the edge of an existing crisis, made conflict more likely, but did not indicate qualitative changes. They did however require a shift of emphasis and some re-orientation of activity by committed revolutionaries to succeed all the previous tactical switches demanded by fresh circumstances. For many the deftness of improvisation has itself become a test of revolutionary purpose and the group least prepared to adjust its methods, invariably the Communist Party, has been the one least regarded on the left as revolutionary. Throughout the period however the Communist Party has remained the largest single organisation on the far left and has also been the reluctant progenitor of so many other enterprises.

II

A British Road to Socialism?

I

THE COMMUNIST DILEMMA

Few organisations excite so much or such varied comment as the British Communist Party. A view from the left depicts the party as timid, cowardly, Stalinist, even counter-revolutionary, and sums it up in the words of a Labour Member of Parliament as 'a tired, worn-out, elderly organisation which has a doubtful future'.[1] Those who so regard the party point to the absence of a Communist intelligentsia, the desertion of the young and active in favour of Trotskyist, Maoist or anarchist groups and the ever more disastrous electoral excursions. From the right however another view prevails. Seen from here the Communist Party is a subversive threat to parliamentary government and a disruptive menace to the nation's economy, evidenced by its successful wooing of sections of the Labour left to join with it in common cause, and, in particular, by its disproportionate influence among many of the larger and more powerful trade unions.

Such conclusions may reinforce the existing prejudices of the observers but they do suggest something about the observed. Whether the Communist Party is revolutionary, whether it faces the task of overthrowing capitalism realistically and the efficacy of the methods it chooses are at the heart of a problem which has faced it since its birth: should it grasp the nettle of Marxist-Leninism and pursue whatever means are necessary to achieve its end, courting illegality and repression, or should it participate freely in the existing political system as an open democratic party, operating within the rules of the system, tolerated by it (while offering no threat) but ultimately resolved to dismantle it.

The choice rests between overthrowing capitalism and transforming it, between revolution and gradual change, between violence and peace. The left is critical of the Communist Party because it has opted for the second course and has failed, the right continues its distrust of communism because although the party appears superficially to have

25

renounced a violent path to revolution its final goal, Soviet dictatorship, remains in their opinion unchanged. In fact the British Communist Party has never successfully resolved these conflicting elements in its make-up, and throughout its history it has constantly wrestled with them, searching for its identity and the kind of party it wanted to become. It has rarely been fixed or even certain in its strategic analysis of how it should confront the situations facing it.

At the beginning of the 1930s for example the Party offered 'the revolutionary overthrow of capitalism' rather than 'parliamentary humbug' as its solution to the economic and political crises of a troubled age. It envisaged workers' councils elected from the 'propertyless masses', and urged the proletariat 'Forward to the Workers' Dictatorship, to Soviet Britain, to the Victory of Communism'.[2] Rarely has the party depicted the coming of socialism in such dramatic colours; indeed those fervent exhortations to revolutionary action in the manner of Russia in 1917 went unheeded and died away, representing just one brief moment on the Communist journey to socialism. Stretching over half a century then, that journey has been one of many changes of course, diversions, blind alleys and retracing of steps, which has brought the party to a position from which the prospect of further rapid advance presents itself only to the faithful—but even they are uncertain of the way ahead and how the terrain might be crossed.

At the outset, in its attempts to discover the means of applying its Soviet-derived doctrine to Britain, the Communist Party attended to the question of organisation, with effects that have lasted until today. The small groups who came together in 1920 to form the Communist Party of Great Britain failed, either singly or collectively, to meet the Leninist requirements of organisation. The British Socialist Party, the Socialist Labour Party, Sylvia Pankhurst's Workers' Socialist Federation and the elements of Scottish and Welsh shop stewards' movements had to be knit from a loose collection of propaganda clubs into a centralised, coherent organisation, trained in Marxist theory and practice. This process was carried out in the 1920s, when it came to mean Stalinising the party. An authoritarian leadership stifled internal debate, brooked no dissent from the line it laid down, and perpetuated its own succession. The party has had only three general secretaries in forty years, each carefully groomed through many years of experience in the party organisation.

For the first quarter-century of the party's life, at least, that kind of leadership entailed the subservience of the party to the *realpolitik* of Moscow. Switches in tactics and doctrine were all made by the British leaders at the behest of the Soviet Union, either on direct orders or indirectly through the Comintern, the Third International. As a historian of the party's early history has noted, adherence to the Comintern offered the only practical basis for the establishment of a Marxist party in Britain and 'it was from the Communist International that the British Communist Party acquired its sense of purpose and during the twenties the necessary funds for extensive propaganda and agitation'.[3] The party's fluctuating fortunes in the 1920s and 30s were exacerbated by the demands of this one-sided relationship, and its capacity for independent thought irreparably harmed. It was not until the dissolution of the Comintern in 1943, and the concession by Khrushchev thirteen years later that the ways to socialism were many and varied, that the party was able to shake off its total dependence on Russia. But even today, when the British Communists acknowledge Soviet leadership of world socialism, the suspicion remains on left and right that Moscow retains some influence over their affairs, in theory and practice.

This Stalinised predominantly pro-Moscow party has hardly been advantageously placed for finding its niche in British political life. To try to do this it has had to try to move steadily away from the Soviet sources which had, historically, governed its beliefs, structure and behaviour. The party understood from an early stage that it was isolated from the mass of the working class, politically and ideologically, and also appreciated that it was not going to attract their support by preaching violent or conspiratorial revolution. It tried various ways of overcoming the established organisations which claimed their loyalty: it sought affiliation to the Labour Party early on but faced rebuff, and its unofficial workers' organisations encountered the hostility of trade union leaders. After a flurry of activity during the general strike, the party's membership fell away and at the end of the 1920s Communists entered a period of extreme sectarianism, symbolised by the slogan 'Class Against Class'. This gave way to the directly opposite conception in the 1930s, the Popular Front, in which Communism became a moral force, fighting the evils of fascism and nazism and backed by the testimony of writers and intellectuals who became converted to it, while the terrible truth of Stalin's Russia was hidden from their view. This strategy was so successful that after a period of agonised ideological in-fighting, the party supported the war effort and reached a record 56,000 members in 1942. It envisaged a prominent role for itself in the post-war world as a respectable political party, renouncing violence, contesting elections, and preaching a generally acceptable progressive morality on the evils of wealth and militarism.

It was however the welfare state and six years of Labour government that swept the ground from under the party's feet. Its hopes appeared utterly demolished in 1956, when Mr Khrushchev revealed something of the true nature of Stalinism and the Soviet army suppressed the Hungarian revolt, while at home a Committee on Inner Party Democracy reaffirmed the principles of its organisation and killed all hope of any relaxation of its traditional rigidities. By 1958 a third of the party's members had resigned and the future looked bleak. In the quarter-century since that traumatic period the Communist Party has never seemed as though it would make any dramatic breakthrough: its membership has stagnated and its electoral performance declined further, a whole range of new organisations has sprung up on its left, but it has in other ways recovered much of the ground it had earlier lost, among trade unions, students and through various single issue campaigns where it has found sympathetic elements outside the party.

There is no escape from the paradoxes of modern Communism, as one glimpses for an instant the image of a pale shadow, a hopeless figure drifting aimlessly across the political scene, to be revealed in a different light as a skilful hunter, tracking down its quarry and slowly stealing upon the defences of capitalism, preparing itself to pounce.

For most of the post-war period however the party has adopted this preparatory stance, prepared to bide its time and wait on events, painfully aware that it has a long way to go to reach its destination. Its programme constructs an intricate web that takes into account the problems that bear down on it, balancing the disciplines and exclusiveness of Leninism against the need to compromise for political respectability on a progressive platform that would command wide support, and balancing the assumptions of Marxist theory against the values and needs of a generation of affluence. The historical problems of the party's identity and its role still haunt its whole existence.

The essential elements of its programme are contained in *The British Road to Socialism*, first published by the Executive Committee in February 1951, revised and approved by Congress the following year, with further revisions in 1958 and 1968. It justifies the need to change society by pointing to a 'deep-seated crisis of the whole economic political and social system [which] affects adversely every aspect of life'.[4]

The programme argues that Britain, as a former imperialist power, tries to maintain its old ascendancy by keeping military bases overseas and investing large sums overseas, all at the expense of the working class taxpayer. Consequently the workers' liberties and standards at home are attacked by the employers and governments who resist attempts by the workers to improve their lot. A new kind of capitalism has arisen presenting new dangers: monopoly capitalism which binds together government, financial institutions and industrial corporations, nationally and internationally, so that all power is confined to a few hands who seek to preserve it for their own narrow ends. Through parliament and the executive the small ruling class holds political power; through the ownership of property and wealth, economic power; and through control of education and the press, ideological power. But because the system is in crisis and is forced to repress the working class, it will, according to the Communist prognosis, inevitably lead to disequilibrium, conflict and its collapse. The relative calm and prosperity of modern British society changes only the manner of the collapse, not the fact of collapse itself. At an undefined point the capitalists will be in retreat, the working class will become an unstoppable force, and they will 'have to make a revolutionary change, end capitalism and build a socialist society'.[5] Because Britain is a sophisticated parliamentary state, work towards this change can begin without waiting for a cataclysmic economic crash, so that the transition to socialism can take place in comparative peace. Throughout the last twenty-five years, the broad conception of the peaceful 'transformation' of society has remained substantially unchanged, with the approval of Moscow. In the edition of 1952, the party sought to re-assure its audience:

> 'the enemies of Communism accuse the Communist Party of aiming to introduce Soviet Power into Britain and abolish parliament. This is a slanderous misrepresentation of our policy. Experience has shown that in present conditions the advance to socialism can be made just as well by a different road; for example through People's Democracy without establishing Soviet Power, as in the People's Democracies of Eastern Europe.'[6]

By the 1958 revision of *The British Road to Socialism* the value of such a guarantee was somewhat doubtful and any comparison between the establishment of socialism in Britain and Eastern Europe was tactfully dropped.

Opposing the monopoly capitalists the Communist programme envisages the vast majority of the population who share a community of interest. This includes not only industrial workers but farmers, shopkeepers, housewives, students, young people, immigrants, office-workers and pensioners. They should work through trade unions, the co-operative movement and Labour and Communist Parties. This is the raw material for the 'unity of the left', that 'broad popular alliance' whose creation is at the heart of the strategy of modern Communism.

Within this alliance, the relationship between the Labour and Communist Parties is the crucial one and because of their clear historical failure to compete effectively with Labour as a mass organisation the Communists have resigned themselves to accept existing side by side with it. The 1958 edition of *The British Road to Socialism*, drawn up in the re-think of policy after the disasters of the previous two years, spoke of Communist and Labour Parties working together in pursuit of common aims, which include opposition to Labour's right wing, the reformists: these are defined as those who accept 'the framework of the capitalist economy and state, the continuing of capitalist foreign policy, the renunciation of socialism'.[7] At their door is laid the responsibility for the failure of successive Labour governments and the subjugation of the interests of the working class to capitalism through wage freezes, incomes policies and a managerial concept of government. Once the Labour Party is purged of reformism and socialism is being built, the Communists say that they do not seek exclusive leadership of the united left, but that they and Labour will be the political organisations of the working class.

Unity begins however 'wherever there is common action on the immediate issues that face the working class'.[8] These are the single issue campaigns where the party hopes to bring together as many as possible of the components of its alliance. From there the campaigns should proceed by the 'continuous use and development of all the traditional democratic means of struggle among all sections of the people, understanding that all aspects of the struggle hang together—whether demonstration or strike, parliamentary or extra-parliamentary pressure'.[9] And out of this would grow a broad socialist programme covering the main areas of struggle—the protection of living standards and trade union rights; public ownership; dissolution of NATO 'ending as a result the Warsaw Pact'; opposing American Imperialism and West German militarism; extension to the welfare state in better housing, education and health services; public ownership of the mass media and the creation of Welsh and Scottish parliaments.

On the basis of this kind of programme the party envisages that socialism can come without civil war, through the election by the majority of a socialist government united on these policies and determined to carry them through. But the party sounds a warning: the winning of a parliamentary majority is an essential step, but attaining that and then power will be an intense struggle of many forms and phases and the parliamentary majority will have to be supported by the mass movement outside parliament.

'The strength of the mass movement will be felt in Parliament, and the strength of the socialist movement within Parliament will strengthen the movement outside. The one supports the other.

In this way, by political action, using our democratic rights to transform traditional institutions, Parliament can be made into the effective instrument of the people's will, able to carry through major legislation to challenge capitalist power and replace capitalism by socialism.

These developments, this programme, will have to be fought for by the mass movement at every step, with conscious understanding of the issues at stake. The ruling class will not easily surrender wealth and power. On the contrary, it will strive, by every means, direct and indirect, constitutional and unconstitutional to restrain and impede the popular movement, to break its strength or sap its unity. Against all such attempts, popular vigilance and mass action will be essential.

The working class and popular movement will need to be ready to use its organised strength to prevent or defeat attempts at violence against it, its organisations or representatives, or other illegal actions by reactionary forces at home or by agents of their foreign allies.'[10]

Thus the peaceful transformation through parliament is backed by mass direct action and by the suggestion of organised force. The extent to which these will be necessary and at what point they will be used, either on the taking of power or after in its consolidation, are problems which leading Communists have discussed, but have left the answers open. In 1966 the then party general secretary, John Gollan, outlined the prevailing orthodoxy on this delicate problem.

'We seek to get the transition to socialism in conditions of peace in the existing political conditions of Britain with its variety of political parties. We Communists in Britain do not stand for a one-party state.

For Marxists the question of whether the transition to socialism is by insurrection or can be achieved by democratic and comparatively peaceful means depends on the historical circumstances, political institutions and background and degree of working class organisations in each country. Communists have always preferred the peaceful way where it has been possible.

Here in Britain we think it is possible with great mass movements involving the overwhelming majority of the people and with a unified labour movement which has defeated the right wing, to use democratic institutions for the advance to socialism. We see the possibility of a new type of Parliament with a majority of socialists and communists carrying through the decisive political, economic and social measures for the socialist transition.

But there is no painless transition; there will be no easy sliding into socialism. Great mass struggles will be necessary on the way to political power and to defend it when it is won.'[11]

The Communist leaders speak of transition rather than revolution, of transforming the system rather than smashing it.[12] But the relationship between the forces within parliament and those without would nevertheless bring about 'a very different parliament from the one we have today'.[13] It would be part of what *The British Road to Socialism* describes as a 'socialist state machine'.

Constitutionally this machine would abolish the monarchy and the House of Lords and would arrange that 'those in commanding positions in the armed forces and police, the civil service and diplomatic service are loyal to the socialist government'.[14] This would be carried out in addition to the economic measures of nationalisation and planning, and the re-orientation of foreign policy and defence. At the same time, the party stresses its respect for traditional rights of individual liberty and 'freedom to think, work, travel, speak, dissent, act or behave, subject only to those limitations required in any ordered and just society to protect citizens from interference and exploitation by others and to safeguard the state'.[15]

It is often argued on the left that such a programme, carried out in this way means the Communist Party is no longer revolutionary: that its ideology is sterile and lacking in originality, its methods, relying on existing institutions, are inimical to radical change, and are optimistic in renouncing the inevitability of violence. Certainly the party has long since dispensed with the bomb and the barricade as an integral part of the revolution and is attempting to build a unique concept of open, legal revolutionism. But it does not discount the possibility that a certain amount of organised, institutionalised force would have to be used at vital moments. Indeed the undefined division of power between representative and mass arms of the working class is a revolutionary change in the manner in which governmental decisions are arrived at and enforced. The dismantling of the constitutional structure of the old order is likewise revolutionary, and so is the party's vision of a socialist state in which the fundamental aims and purposes of society are redirected in the interests of one social group and its ideology. It is a concept of revolution which buries much of the formal Leninist schemes, but which does not lend itself to radicalism in a British pragmatic tradition. It seeks to blend the two parts but fails to resolve clearly and unequivocally the central dilemma of the party's identity and its relationship with those around it.

It keeps open its options between the peaceful transformation carried out in conditions of peace watched over by a left majority in parliament and Communist-dominated unions, and the possibility, which has not been altogether discounted in theory, that capitalism may yet come crashing down, leading to a revolution of tumult and conflict where the emphasis is overwhelmingly on mass extra-parliamentary struggles.

The practical application of this programme takes place in a wide variety of areas: firstly there is the task of building the party itself as an accepted organisation, and secondly putting it to the test in parliamentary elections, success in which it regards as vital; thirdly, complementing the latter with the creation of a mass movement; fourthly bringing together as many groups and interests on the left on policies acceptable to itself, and fifthly placing this united left behind a 'progressive' foreign policy of solidarity with other socialists and in particular with the aspirations of the Soviet Union.

2

THE STATE OF THE PARTY

During 1974, when much attention was being given in the press and by politicians to Communist influence in the trade union movement, party membership was at its lowest figure for fourteen years.[16] Whatever influence it may possess in some quarters, the party has made no attempt to disguise the fact that its direct appeal is diminishing both for committed socialists and for the electorate at large. The British Communist Party has always been one of the smallest and least powerful of such parties in post-war western Europe. From the all-time peak of 56,000 members recorded in December 1942, support fell in twenty-three of the following thirty-three years. As the party's hopes of playing an active role in the reconstruction of post-war Britain faded, membership dropped to between 33,000 and 35,000, but fell away dramatically after the events of 1956. A third of the members left in two years, including prominent academics such as Professor Hyman Levy, Christopher Hill and John Saville, as well as others who became active in other spheres—Lawrence Daly of the mineworkers' union, Peter Cadogan in the Committee of 100, Ken Coates of the Labour Party and Institute for Workers' Control and Pat Jordan of the International Marxist Group. In the six years after 1958 however some recovery was made so that by 1964 the party had over 34,000 members, a figure never reached since. For in the following eight years, a period of intense radical activity, the figures fell slightly every year, with a 10 per cent loss between 1968–70 when 'New Left' revolt reached its zenith. A modest recovery was made in 1973 and then the downtrend was resumed so that by May 1974 the record showed only 27,400 card-carrying members.[17]

The electoral disasters are further evidence of the Communist

33

Party's failure to make any kind of popular impact. In general elections since 1959 the number of Communist Party candidates standing on each occasion and the total votes received is as follows:

1959	18 candidates	30,089 votes
1964	36	45,086
1966	57	62,092
1970	58	37,910
Feb 1974	44	32,741
Oct 1974	29	17,426

In the second general election of 1974 only four candidates reached four figures, two in South Wales and two in Scotland, including Jimmy Reid in Dunbartonshire Central, who polled 3,417 votes. The party puts most of its parliamentary candidates in these two areas, from which traditionally it has drawn much of its support: in the two 1974 elections, nine candidates stood in South Wales (six in February and three in October) and twenty-five in Scotland, mainly in the Glasgow area (fifteen and ten at each election respectively). At local elections, the close involvement of Communist party activists in bread-and-butter economic and social issues, such as housing, rents and welfare services, ensures a marginally better return. The party has generally secured a small amount of representation on borough and county councils in the west of Scotland, South Wales and the East End of London. Contesting an average of between 500 and 550 seats over the last ten years, the party secured the election of 24 councillors in 1964, 28 in 1968, 27 in 1970, and 23 in 1973, the majority of whom were in west Scotland.

In view of this record it is something of a mystery why the party should continue to attach so much importance to elections. It insists however, at party congresses, in all main statements of policy and speeches by its leaders, that electoral success is vital for the advance towards socialism. As a pamphlet for use in branch education classes states: 'the electoral fight is of enormous importance, for in Britain traditionally the progress of a political party is measured by its parliamentary and local government votes',[18] and it is the party's eagerness to be accepted as a sincere participant in the mainstream of political life that compels it to persist with the exercise. But the failure is evidence also of the lack of appeal for the British people of a scattered minority party when their main concern is to choose a party of government.

Some criticisms of this effort also attribute its failure to the character of the party's leadership, that it consists largely of ageing men and women who are out of touch with reality and unable to formulate relevant, attractive policies. Some indication of these factors is given in the reports of the party's biennial congresses, which state, among other details, age-group of delegates, their sex, length of party membership, and occupational background. For the five congresses from 1967–75, taken as examples, the personal statistics for these top $1\frac{1}{2}$ per cent of active Communists are as follows: 1967009

	Total Delegates	Women	Under 25	25–40	Over 40	Years membership[19] Under 2	Over 10
1967	424	59	40	169	215	46	252
1969	435	69	52	155	226	59	227
1971	422	63	67	182	173	57	201
1973	459	61	67	214	178	53	198
1975	425	77	46	233	146	58	153

The average age of delegates in 1975 was 36·25 compared with 34·8 two years earlier and 38·6 in 1971; the proportion aged over 40 had declined from over half at the end of the 1960s to just under 35 per cent in 1975, but the representation of the under 25s—between 9 per cent and 15 per cent—supports the view that the party lacks appeal for the young. The plight of the Young Communist League confirms the relative weakness of the party in this area, where Trotskyists and anarchists have captured the imagination. YCL membership dropped by a half in the years following 1956, but climbed up from a low of 1,700 in 1959 to nearly 6,000 in 1967, since when it has declined consistently. In 1973 the Communist leaders acknowledged that a membership of 2,890—to fall another 500 in the next year—was 'completely inadequate for the job'.[20]

The Young Communists have suffered badly then in the face of 'New Left' competition. But this pattern has not occurred in the same way among student activists. As Henry Pelling observed in 1958, the party appeared to hold little for students in the immediate post-war period,[21] for, as with the intellectuals who departed in 1956, the orthodoxies of such a bureaucratic oligarchy did not reflect their aspirations or ideals. By 1965 there were only four student Communist branches throughout the country and the party was unable to exploit the stirrings of discontent and the search for a radical socialist faith. Neither the party in general nor the YCL played any significant role in the 'student movement' of the late sixties, and indeed in many respects they deplored the new élitism of the 'red base' theory.

But as that wave of protest died the Communists began to increase their role in student politics. By 1971 the party's nominee, Digby Jacks, was president of the National Union of Students and since then it has secured a sprinkling of posts on the union's executive, including the key position of secretary, filled by Steve Parry from 1974–75 and Susan Slipman in the following year.

The number of Communist student branches has also grown steadily:

1967	16 branches
1968	25
1969	28
1972	37
1973	43
1974	50
1975	55

The number of party members included in these branches has increased from 270 in 1969 to over 1,000 in 1974, but in addition there has always been a number of individuals scattered throughout universities with no branches of their own; the party claimed up to 500 'unorganised' student members in 1969 and 800 in 1972. Since the 1920s, when the YCL was formed, the involvement of young people within the party's spheres of influence has been accorded a high priority, but as the modern picture shows the results have been patchy and the staidness of the party easily outmatched by more attractive alternatives.

Similarly the Communist Party has from its earliest days paid special attention to the role of women, in society and in its own ranks. The number attending congresses in recent years has remained constant with between six and eight on the forty-two strong executive committee. In addition there is a separate Women's Department in the party organisation, a newspaper for women, women's district committees, but only twenty-seven local women's branches. The party's executive reflects to a certain extent its social composition, or at least those groups and interests to which it directs its propaganda and recruiting efforts. In recent years, for example, the committee has included one West Indian member, Asquith Gibbes, who is the Community Relations Officer for Lambeth, and Vishnu Sharma, a former member of the now defunct Campaign Against Racial Discrimination. At local level however the party has few immigrant members, although it has some supporters in the Indian Workers Association, which is divided between pro-Moscow and pro-Peking Marxists.

Whatever importance is attached by the party leadership to recruitment among particular social minorities, its ability to draw in a clearly definable and substantial element of 'workers' is the primary test of its effectiveness. Again, the Congress returns, though variable in form and content, offer some indications of changes in the social pattern of membership. Taking the 1967–75 Congresses, the broad category of engineering, metal and shipbuilding trades accounted for an average of a fifth to a quarter of delegates, with power and building workers, miners and railwaymen each covering from 5% to 8% of the total.

Of individual unions represented during this period, the Amalgamated Union of Engineering Workers, or its equivalent, has been the largest by far with 78 members present at the most recent Congress. Of others, the Transport and General Workers' Union increased its representation from 20 to 38 delegates. Behind them the National Union of Mineworkers, the Electricians' unions, and the Union of Construction and Allied Trades Technicians have been strongly represented while others such as SOGAT, the printworkers' union, the shopworkers' USDAW, and the Associated Society of Woodworkers and the Clerical and Administrative Workers Union, both merged into larger unions, have faded. The National Union of Railwaymen and the General and Municipal Workers Union, despite their size, have each provided an average of only ten members at Congresses.

It has been among the white collar unions, opening up previously dormant sections of the working population to a new militancy, that some of the major increases have taken place in recent years. The proportion of non-manual workers at Congresses has increased from a fifth to a third, with teaching the largest single professional group among the white-collar sections. The Association of Scientific, Technical and Managerial Staffs had only three members present at the 1969 congress, but 26 two years later and 22 in 1975; the Association of Teachers in Technical Institutions rose from two in 1967 to 22 in 1973 and 18 in 1975, and the National Association of Local Government Officers from 7 to 18 over the period. Non-membership of a union is frowned upon among Congress delegates, very few of whom in recent times have been unemployed. The executive committee shows a slightly higher proportion of white-collar to manual workers, which is emphasised by the inclusion of full-time party workers, officials and propagandists, who comprise, on average, a quarter of the committee's total.

These activists include many skilled and semi-skilled workers who are not drawn to communism by their down-trodden economic status. Indeed they include some relatively highly-paid categories. But many of them have been affected by rapid changes in technology, in social status or job security and have perhaps come to communism through an understanding of the uses of militancy to preserve their economic status, which then develops into a critique of existing society. For traditionally quiescent white-collar workers, roused to action by others' success and by the ravages of inflation, communism supplies a creed to justify their actions, as it fortifies also miners or railway workers, for so long in declined and troubled industries.

Many varied motives prompt individuals to join the Communist Party—psychological, economic or a generalised idealism to bring about fundamental changes in society. Ordinary membership necessitates activity in furthering the aims of the party, but it does not at first presume or entail a detailed knowledge of its ideology. This is revealed gradually to the new convert as he becomes more deeply involved in the work and organisation of the party. Formal education is undertaken through schools and courses, at branch, district and national level, in lessons on Marxist philosophy, its application to Britain, and the ultimate purposes of the party. Of those attending congresses, for example, an average of more than half had attended national schools and over two-thirds branch schools. Those versed in the full rigours of this process constitute what have been described as the party's 'steel-hardened cadres',[22] who dominate its activities.

The organisation which serves their ends can be divided into four levels: the Congress; the Executive and its associated committees and departments; the Districts; and the Branches, at local and factory level. It has remained substantially unchanged for many years. Local rather than factory branches became the primary basic unit after the last war, and Area Committees (between Branch and District) have gradually fallen into disuse in the post-war years. Constitutionally the highest authority of the party is the Congress, which meets every two years to receive reports from party officials reviewing activities since the last gathering, consider documents setting out party policy and recommendations for future activity, and elect the forty-two members of the executive. The delegates, who represent districts and branches, are however very largely rubber stamps for the party leadership: although some vocal opposition on major issues does occur particularly from groups representing Kent and the Surrey District Committee, the recommendations of the existing executive, which include policy programmes and lists of approved candidates for further election, are simply never defeated.

Between congresses, the executive holds together the strands of power within the party. It dictates the involvement and activity of the party on particular issues and chooses from its number members of specialist committees and the full-time heads of the departments working from party headquarters in King Street, Covent Garden. The executive selects a Political Committee, the party's innermost council: it contains the party general secretary and assistant secretary, chairman, national organiser, industrial organiser, the editor of the *Morning Star*, and others including prominent trade unionists and departmental heads to a total of sixteen. The departments, of which the Political Committee members are in charge, are Press and Publicity, Organisation, Industrial, International, Education, Electoral and Women, with separate committees for work concerned with youth and on racial issues. Appointments to these positions are not made by election but controlled strictly within the ruling circle.

Moves between departments occasionally occur: in 1974, for example, Tony Chater, a former college lecturer and parliamentary candidate who had been head of the Press and Publicity Department and a former party chairman, exchanged places with George Matthews, for fifteen years previously the editor of the *Daily Worker* and *Morning Star*. And in the next year John Gollan retired at the age of 64 after nineteen years as party secretary, to be succeeded by Gordon McLennan, formerly the national organiser, a post taken over by Dave Cook, previously student organiser.

At the centre the Communist Party is intensely active and dedicated, but below the main committee and departments little authority is delegated and independent activity is discouraged. At the lower levels one obtains a different picture of the energy and efficiency of the party. The nineteen Districts, half of which have full-time organisers, act as the channel of communication between the leadership and the rank and file. There is enormous variety in the size and activity of the Districts. Scotland, for example, has over 7,000 members, London 5,000, the North West 4,000, with just under 2,000 in each of Middlesex, Yorkshire and Wales. Three-quarters of the party's membership is in eight districts, while in the other eleven districts the party's support is so scattered it is quite ineffectual and in some cases virtually non-existent. In Devon and Cornwall District there are approximately 200 members in six branches, and in the South Midlands District, encompassing Oxfordshire, South Warwickshire, Berkshire and Buckinghamshire, the party has 280 members grouped into eleven branches, one of which is non-functional and only six of which have working committees. In contrast Glasgow alone had in 1970 2,153 members with a full-time organising secretary.

All individual members belong to a branch, either a local one covering an area in size anything from a housing estate to a small town, or a factory branch by which is meant a group of members based on any single workplace. Upon the activities of these the health and appeal of the party ultimately depends. An average total of branches at any one time in recent years has been around 1,000, the vast majority of which are local branches. They are expected to engage in a wide range of activities, particularly to try to strike up contacts with sympathisers in trades unions, Labour Party branches, co-operative societies, peace committees, friendship societies, ex-service organisations, women's groups, youth, sporting or cultural organisations.[23] Through these they are expected to involve themselves in campaigns on housing, race, burning local issues, act as pressure groups on local councils and authorities as well as provide the rank and file support for major national campaigns. In addition the interests of the party itself play a major role—boosting the sales of the *Morning Star*, recruiting members to the branch or to the Young Communist League. The party organisation lays down guidelines for the structure of branches, the kind of meetings it should hold, their frequency, and the composition of a Branch committee, which should consist of between seven and ten members, including a secretary (to act as the branch leader and link with the higher echelons of the party), chairman, treasurer, education secretary, literature secretary, recruitment organiser and *Morning Star* sales organiser.[24] In an average branch of thirty to forty members this imposes a high degree of committed activity upon individuals and only the larger branches can manage the full range of work or include special sections for young people or women.

The effectiveness of the factory branches has caused the party greater anxiety. The official line has been to stress their importance: 'We need Communist organisation in the factories', declared a handbook for party members in 1962, 'in order to see that the militancy and decisive strength of the industrial workers is brought into the heart of the political struggle'.[25] To strike at capitalism at its very nerve centres, to bring the workers to socialism, have been objectives central to the Communist purpose which the factory branches have been intended to achieve. But they have become a definite weak link in this effort. John Gollan conceded at the party's 29th Congress in 1965 that there had been 'a decline in our attention to the factories',[26] and the following year a special factory branch conference was convened.

The then party chairman, Frank Stanley, told the meeting that 'factories are the key point in the struggle against the government's incomes policy ... The factories are decisive for generating mass action on all the major issues and in influencing the trade union movement in a left progressive direction'.[27] Some Communists had argued that they were superfluous in the context of left unity and parliamentarianism, but the view was resisted by the leadership, who accepted the report of a committee on party organisation in 1966 which argued that to 'abandon the organisation of factory branches would seriously weaken the fight to build the party among the key sections of the British workers'.[28] On the other hand some militants have queried the seriousness with which this task has been undertaken, regarding the *British Road to Socialism* programme as inevitably entailing a diminution of effort in the factories. Among those who adhered to this view were small groups who expressed their opinions in terms of a pro-Chinese ideology—such as Michael McCreery, who left the party in 1963 to form the first separate 'Maoist' group in Britain, and Reg Birch, an executive member who was expelled three years later and set up his own pro-Chinese party.[29]

Stagnation at the lower levels of the party organisation is a direct result of its principles and structure. One of the basic reasons for this is the application of 'democratic centralism', the guiding principle of party authority since the 1920s and which the 1956 commission on inner party democracy reaffirmed in all essential elements. It permits the right of members to participate in discussion of policy and to stand for office and be represented at the higher levels; that is the democratic aspect. Centralism entails the right of higher organisations to take decisions binding lower ones and compels all members to unite behind a decision once taken and fight for it as a disciplined body. Democracy is constrained by the ban on 'factions', defined as 'a grouping of members outside the recognised organisation of the Party'.[30] That is to say that members in one branch cannot join forces with members in another to press a particular point of view. Each separate branch must submit its proposals through the appropriate District Committee and accept its verdict. To allow factions and groups of members to disagree with policy and campaign for changes would in the official view lead to the establishment of 'alternative political centres and leaderships, alternative policies and alternative group loyalties. The party would be torn asunder, its unity and effectiveness destroyed if this were allowed to happen'.[31] In addition, to preserve the coherence of leadership the formation of cadres is encouraged, to include the key members in branches or on committees taken from the most experienced and reliable members on whom leadership and the generation of activity falls, and this invariably leads to a concentration of decision-making to the exclusion of the rank and file. In 'democratic centralism' therefore centralism is the dominant partner.

Besides this, the allocation of the party's financial resources works directly against the interests of local branch initiative in favour of the centre. At the end of 1973 membership fees, paid directly to the branch, were raised to 25p per month per head (£3 per year) and distributed in the proportion £1 to the Executive Committee, £1 to the District Committee, 80p to the Branch and 20p to the Central Election Fund. If, for example, 20,000 full fees were received in a year—allowing for the non-payment and reduced fees for students, housewives and pensioners—the £60,000 collected would be divided in the sums of £20,000 to the Executive Committee, £20,000 to the nineteen District Committees according to the membership totals of their component branches, £4,000 to the election fund, and a mere £24 for an average-sized branch of thirty members. Thus the branches are stranded and the executive given a considerable sum to dispense as it sees fit.

The money is used to pay the wages of more than fifty full-time party workers, for the organisation of conferences, rallies, weekend schools, speaking tours around the country by leading members, and in a prodigious output of propaganda. In 1972, a year of numerous industrial confrontations between unions and government, a total of $3\frac{1}{2}$ million leaflets were printed. Quantities of half a million leaflets are printed at a time for specific campaigns, such as opposition to income policies. The party maintains a constant output of pamphlets for recruiting, guidance on policy, reprints of speeches and for party education classes. It also publishes a wide variety of magazines: *Comment*, a fortnightly paper which began as a weekly in 1963 in succession to *Workers Review*, but was forced to reduce its frequency in 1971 because of low sales, then about 10,000 copies per issue; *Marxism Today*, a monthly theoretical journal; *Challenge*, the Young Communist newspaper, whose circulation has also been dropping— from 11,000 in 1965 to 7,500 in 1971; *Cogito*, a Young Communist theoretical magazine; and *Link*, a journal for women.

The party's main propaganda weapon, the *Morning Star* (formerly the *Daily Worker*) is not included in the main organisation but belongs to a nominally independent company. It does however faithfully reflect the prevailing party line and is regarded as an integral part of its effort to appeal and organise among the working class. It is the front line of major campaigns, such as those on the Shrewsbury Pickets, or opposing the Common Market, and is able to draw on contributions from left-wingers from outside the party's ranks, including leading Labour Party politicians. But it too has been struggling and its average circulation in the 1970s, 50,000 to 60,000 copies per day, is less than half the figure in 1945. It does however manage to afford three full-time District organisers, in Scotland, the North West and London, as well as nearly 200 organisers attached to party committees and branches throughout the country.

Over the years, the Communist Party has developed a wide range of business and political interests, many of which, although ostensibly beyond its control are closely connected with it. There are for example, Central Books Ltd., which distributes *Comment* and stocks the party's literature; Lawrence and Wishart, a publishing house; Fasleigh Press and London Caledonian Press, printing firms; Rodell Properties Ltd, whose directors include party treasurer, Denis Ellwand and Tony Chater[32]; Progressive Tours Ltd, to arrange holidays in Eastern Europe; the Marx Memorial Library in east London, and the Labour Research Department, which publishes the 'left-unity' journal, *Labour Monthly*.

Of all the fringe activities of the Communist Party the best known are those of the numerous 'front' organisations which sprang up mostly between 1945 and 1952. They include Friendship Societies, Leagues and Association for the Soviet Union and individual East European Countries, the World Peace Council, British Peace Committee, Artists for Peace, Musicians for Peace, Teachers for Peace, the British Youth Festival Committee, and the National Assembly of Women. Fellow-travellers and non-card-carrying sympathisers are often more prominent in these organisations than Communist Party members, although the party's guiding hand is never far away. The intention of spreading the Communist gospel in this manner was largely thwarted early on when the Labour Party proscribed such bodies. An annual list of prohibited organisations was published until 1972 by which time it was out of date, many of the organisations were moribund and attitudes to Communists had softened.

The elaborate structure of the Communist Party, although cumbersome and stultifying, enables it to remain the most highly organised national group on the far left. Authority rests firmly at the centre, wedded to doctrinal orthodoxies many rejected a generation ago. It is hardly surprising that the party's thunder has been stolen by more adaptable radical groups with energetic and independent grass-roots membership. The party places high demands on the obedience and hard work of its members, but as the report on party organisation in 1965 observed, has failed to accept variations in individual contributions, which is implicit in a mass party. The corollary of moving from a small party of dedicated committed activists to a broadly based popular party—the basic aspiration of *The British Road to Socialism*, is 'humanising the appeal and aims of the party'.[33] This process has been undertaken in seeking the unity of the left.

3

THE UNITY OF THE LEFT

Left unity assumes many forms with three distinct dimensions: political, social and international unity which have become interwoven in the grand design of Communist long-term aims.

Political unity means the party working in co-operation with members of other 'progressive' organisations: the Labour Party, Labour Party Young Socialists, Young Liberals, Peace Pledge Union, Campaign for Nuclear Disarmament, Anti-Apartheid Movement, United Nations Association, Student Christian Movement and Liberation (formerly the Movement for Colonial Freedom) are bodies with which the party leadership encourages its members to have contacts, local and informal where they cannot be national and official. The list of single issue campaigns which Communists and members of such groups have pursued together, is lengthy and has been the staple diet of radical protest over the whole of the period since the beginning of the 1960s: it includes the 'ban-the-bomb' campaign, wage freezes, industrial relations legislation, Vietnam, Ireland, Chile, the Common Market, Southern Africa, the Shrewsbury Pickets and the National Front. Generally left unity has not embraced what the Communists describe as the 'Ultra-Left', the Trotskyist, Maoist and Anarchist groups, although the party has worked with International Socialists and the International Marxist Group in, for example, the Liaison Committee for the Defence of Trade Unions and the Chile Solidarity Campaign. But when they have attempted to join forces bitter squabbles have broken out in which the 'Ultras' have accused the Communists of refusing to build a genuine mass movement for direct action and of being more interested in cultivating left-oriented trade union leaders and politicians, whom the 'Ultras' despise.

The Communist Party is however more interested in connecting itself with the mainstream of the Labour movement and developing these campaigns into a more permanent relationship than in staging dramatic demonstrations and related activity for their own sake. Its conduct in these campaigns has always been restrained and the party has pointed an accusing finger at the antics of Trotskyists and others in provoking unnecessary violence which damages the overall cause for which they are working. The party's moderate image in such matters is another aspect of its desire to be acceptable as a democratic party and an integral part of British politics and society, the true friend of the working class. It concedes that it can never altogether overcome the workers' allegiance to the Labour Party so it tries to win support among that party on policies acceptable to itself. The 'unity of the left' between Communist and Labour parties stems from the former's assumption that it has a role to play, but it is also a product of its failure to find that role in practice: it clutches at the Labour left which is a lifeline to prevent its being submerged and washed away. Indeed the drive for unity with Labour went into full swing in the years after 1956 when its own membership had fallen so dramatically. The Communists therefore approach left unity from weakness rather than strength and are hardly in a position directly to dictate to the Labour party or any section of it.

Officially Labour remains as hostile to the Communist Party as it has done since it rejected the first of its six applications for affiliation in the 1920s. Since the middle of the 1960s numerous factors have contributed to break down some of the old barriers between the two parties. In constituencies dominated by the Labour left the contacts forged in campaigns have been extended to co-operation in elections where parliamentary candidates have been acceptable to both organisations. After the general election of October 1974 the Communists, Assistant General Secretary, Reuben Falber claimed in the *World Marxist Review* that

> 'in many constituencies where no Communist was standing our branches helped the Labour candidate, in some instances taking charge of organising the campaign in whole sections of the constituency. This was of particular importance in marginal constituencies where the difference between Labour and Conservative votes in February had been narrow. A number of Communist Party branches were publicly thanked by local Labour Party officials for the help they rendered.'[34]

Nationally the Communist Party can count upon the public support of a few Labour Members of Parliament and National Executive members in the columns of the *Morning Star* or at the newspaper's occasional rallies, alongside Communist leaders. Among the most prominent in these respects have been the former chairman of the *Tribune* group, Sydney Bidwell, former cabinet minister Judith Hart, Renée Short and Joan Maynard, whose contacts with Communists and Trotskyists are among the most extensive of any Labour politician: a member of the National Executive Committee of the Labour Party since 1972, and an MP since February 1974, this former vice-president of the National Union of Agricultural Workers has been chairman of the Communist front organisation, the British Peace Committee, a council member of the Institute for Workers' Control, supporter of the National Assembly of Women, the Troops Out Movement, the National Abortion Campaign and a visitor to North Vietnam for the British Campaign for Peace in Vietnam and to East Berlin with the British Youth Festival Committee. The latter together with the National Assembly of Women and the British Peace Committee were among approximately thirty organisations—largely Communist-dominated—proscribed by the Labour Party for their undesirable connections.

45

It is symptomatic of the reduction in Labour's historical antipathy to Communism and the increase in the influence of its own left wing that the list was discontinued in 1973 leaving no barriers to co-operation between Labour members, branches or indeed the party nationally and the Communist Party or its agencies. The Communists' greatest hope for a profitable liaison with Labour comes, as will be described later, through the trade union movement, whose block votes largely determine Labour policy and where industrial action may be threatened as a political lever.

At the same time as the Communists have been working to increase their influence in the Labour Party there have been enormous social changes affecting the sources and nature of discontent. In the 1960s orthodox Communism was slow to adjust to the presence of a radical movement on its left and some of the newer concepts of revolution. It was critical of the student 'red base', Debray's Latin American 'Foco' theory and the whole apparatus of New Left sociology as expressed by Marcuse and Mandel.[35] Since then, many of these theories have been discarded and the Communists have seen the wheels of fashion turn full circle to come back to a starting point which they, standing still, had never left.

The party has however grasped the importance of youth in generating revolutionary activity. Despite its weakness, the YCL has always been very active and some of the party's leading members, such as John Gollan, Mick McGahey and Jimmy Reid, have come through its ranks. In the 1960s the League was instrumental in creating a youth section to the Campaign for Nuclear Disarmament, later a Youth for Peace in Vietnam which became a section of the British Campaign for Peace in Vietnam, and then a subsidiary of the Movement of Colonial Freedom (now Liberation) for young people. In this area it worked closely with Labour Party Young Socialists and Young Liberals, so that by 1970 it became a part of the Young Liberal-led Stop the Seventy Tour Committee, whose spokesman, Peter Hain, invited 'the active support of young workers and particularly Young Communists'.[36] Such exercises are evidence of one of the Young Communist League's main tasks described in *The British Road to Socialism* as helping 'young people move from radical rebellion against the capitalist establishment to positive socialist ideals'.

In the National Union of Students the 'Broad Left' alliance of Labour Marxists, Communists and unattached socialists that has dominated its affairs for most of the 1970s has been one of the most successful applications of left unity. Trotskyists and International Socialists have been reduced to a rump opposition and the Union's concern for economic matters, its attempt to be regarded as a trade union, and its policies over a wide range—grants, Ireland, anti-racialism—owe much to Communist influence. Attempts to extend this further in the academic field have been made through a series of annual Communist 'Universities', first held in 1968, and each lasting a week during which party members and intellectual sympathisers gather to discuss labour history, Marxist philosophy and economics to relate them to each other, to the party and to the overall cause of the industrial working class against the common enemy of 'monopoly capitalism'.

Left unity has many layers and interlocking areas of activity and nowhere is this more evident than in the context of international unity. Here the party's intention is manifold: to forge a domestic movement to campaign for acceptable policies on foreign issues, to bring together British and overseas socialists, to demonstrate solidarity with orthodox Communists throughout the world, and ultimately to further the interests of Soviet-led communism.

The Communist Party has traditionally stressed the evil intentions of its enemies whose unscrupulous machinations threaten world peace: American and NATO's imperialism; West German militarism—in the days of the Cold War a major propaganda target; South African racism; Spanish, Portuguese, Greek or Chilean fascism; and British colonialism. In contrast it proclaims the peaceful policies of the Soviet Union and its allies as a shining example to progressive people everywhere. The latter message may not have penetrated the public consciousness, but the former issues constitute the unchallenged assumptions and obsessions of a generation of dissent. The Communist Party has therefore attempted to turn these issues to its advantage, to earn for itself moral superiority and political acceptance, beginning in the campaigns of what it describes as the 'Peace movement'.

In May 1960 the party reversed its policy and declared its support for the Campaign for Nuclear Disarmament, trailing as it so often is, behind the idealists and the revolutionary sects; it had entered a movement already near its peak and on the verge of sharp decline.[37] Indeed the encroachment of Communist influence was at first harmful to it, but, in the present decade, when public interest has dropped away, it is largely the support of the party which keeps it going. From 1965 the thoughts of the Communists as well as other CND supporters turned to Vietnam and gradually that supplanted the bomb as the burning issue at meetings and on marches. In that year the British Campaign for Peace in Vietnam was formed, with Fenner Brockway, churches, some liberals and Labour members among its following, but gradually the BCPV was turned into another agent of Left Unity with Labour and Communists working side by side. The cultivation of

47

'responsible' politicians in restrained lobbying was deliberate, to highlight the alleged irresponsibility and adventurism of the 'Ultra-Left'.

In campaigns concerned with the peace movement and with international solidarity, the 'front' organisations have a prominent part to play. Many of these were formed after the Second World War as propaganda agents of the Communist Party but their efforts were quickly nullified by Labour Party proscription. They have however continued to attract some support from outside the party, which prefers to take a back seat. One of the more resilient of such bodies has been the British Peace Committee, established in 1949, which calls itself a 'non-exclusive and non-sectarian' organisation.[38] Its 1974 National Peace Congress for example, calling for the recognition of the Provisional Revolutionary Government in South Vietnam, was sponsored by ten Labour Members of Parliament, as well as trade union leaders and peace activists, and it demanded also British defence cuts of £1,000 million and withdrawal from NATO, proposals which later in the year the Labour Government was at some pains to resist from its own national conference. In recent times the Committee has campaigned on Chile and in favour of the withdrawal of British troops from Northern Ireland. The Committee is the British section of the World Peace Council which was also set up in 1949, under considerable Communist influence from Eastern Europe. Tony Chater is a member of its main committee and in 1972 sponsored a Committee for European Security, on which most western European Communist Parties were represented.

Such domestic campaigning bodies soon acquire—or indeed are born with—particular international affiliations. In 1968, for example, 800 British supporters of the British Campaign for Peace in Vietnam, including many trade unionists, Labour and Communist supporters, visited France to meet Viet Cong and North Vietnamese representatives. And in 1974, the 10th World Youth Festival, organised by the East German government and held in East Berlin, drew not merely the support of the Young Communist League but the sponsorship of Young Liberal Peter Hain, Graham Tope, the Liberal MP, Renée Short, Joan Maynard, Lord Brockway, Mrs Betty Ambetilios and former party stalwarts Jimmy Reid and Eddie Marsden, who died in 1975. A number of other organisations were also eager to hear speakers such as Palestinian guerrilla leader Yassar Arafat and American Black Power Marxist Angela Davis, including the Student Christian Movement, the United Nations Youth Association, National Union of Students, the British Campaign for Peace in Vietnam, and Liberation.[39]

More exclusive links are developed between the party and both its

48

ruling and non-ruling counterparts abroad. The British Communists receive many visits and delegations from overseas parties—at the 1973 congress representatives from Chile, North Vietnam and Portugal were present and 'fraternal greetings' were received from the Communist parties or their equivalents in over forty countries. In return, prominent British members visit their comrades overseas: in recent years delegations have been to the Soviet Union and most Western and Eastern European countries, Cuba, Iraq, India, North Vietnam and Mongolia. Similarly the Young Communist League has made exchange visits with Komsomol, the Soviet Youth organisation. These contacts are placed on a more formal footing at mass gatherings of parties. When twenty-one Western European Communist Parties last met in Brussels in January 1974 they reaffirmed left unity as a strategy applicable across the whole continent by 'seeking out similarities of approach and common action and initiative with Socialist and Christian parties'.[40]

The Soviet Union wishes to be regarded by all of these parties as the principal model of the socialist state and moral leaders of the world communist movement. On occasions, as in 1956, the association is damaging to the British party's interests, but despite the events of that year it remained loyal to Moscow and took its side in the Sino-Soviet dispute which came to the surface in 1962–63. In 1968, however, after the Soviet-led invasion of Czechoslovakia, the British party denounced the use of force as a 'gross violation of the democratic rights of Czechoslovak Communists',[41] for at a time when the party was losing ground to heterodox factions it was anxious to make some gesture of independence from Moscow. It has since criticised the treatment of some dissidents in the Soviet Union, and is cautiously following the French and Italian parties in developing a more individual line. In other respects it encourages the association. An international series of front organisations, run mainly from East European countries, maintains contact between Communists and non-Communists in different countries in a manner easily controllable by the Soviet Union. These bodies include the World Federation of Trade Unions, the International Union of Students, the International Organisation of Journalists, and the International Association of Democratic Lawyers. The international role of the front organisation is captured in a symbolic way by a ceremony held in November 1973 by the British Soviet Friendship Society to celebrate the Bolshevik Revolution of 1917. The Soviet Ambassador, with John Gollan sitting at his side, received from Ray Buckton, general secretary of ASLEF, a bound volume containing signatures of greeting, and heard William Wilson, Labour MP for Coventry South, praise the amicable way in which peoples of different culture and race lived together in the Soviet Union (to judge from his recent visit there).[42]

The Communist Party's strategy of the unity of the left has made some noticeable advances on the position of clinging to coat-tails for salvation, in which attitude the operation was begun. The ultimate aims of international left unity—for a Britain with no overseas military commitments, a re-orientated foreign policy, economic co-operation with Socialist states rather than capitalist ones, and active support for approved revolutionary movements in Africa and Asia—are distant targets that will only be realisable if domestic unity comes first to fruition. Above all the core of the united left at home is the organised, industrial working class.

4

UNITY, THE UNIONS AND MASS ACTION

Of all aspects of British Communism the industrial field is the most discussed. The questions of the nature of Communist influence in the trade union movement, its extent and the uses to which it is put, are so closely bound up with political controversy that the truth is elusive. From the right, the tentacles of Communism are seen in trade unions to grasp democracy by the throat. Even on the left, the presence of Communist trade union leaders in relative strength is not denied—Tariq Ali concedes that the party has more industrial militants than all other left groups combined[43]—but argues that its influence is inimical to the revolutionary cause: it concentrates too much on trade union bureaucracies and not enough on building rank and file movements capable of launching general strikes or factory occupations. To the radical left then the Communist influence, although extensive, militates against the direct disruption of capitalism. Only the centre derides the suggestion that Communists are in any way to blame for industrial friction or indeed that their presence—even if it is there—constitutes any kind of challenge to liberal parliamentary government.

For the party itself industry is the primary battlefield, where socialism, by the workers for the workers, is to be made or broken. All its propaganda resources and organisational apparatus are brought to bear: 'Smash Heath—At a Stroke' and 'McGahey's Warning: Phase 3 or Coal' proclaim the headlines of the *Morning Star*, while its members work away with dedication to secure the election of Communist or fellow-travelling officials from branch and factory level to the national executives of the major unions of the country's key industries, coal, engineering, transport and railways. From there the path leads to the Trades Union Congress General Council and the Labour Party National Executive Committee. The prize is not merely the potential power to mobilise thousands of workers in support of economic demands or to oppose government; it is the culmination of left unity in the ability of trade union block votes decided by Communists and their supporters to determine the policies and leaders of the Labour Party. It is in this context, broader and more long-term than the naïve encouragement of strike action for its own sake, that the role of Communists in industry should be considered. Success offers the party both the raw material of socialism and the political means to its end, and like other aspects of left unity and of other mass movements it begins on specific issues in campaigns of propaganda.

Formed in 1966, the Communist Party's chosen instrument for organising such campaigns has been the Liaison Committee for the Defence of Trades Unions. The year is significant for it was that of the seamen's strike in which Mr Wilson attacked the sinister influence of Communism, the year in which after Labour's second election victory, the Prices and Incomes Board and the pay freeze were introduced, and a time when the first stirrings of student radicalism were manifesting themselves. It was in a short time when the left's disillusion with the Labour Party and the sense of endemic economic crisis were mounting. The immediate origins of the Liaison Committee were the London Industrial Shop Stewards Defence Committee formed earlier that year, following a strike at a north London engineering factory. Many militants rallied to the Committee's banner but immediately upon its conversion into the LCDTU, when the hand of the Communist Party began to make an impression, it divided into four opposed groups. Based on Oxford, a breakaway branch helped form the All Trades Union Alliance, the agent of the Workers Revolutionary Party; a second section consisted of International Socialist sympathisers, many of whom continued with that group through to its Rank and File Movement of the 1970s; a third smaller group in the Engineering Union centred around Reg Birch, who supported the initial strike, which became the nucleus of his pro-Chinese party,[44] and the remainder, the largest group, remained as the Liaison Committee under the guidance of the Communist Party but embracing the 'Broad Left' of sympathetic non-party members and militants.

Together these bodies have constituted the basis of a semi-permanent extra-parliamentary industrial opposition, attempting by propaganda and various forms of direct action to put pressure on governments to stop policies they oppose. Between 1966 and 1972 the Liaison Committee for the Defence of Trade Unions was the most active of them.

With both a Communist Party chairman in Kevin Halpin, a former employee of Ford's at Dagenham and general election candidate there in 1964, and secretary Jim Hiles, the party has been in a dominant position, although the LCDTU has not been an exclusively Communist affair. At its conferences, among up to 1,200 trade unionists, leading figures like Ray Buckton, Lord Briginshaw, the general secretary of the printworkers' Union NATSOPA, and Hugh Scanlon of the engineers, have attended, together with National Union of Mineworkers' members from Kent, South Wales and Scotland, representatives of many trades unions, trades councils and shop stewards committees.

By 1969 the Committee opposed Barbara Castle's proposals for *In Place of Strife*, and after the election of Mr Heath's government in 1970 the Communist Party and the LCDTU turned its fire on the Industrial Relations Bill hoping to stop that also by protest demonstrations, one-day stoppages and the sheer force of the whole trade union movement in opposition. But the campaign failed, in the words of the Communist slogan, to 'Kill the Bill' and after it passed into law only individual unions, especially the engineering workers', continued their fight and the concerted movement evaporated. The Liaison Committee faltered also and by 1972 those Trotskyist and International Socialists who had previously supported it withdrew in protest at the Communist Party's refusal to develop local rank and file branches to step up direct action.

It was not until the end of 1973 and into 1974 that the Committee found another issue to stir it back into action. This was the case of the building workers who were sentenced in December 1973 to prison sentences as a result of violent incidents in the building strike the previous year: the notorious Shrewsbury Pickets. An energetic campaign was mounted and the slogan 'Free the Shrewsbury Two' has entered the mythology of the left as an example of capitalist injustice comparable to the case of the Tolpuddle Martyrs. From the Labour backbenches, Norman Atkinson, Eddie Loyden and Audrey Wise have been among the most active in the assorted company of UCATT, the building workers' union, the Transport and General Workers' Union, the TUC general council, the Workers' Revolutionary Party and the International Socialists. With the Communist Party and the Liaison Committee for the Defence of Trade Unions they have supported the Shrewsbury Defence Committee whose London secretary is Lou Lewis, a former member of the Communist Party executive, a prominent activist in the Building Workers' Charter movement which had been at the centre of the 1972 strike, and a member of the industry's Joint Sites Committee in the 1960s. Other leading Communist building workers supported the campaign including Peter Carter and Peter Kavanagh, both members of the Charter Movement and former YCL leaders. In May 1974 they and the LCDTU helped organise a one-day strike to press for the release of the men and a lobby of parliament at the beginning of 1975, but with no effect and many arguments broke out between Communists and Trotskyists who raised their familiar demands for a general strike to force the government to concede.

Such campaigns are expensive in time and money and have brought little in the way of concrete results except a polarising of opinion and the inching forward of left unity. They are considered no substitute for hard work in the unions themselves. At shop floor level it is less the Communists' politics that count than their doggedness in pursuing men's grievances and upholding their interests. The well-trained Communist unionist does this task well and he can count also on the apathy of the majority working in his favour. But the party line and the shadow of King Street loom at all times. A shop steward in the National Union of Vehicle Builders at Ford's Dagenham plant, and a former party member wrote: 'The "line" was handed down from the Executive to the District Committee, then to the Branch. Certain stewards were informed by hand-delivered letters, others by the group cadre. Group meetings in the factory were always encouraged. A cadre would be delegated to ensure that the members toed the party line'.[45]

Gradually, and particularly since 1966, the Communist Party has thus increased its representation at all levels, up to national executives. Its numbers on the main committees of some major unions by 1974–75 is well known: the National Union of Mineworkers had six Communists on its executive of 27; the Transport and General Workers' Union at least 10 out of the 39 members of its general executive council. In the white collar and professional unions the party has representatives in NALGO and USDAW, the shop workers' union, as well as seven members on the 23-strong executive of the Association of Scientific Technical and Managerial Staffs and three on the executive of the National Union of Teachers including the president until 1975, London headmaster, Max Morris. The president of ASLEF, the train drivers' union is also a Communist, Bill Ronksley of Sheffield, a party member since 1945, giving the militant 'Broad Left' a majority on the nine-man executive. The key position of ASLEF London Area organiser, based at Waterloo, is also held by a Communist, Neil Milligan.

None of these unions nor any others are controlled exclusively by the Communist Party. But in the company of unaffiliated Marxists, the occasional Trotskyist, and those who are simply militant over issues of pay or the threat of unemployment, the party can often find the balance tipped in its favour. It is the coincidence between the aims of the Communist Party and others of different opinion or motivation on these basic problems at a time of economic crisis and inflation that has been the main factor contributing to the relative success it has enjoyed, and a degree of influence which appears disproportionate to its numerical support.

In unions where it does not enjoy support it has encouraged some rank and file movements. In the National Union of Seamen, for example, the party was active in the seamen's Reform Movement of the early 1960s and involved in—though not directing—the strike of 1966. Following that crucial event and the denunciation of Communist involvement by Mr Wilson, the left's fortunes went into reverse until 1974 when Jim Slater, a non-party militant, was elected firstly to the N U S executive and then to the T U C general council. In 1966 the building disputes at the Barbican and Horseferry Road sites in London led to an official Court of Inquiry which sharply criticised the part of the London Building Workers' Joint Sites Committee, in which Jim Hiles, Lou Lewis and Jack Henry, also a Communist, were key members, for its 'subversive and mischievous activities' in leading unofficial strikes and go-slows.[46] The Committee was succeeded in 1972 by the Building Workers Charter group, as a national body to campaign for a 'charter' of demands centred around pay and conditions, and which became one of the most militant sections in the 1972 strike. Similarly in the docks the party is well represented on the National Ports Shop Stewards Committee, whose effective leader, Bernie Steer, was one of the five dockers gaoled in 1972 for contempt of the Industrial Relations Court.

The supreme example of Communist influence in trade unions, either at national level or in unofficial movements, is the Amalgamated Union of Engineering Workers. The major breakthrough came with the election of Hugh Scanlon as president of the then A E F in 1968; a former Communist, he was supported by the party and by the *Engineering Voice*, a newspaper which since 1963 had campaigned on a 'Broad Left' platform supported by Communist and Labour supporters alike. To further Scanlon's cause, a Left Unity Committee was formed in Sheffield, a major engineering centre and consistent source of Communist support. It had 150 members chaired by Cyril Morton, an engineering convenor and member of the Communist Party's inner Political Committee. After the election of Hugh Scanlon, the Sheffield Committee took part in anti-Vietnam war demonstrations and paved the way for the election of Communists to Sheffield Trades Council.

In the next five years the party tightened its hold on the union:

Les Dixon went on to the executive; Ken Gill became general secretary of the white collar TASS section and in 1974 was elected to the TUC general council; John Tocher was Secretary in the Manchester region of the union; Brian Chambers became secretary in the Birmingham region and the late Eddie Marsden was general secretary of the Construction Section from 1968. All of these are card-carrying party members and they can draw the support of other militant figures in the Union such as Reg Birch, the Maoist who serves on the executive, its assistant general secretary Ernie Roberts, a Labour Marxist and supporter of the 'Voice of the Unions' group and the Institute for Workers' Control, and Bob Wright, a 'Scanlonite' executive member. It was these men who led the Engineering Union through its bitter battles with the Industrial Relations court until May 1974. But the 'Broad Left' hold on the AUEW has been neither total nor unassailable. In 1972 a factory-by-factory struggle for a large pay increase collapsed and with it much of the Communist influence in Lancashire and the North West. In elections two years later the 'Broad Left' failed to secure the hoped-for position of general secretary and some of its nominees suffered clear defeats against right-of-centre candidates. By the Executive elections of 1975, in which Bob Wright was removed and Jimmy Reid defeated for the position of Scottish representative, the balance of power on the Executive had swung decisively in favour of the moderate interests, to the detriment of the Communist Party and its allies.

These reverses in the AUEW came after a long period of intermittent conflict out of which the ordinary member had gained little. They confirm the warning that Labour leaders since the nineteenth century have sounded: the strike is a fearsome weapon that can easily misfire. For the Communist Party industrial action is the essential aspect of the 'mass struggle' through which the working class can put pressure on parliament and on government, but it is not to be entered into rashly. It should be used to bring decisive force to bear when the mass of workers are united in their aims, where the goal is limited and definable, or, where it is used for political rather than economic purposes, if it can be sustained by other forms of protest and propaganda. Since the 1920s the party has considerably modified its attitude to the strike weapon. No longer does it call for the formation of Councils of Action to organise food and transport as it did during the 1926 general strike. Indeed it rarely raises the cry of the general strike today as a means of challenging the total authority of government. In these respects the Communist Party is now more cautious than it was, and it is the rival Trotskyist or International Socialists who maintain the old Bolshevik slogans of arming the workers and rely exclusively on mass direct action under a military degree of discipline from the party.

In the 1970s it has however begun to restate the overweening power of industrial action. The Upper Clyde Shipyards crisis of 1971 made a national figure of Jimmy Reid and thrust ideas of factory occupation, work-ins and sit-ins into the forefront of the unions' repertoire. The party eagerly exploited its position and hailed the work-in there, which was securely under its control, as a fundamentally new departure. In the eyes of the ultra-left, it eventually 'sold out' to capitalism by repudiating the feasibility of placing the yard under workers' control, but to attempt to do that, as an isolated case, would have been mere syndicalism in Communist eyes. The innovation of mass picketing in the miners' strike of the following year was also heralded as a new weapon in the class struggle by all the left. For the Communist Party, a building worker, Peter Carter, proudly claimed to have been at the head of the column which blockaded the coke depot at Saltley.[47] Upper Clyde and Saltley are important because they suggested radical variation on mere withdrawals of labour with enormous potential for development and for refinement into political weapons.

These events—and those of the previous seven years—in the rising tide of militancy and Communist influence created by the winter of 1973-74 a new understanding of the potential of mass action, which was placed on the party's agenda with a prominence not seen since the 1920s. The 33rd Congress called for 'a new stage of mass political and social action, over the whole range of issues, and including various forms of direct action, strike action, mass extra-parliamentary activity, local community-based struggles as well as the utmost pressure inside parliament and the local councils'.[48]

The action came to concentrate on the miners' strike where in pursuit of a given aim a union could defy the government. The situation, the cause, the balance of forces were right for a decisive battle. Bert Ramelson, the Communist industrial organiser, hoped the TUC would develop matters a stage further to 'co-ordinate a mass confrontation to bring down this government as well as its policies'.[49] Yet even at this watershed the Communists paused, and at that point the paradoxes and inconsistencies which haunt the party came to the surface. It was unable to grasp the nettle of Marxist-Leninism and usher in socialism by mass action, so firmly wedded to the idea of gradual revolution had it become, and it merely called for the replacement of a Conservative government by a Labour one compelled to socialist policies by the power of mass struggles at some later stage. However the subsequent formulation of the elastic social contract, which satisfied most union needs, completely blunted the kind of large-scale action the Communists had envisaged. This gradualism had been a product of the party's own weakness, its diminishing membership, relative failure to attract youth, and rejection at the polls, for which it has substituted the long slow process of left unity. This has enabled its influence to grow without, ironically, improving its own state of health.

The result has been that the Communist Party is being squeezed between the Labour Left, an adjunct of which it has become, and the revolutionary sects, who reject the parliamentary road, the ideological authority of Stalinist Soviet Union, and rigid centralism. If Marxism is resurgent in the Labour Party, albeit helped by the Communist Party, and if the Trotskyists, Marxists and Anarchists have stolen the red robes of revolution, what need is there for the old King Street orthodoxy? One of the party's most celebrated members, Jimmy Reid, himself provided something of an answer in February, 1976, when he resigned, disillusioned with its performance and its policies. There is keen competition for its original place in the spectrum of socialism, not least among groups whose inspiration, like the Communists' once did, begins in the primitive Bolshevism of 1917 and the idealism of 'proletarian internationalism'.

III

The Prophecy Unfulfilled

The history of Trotskyism is a curious and tangled tale of unrealised dreams. For nearly half a century the followers of Lev Davidovich Bronstein—otherwise known as Leon Trotsky—have anticipated the collective downfall of capitalism, Stalinism and social democracy. Out of this world-wide upheaval they, the true believers of revolutionary communism, would lead the proletariat to final victory and absolute power. The consolidation of Stalinist-type regimes over much of Eastern Europe and the failure of the 'inevitable' crisis to materialise in the West, where it has always been regarded as imminent, have however assigned the Trotskyists to prolonged obscurity, politically isolated from the working class and in perpetual disarray.

In Britain as elsewhere Trotskyism's greatest battles have been fought not on the barricades of revolt but in factious struggles for survival. The curiosity of the movement is how it remained alive at all from the 1930s until the end of the 1950s, when its predictions were proved again and again to be incorrect, and how in the 1960s it was transformed into the most dynamic element of the burgeoning revolutionary left in Britain. In 1957, fewer than 300 people supported three Trotskyist groupings: by 1975 there existed three larger organisations, the Workers Revolutionary Party (formerly the Socialist Labour League), the International Marxist Group and the International Socialists (which although Trotskyist-derived and containing some Trotskyists pursues an independent line), together with six smaller groups, the Revolutionary Workers Party, Workers Fight, Socialist Charter, the Workers Socialist League, the Revolutionary Communist Group, and Militant, which is only partially Trotkyist, with a total following of approximately 14,000 people.

The development of the movement during those eighteen years of unprecedented growth only serves to emphasise its basic characteristics. From the earliest days it has been divided in ideology, organisation and methods. The Trotskyist movement is permanently locked in fierce internal debate which darts from the philosophy of world socialism to tactics for local agitation. Obscure points of theology or semantics presage irreversible schisms which ripple across the world in a prolix scholasticism. The principal areas of dispute have concerned the nature and structure of Soviet and western societies, and, increasingly in the last two decades, the character of newly independent former colonial states. Out of conflicting interpretations on these fundamental problems have arisen differing assessments of the prospects for revolution in those parts of the world where it was deemed necessary, what models of socialism Trotskyists should emulate, how they should organise in countries where the prospects for revolution are remote, and what social groups constitute the leadership of the revolutionary struggle. Some Trotskyists, for example, adhere to the fundamentals of proletarian revolution in the West as the primary objective while others amend the basic creed to 'New Left' concepts of student revolt or Third World Revolution.

The political consequences of these divergent tendencies have been to weaken Trotskyism in countless splits and divisions. Through its preoccupation with theoretical discussion the movement has subjected itself to an endless process of self-destruction whose effects have to some extent been mitigated by a parallel process of re-creation and re-alignment. Trotskyism has never been monolothic nor unbending, and presents many aspects in different situations, adapting, chameleon-like, to its surroundings as new circumstances have arisen and fresh ideas have come forward. The esoteric dogma of the Fourth International is a very different Trotskyism from that found in the Labour Party, where small groups working for the emergence of a strong left wing have rarely admitted their true allegiance, and this faceless 'entryism' contrasts sharply with the strident Trotskyism of building an open revolutionary party. Doctrinal purity is constantly stressed but is often sacrificed to capitalise upon an opportunity to create a mass movement.

Trotskyism began as a form of dissident communism, inherently weak in organisation and appeal. The profundity of its philosophical wrangling has always appeared somewhat incongruous given the movement's limited political importance and its inability to influence the matters over which it argues. Only in the last decade has it been able to escape from isolated theorising to begin to put its ideas into effect, and this transformation from obscurity to growth lies at the heart of the contemporary revolutionary movement in Britain. The Trotskyists remain divided, but their present alignments and the ways in which the various sections have risen to their recent unfamiliar prominence are a product of the movement's international character and its history, beginning with the Russian revolution and the contribution of Trotsky himself.

59

THE ORIGINS OF TROTSKYISM

At first Trotsky was a hero of the revolution.[1] He spent many years before 1917 in exile, but on his return to Russia after the fall of the Tsarist government, resumed the position of President of the St Petersburg Soviet that he had held in the abortive revolution of twelve years earlier. He subsequently headed the Military Revolutionary Committee, which organised the coup of November 1917, when his popularity and international reputation were second only to Lenin's. In the Bolshevik government Trotsky became Commissar for Foreign Affairs, negotiating the peace treaty with Germany at Brest Litovsk in 1918, and then he took on the job of Commissar for War, to build and guide to victory in civil war, the first Red Army.

Differences soon emerged between some sections of the Bolshevik leadership and the independently minded Trotsky, who had only joined the party in July 1917. But it was shortly after Lenin's death in 1924 that Trotsky's fate was sealed as the regime fought for its survival in power struggles and economic crises which permitted no compromise. Party Secretary Joseph Stalin was determined upon supreme power and the consolidation of the revolution within Russia, and Trotsky stood in his way. In 1925 Stalin secured Trotsky's removal from the Commissariat for War and two years later Trotsky and 1,500 supporters were expelled from the Party. In the following January the fallen hero, outmanoeuvred and isolated, was exiled to Central Asia and within a year, in January 1929, he was expelled from the Soviet Union.

The source of the decisive struggle which had become personified in Trotsky and Stalin concerned the problems of building on the 1917 Revolution inside Russia, and of extending its influence throughout the rest of the world. Trotsky adhered to the view, first expressed by him in 1905, that the revolutionary process must be 'uninterrupted', or to use the more familiar term, 'permanent'. By its own momentum and logic, revolution in a country like Russia, with a relatively small middle class, would proceed in the Marxist scheme, straight from its bourgeois phase to its proletarian phase, from democracy to socialism. Such revolution would not mark time between the stages, nor once begun in this way could it stop at national boundaries; indeed it could not, said Trotsky, survive in one country. He anticipated that from underdeveloped Russia revolution would spread to the more industrialised capitalist countries of the west.

In this prognosis Trotsky emphasised the role not of the peasantry who formed the majority of the population in Russia but of the urban working class, since socialism could only emerge from a capitalist society. If the Russian revolution was forced to rely on a population that was essentially counter-revolutionary, as Trotsky believed the peasantry was, then it was doomed. To exist at all the revolution needed proletarian internationalism, but if it was to have any value it also meant to Trotsky the involvement of the masses in making decisions. The bureaucracy that was gaining a stranglehold in the Soviet Union without encouraging revolt in the west was therefore doubly damaging. Stalin on the other hand formulated the doctrine of Socialism in One Country—putting the Soviet Union first and the rest of the world second—against which Trotsky's ideas were successfully portrayed as those of an unrealistic leftist heretic. After his banishment Trotsky's supporters were soon also expelled, exiled or liquidated.

By 1930 Trotskyism had ceased to exist in the Soviet Union and the movement was forced to organise elsewhere. From his expulsion until 1940, when he was murdered by a Stalinist agent with an ice pick, Trotsky lived in turn in Turkey, France, Norway and finally Mexico, and during those eleven years he consolidated the ideas which had brought him into conflict with Stalin. His works, *The Permanent Revolution* (1929) and *The Revolution Betrayed* (1936) provided those Marxist-Leninists disillusioned with the course of events in Russia with both a theoretical and a practical starting point for the regeneration of revolutionary communism. At first they were small numbers of socialist intellectuals scattered across the world but mainly in France, Poland and the United States. They organised themselves into an 'International Left Opposition', whose British section emerged in May 1932.

In that month an anonymous journal called *The Communist* appeared. It was the work of the Balham group of the Communist Party of Great Britain and its source was soon revealed. In August 1932 two of the group's members, Reginald Groves and Harry Wicks, were expelled from the party, a third, Henry Sara, was suspended and the Balham group, no more than twelve people in all, was liquidated. British Trotskyism was born.[2] The infant movement fell immediately into ideological and personal squabbles. Two of the arguments which began in the 1930s continue today: whether the Soviet Union remains, even in a limited sense, a workers' state or whether the Stalinist dictatorship has destroyed the achievements of 1917; and whether Trotskyists can hope to create their own independent parties in Britain or whether they should work inside the Labour Party to move it in a leftwards direction. Groves himself adopted the latter course, leaving Wicks and Sara in one Trotskyist group, ranged, within five years, against three others. These were the Workers International League, whose direct descendants are the Workers Revolutionary Party; a Labour Party faction which published a magazine called *The Militant*; and a Marxist League, led by the writer C.L.R. James, producing a journal entitled *Workers Fight*.

None of these groups had more than a score of supporters, drawn mainly from the ranks of the Communist Party and the Independent Labour Party, which had disaffiliated from the Labour Party in 1932. They had no influence and no popular appeal in the years before the outbreak of the Second World War. Indeed in the political history of the 1930s, with slump, national government, the rise of Fascism and its battles with Communism, the Trotskyists do not deserve a footnote.

The historian and biographer of Trotsky, the late Isaac Deutscher, has described the predicament of all the European Trotskyists during their first decade:

'The new converts to Trotskyism started out with a determination to shake the party they loved and to make it see the light which they themselves studying Trotsky's writings, had excitedly seen; but soon they found themselves shut within small hermetic circles, where they were to accustom themselves to live as noble lepers in a political wilderness. Tiny groups which cannot hitch themselves quickly to any mass movement are quickly soured with frustration. No matter how much intelligence and vigour they may possess, if they find no practical application for these they are bound to use up their strength in scholastic squabbling and intense personal animosities which lead to endless splits and mutual anathemas. A certain amount of such sectarian wrangling has, of course, always marked the progress of any revolutionary movement. But what distinguishes the vital movement from the arid sect is that the former finds in time and the latter does not, the salutary transition from the squabbling and splits to genuine political mass action.

The Trotskyist groups did not lack men of brains, integrity and enthusiasm. They were unable to break through the ostracism which Stalinism had imposed upon them; and, in their beyond-the-pale existence they could never rid themselves of their internal dissensions.'[3]

The first attempt to escape from this cocoon of stagnation came in 1938 with a gathering of twenty Trotskyists near Paris, which has entered Trotskyist mythology as the Founding Congress of the Fourth International, otherwise to be called the World Party of Socialist Revolution.

THE FOURTH INTERNATIONAL:
WORLD PARTY OF SOCIALIST REVOLUTION

Since internationalism was a fundamental canon of Trotskyism it was natural that the movement would soon acquire a formal, international political dimension. The establishment by Trotsky of a new Communist International, the Fourth, was the outcome of many years thinking about the Soviet Union and the part the Soviet Communist Party could play in advancing world revolution. However the attempt to revitalise the international movement was premature: the outbreak of war in 1939 and the Trotskyists' capacity for internal strife destroyed it before it had begun. It re-formed after the war, since when it has exercised a decisive influence over its British affiliates in determining their ideological programmes and the orientation of their activities. The present day divisions of Trotskyism derive largely from this international context.

The Foundations (1933–45): During the early years of exile Trotsky believed that the Communist Party of the Soviet Union was capable of reform and that it and the Third International, the Comintern, should be influenced from within, without creating a new party nor a new International. But by 1933 Trotsky had begun to change his mind. Under Stalin's leadership the Third International had been unable to prevent the defeat of communism in Germany, where the party had been destroyed and would need rebuilding. Trotsky concluded that so also would the Soviet Union's Communist Party need reconstruction and consequently the Soviet-dominated International too. He was in no position to influence affairs within Russia but he could declare a new International.

The first congress of the Fourth International assembled on September 3, 1938, at the home of a French Trotskyist, Alfred Rosmer, in the suburbs of Paris. It comprised twenty people from eleven countries, including C.L.R. James of the Marxist League and J. Harber of Militant, representing Britain.[4] The occasion had persuaded the British groups, with the exception of the Workers International League, to unite in an organisation known as the Revolutionary Socialist League. The alliance was short-lived. On return from this suburban journey disputes arose over the way the International should be supported and over the meaning and implementation of the agreed programme.

There was however a somewhat limited organisation to support. Most of the principal political agencies of the International had been set up some years before the congress, but according to one French delegate the whole organisation 'was little more than a fiction: none of its so-called Executives and International Bureau had been able to work in the past few years. The "sections" of the International consisted of a few dozen or at most a few hundred members each'.[5] Only the American section, the Socialist Workers Party, whose leader, Max Schachtmann, presided over the congress, approached a four-figure membership. Indeed the Polish delegation opposed the whole idea of a new International because they regarded it as so weak as to be worthless. That the International was born out of 'the greatest defeats of the proletariat in history'[6]—the rise of Mussolini, Hitler, Franco and Stalin—was precisely what commended it to Trotsky, for he imagined these defeats would be followed by a 1917-type workers' uprising across the whole of Europe against Fascism.

One of the reasons why the International had not gathered earlier, since its organisational structure had been for some time drawn up, was that it lacked a concrete political programme. Then Trotsky himself wrote one, in the summer of 1938, a 15,000 word document entitled 'The Death Agony of Capitalism and the Tasks of the Fourth International'. This was adopted at the Paris meeting and has remained the bible of Trotskyism since then. It depicts a disintegrating capitalist system with the mass of the people 'threatened now more than at any other time with the danger of being cast into the pit of pauperism'[7] and the middle class retreating to the last redoubt of fascism.

Trotsky described the Soviet Union as a 'degenerated workers' state' in which a new revolutionary upsurge was needed to overthrow the bureaucracy and the oppression of 'Stalin's Bonapartist clique'. The 'Death Agony's' proposals for proceeding to international revolution varied according to the existing kind of regime. For the capitalist countries, upon which the programme concentrates, it describes a mode of action which Trotskyists adopt today and the terminology of which—opening the books of capitalist concerns, a sliding scale of wages and hours, workers' control and armed pickets—is still used.

The political strategy of Trotskyism in capitalist countries begins with the Transitional Demand, which a modern exponent has described as 'putting forward demands which seem important and reasonable to the working class at a particular time and a particular level of political consciousness but which are incapable of being met under capitalism'.[8] Such demands would in the present day include the absolute assurance of full employment, a constantly rising standard of living and good cheap housing. The application of the transitional demands is most appropriate in the economic arena and the 'Death Agony' regards the trade unions as principal agents in the transition from capitalism to revolution, but ultimately subordinate to the dictates of the party machine.

The programme develops in some detail the road to socialism in an industrial society. Its theme is organised activity, building on strikes and factory occupations to challenge firstly employers in factory committees, then, as the revolution moves on to the streets, through soviets, which challenge directly the existing institutions of government. This situation of dual power between the establishment and the soviet can only be resolved by force and the Trotskyist programme emphasises the importance of developing a proletarian army at an early stage, around the nucleus of strike pickets: 'In connection with every strike and street demonstration it is imperative to propagate the necessity of creating workers' groups for self-defence. It is necessary to write this slogan into the programme of the revolutionary wing of the trade unions. It is imperative whenever possible, beginning with youth defence groups, to organise groups for self-defence to drill and acquaint them with the use of arms.

'A new upsurge of the mass movement should serve not only to increase the number of these units but also to unite them according to neighbourhoods, cities, regions ... It is necessary to advance the slogan of a workers' militia as the one serious guarantee for the inviolability of workers' organisations, meetings and press.'[9]

Thus equipped, the working class would be in a position to expropriate the resources of capitalism, expose the secrets of big business and place industry under workers' control. But the programme says little of the mechanics and government of a workers' state, nor does it describe the role of the party, to which it states that the trade unions and soviets are subordinate. The Fourth International's plan, in fact, is only a 'Transitional Programme'—by which title it is most generally known—and it describes the destruction of the old regime, not the creation of socialism. The Trotskyists' reputation for being explicit about the evils of capitalism and how it would end them, but less forthcoming about what would replace them, began here.

The outbreak of war soon after the Fourth International had come into being shattered the movement. Its international agencies never began to operate, most national sections were forced by occupation or emergency restrictions to cease activity—although some French Trotskyists joined the resistance—and others relapsed into the self-defeating theorising which engendered further splits. The American Socialist Workers Party was an early casualty. In 1940 a minority led by Schactmann broke away, in the belief that the Nazi-Soviet pact had confirmed that the Soviet Union had ceased to be a workers' state, although the majority remained convinced that it retained that status and should therefore be defended.

In Britain the war further divided the Trotskyists. The Revolutionary Socialist League split into three factions, all of which decided against any open activity during the war, while the Workers International League remained in overt and vigorous opposition to the war throughout its duration. By 1944 it was able to take over the moribund RSL in a unified Revolutionary Communist Party and acquire, for what it was worth, official recognition as the British section of the Fourth International.[10]

Under the title of the RCP, which effectively brought together all the active Trotskyists in Britain, the movement came out of the war less pessimistically than it had entered it. In 1945 Jock Haston, the general secretary of the RCP, contested Neath in the general election. He polled 1,781 votes against 6,290 for a Nationalist candidate and 30,847 for the Labour victor. The Trotskyists were soon to discover their place in the welfare state of post-war Britain.

The Post War Crisis of Trotskyism (1946–53): Immediately after the war, the Fourth International held high hopes both for revolutionary prospects and for the future of its own organisation, only to have these quickly dashed. The International began with the essential task of re-forming itself. A pre-congress conference in 1946 elected a new International Secretariat with a Greek factory worker, Michael Raptis (more widely known as Michael Pablo) as its secretary, chose a ten-man Executive Committee representing eight of its 22 countries and formally recognised the RCP as the British section. The second World Congress of the Fourth International took place in April 1948, attended by 50 people from 22 countries. It reaffirmed its analysis of the Soviet Union as a 'degenerated workers' state' but considered there had been no socialist revolution in the emergent People's Democracies of Eastern Europe or in North Korea. For the west, the International declared: 'there is no reason to suppose that we are facing a new epoch of capitalist stabilisation and development'.[11] In other words it believed revolution was on the agenda but by the third World Congress of 1950, at which it recategorised the emergent People's Democracies and North Korea as 'degenerated workers' states', it accepted that there would be no revolution in western Europe or North America.

These shifts in ideology and political strategy had fundamental repercussions among British Trotskyists, which are still important today. In June 1946 the International Executive Committee had suggested 'the decisive orientation of the British Trotskyists towards essential work in the ranks of the Labour Party'.[12] This became known as entryism: penetrating a social democratic party to build a Trotskyist current of opinion which would capitalise upon any leftward swing in that party and would work for the replacement of 'right wing' leaders and policies by Marxist ones.

There are three main reasons for adopting the entryist strategy: firstly in anticipation of an imminent crisis which does not permit time to build an independent party, but which will cause the social democratic party to fall behind the Marxist leadership as its right-wing leaders become discredited; secondly, for the very opposite reason, because revolution is distant and a separate revolutionary party would not survive in such an unfavourable climate, and thirdly where entryism is the preliminary step to forming a party and is used to win support from a traditional organisation to secure the political base of the new party.

In 1946 a minority of the RCP, at most fifty people, led by Gerry Healy, wished to adopt entryism for the first purpose, which corresponded with the expectations of the International Executive Committee. This division fatally injured the remainder of the open RCP, of about 150 people, for it could not compete against the Communist Party now that it had resumed full-scale political activity after supporting the war effort, let alone against a Labour government. The RCP declined in spirit and in numbers and in 1949 dissolved itself to allow individual members join Healy's group inside the Labour Party. By this time the motivation for entryism had changed to the second reason—that of the extreme weakness of the revolutionary position. Indeed some of the RCP members left active revolutionary politics altogether.

One group of British Trotskyists, only thirty-three strong, was prepared for entryism but not with Healy and not under the aegis of a Fourth International which regarded the Soviet Union and the People's Democracies as workers' states. Led by Tony Cliff, they followed the line of Max Schachtmann that the Soviet Union was a capitalist not a proletarian state, with the ruling bureaucracy fulfilling the capitalist function. The group began to publish a journal, Socialist Review, in the autumn of 1950 and became known by that or as the 'State Capitalists'. At its founding congress at Whitsun 1951, it declared the intention—which was never carried out—to 'fight for the building of the Fourth International, being a genuine Trotskyist organisation. We shall apply for membership of the Fourth International'.[13] Today it is known as the International Socialist group and has severed its connections with the Fourth International.[14]

With the exception of the tiny groups around Gerry Healy and Tony Cliff, organised Trotskyism effectively ceased to exist after 1949. Those Trotskyists that remained were preoccupied with entryism and did not emphasise too openly their affiliations for fear of being cast out into a wilderness in which they might perish. Clearly the Fourth International, by permitting the division of the RCP and by its own theoretical juggling, had greatly contributed to the demise of its organisation in Britain. The movement, internationally and in its national sections, had failed to adapt to the new situation. The divisions of individual groups such as the RCP were soon superseded by more splits in the Fourth International itself, when the fortunes of Trotskyism reached their nadir.

A Movement Divided: (1953–63): At its fourth world congress in 1954 the Fourth International split into two sections which remain opposed to this day. The immediate cause of the division was whether the Soviet Union after Stalin's death could be reformed in a way which would satisfy Trotskyist puritanism and remove the need for a new Russian Revolution. The majority, led by Pablo, argued that this was the case. Behind Pablo stood an International Secretariat, which inherited most of the Trotskyist movement administrative apparatus but which, from that point on, has displayed greater doctrinal flexibility; against him emerged an International Committee which has represented a more rigid concept of Trotskyism. Supporting the Secretariat were the French, including Pierre Frank, a former colleague of Trotsky himself, who spent much of the Second World War interned in the Isle of Man, and aligned with the Committee were Gerry Healy and the American Socialist Workers' Party. In most countries, including Britain, the already miniscule organisation split down the middle over the issue.

The programme of the International Secretariat as developed from the fourth Congress until its ninth congress in 1969 rested on three main points: first, it marked a partial return to a Trotskyism of the pre-Fourth International phase in suggesting that reform rather than new revolution could overcome the degeneration of workers' states, which now included Yugoslavia and China as well as the Soviet Union. Secondly, the Secretariat regarded colonial revolution as the 'predominant factor in the world'.[15] It lent its unconditional support at its fifth Congress in 1957, to 'all struggles of the colonial peoples against imperialism regardless of their temporary leadership'.[16] Thirdly, hopes for revolution in the west had vanished completely and the International Secretariat clung to deep entryism. At the sixth World Congress in 1961 its manifesto stated: 'In western Europe the general task remains essentially through the work of entryism, to build up inside the mass organisations and the Labour movement strong left wings which are capable of playing the role of rallying points and centralisers for various left-wing initiatives . . . Special attention must be paid to the situation in Great Britain where today the strongest left-wing tendency in

68

western Europe is developing under extremely favourable conditions for a decisive intervention by revolutionry Marxists'.[17]

In reality, the British Section, the Revolutionary Socialist League, was extremely weak. It was formed in 1953 out of those former RCP members who followed neither Healy nor Cliff, but was at no time in any way influential or numerous. Until 1958 it produced a *Workers' International Review*, but when that was wound up it relied for the next four years upon the *Fourth International*, the English language version of the organisation's magazine run from Paris, and it possessed no journal of its own. Indeed its entryism inside the Labour Party became so deep that when the International Secretariat cast off entryism in 1968 the RSL had so completely changed its form that it was incapable of fulfilling its obligations to come into the open: it had vanished from sight.[18] The International itself however showed a slow but steady growth: at its 1957 Congress in Italy 100 delegates from 25 countries attended, and at the next gathering, in Switzerland in 1961, 170 people represented Trotskyist supporters in 30 countries. In 1958 organised and active sections existed in Argentina, Brazil, Germany, France, Italy, Greece, Japan and Uruguay.[19]

The International Committee on the other hand had fewer sections but they were at this time individually stronger and more active. Besides Healy's group they included members in Argentina, in France as well as the Socialist Workers' Party in the United States. But it possessed no effective secretariat and was internationally insignificant. The International Committee as represented by Healy opposed the shift in emphasis of the 'Pabloite' International Secretariat particularly on the questions of colonial revolution, the primacy of which it believed was a distortion of Marxism, and on entryism. Healy had found unrelenting opposition from the right of the Labour Party and from the more cautious entryists of the *Socialist Review Group* and the RSL whom he accused of 'liquidating' the development of his organisation by their opposition. The 'Pabloite' concept of entryism, he believed, consisted 'essentially of an abandonment of the perspective of constructing independent Marxist parties, relying instead on the inevitable left development of the petty bourgeois revisionists of the Labour bureaucracies'.[20]

Because of its more strident tone the International Committee was eventually forced to abandon entryism. In 1957 Healy was able to gain recruits from among former members of the Communist Party who left it after the invasion of Hungary and in 1959 he created the Socialist Labour League which effectively ended his entryist period. The International Secretariat with its deep entryism was unwilling to exploit these events. For a decade its strategy seemed to stifle any

69

tangible progress and it was not until the middle of the 1960s that its flexibility enabled it to be joined to an independent revolutionary movement and one which the International Committee failed to harness.

Realignment and Revival (1963–75): Following this period of weakness, the last decade has been one of unique expansion for the Trotskyist movement. This advance has entailed both a numerical increase in support and a lessening of dependence on the Labour Party. The upsurge has however been less uniformly beneficial to the Fourth International for while some international bodies have flourished others have virtually collapsed and although they may consist of large separate national sections are irrelevant as a coherent international movement. The International has divided in a time of comparative strength just as it did during periods of undoubted weakness.

This era began with renewed ideological disputes which led to a further realignment of the forces of the Fourth International in an arrangement which has remained substantially unchanged since. The arguments were occasioned by the successes of the Cuban and Algerian revolutions, which the Secretariat wholeheartedly supported.[21] It also backed the Lanka Samaja Party in Ceylon which had consistently received up to 10 per cent of votes in general elections and joined in 1964 a government led by Mrs Bandaranaika.[22]

None of these developments met with the International Committee's approval and it was particularly scathing about Cuba, where it argued there was no Leninist Party and where the leadership was 'petty bourgeois'. To the Committee, Cuba was not a workers' state, but it was not unanimous in this opinion. The American Socialist Workers' Party shared the view of the International Secretariat and after a prolonged debate the Americans discovered how politically far removed they were from the Socialist Labour League and joined the International Secretariat in 1963, which then became known as the Unified or United Secretariat.

Since 1963 the International Committee has struggled, unable to shake off its inherent weaknesses, and its subsequent efforts to revitalise its activities have only courted further disasters. Its aims have been the 'reconstruction' of the Fourth International and 'the centralised leadership of the world revolutionary party'[23] on a programme which rejects the 'Stalinism' of the conventional Communist Parties and the 'Third Worldism' of the Pabloite Unified Secretariat, and emphasises doctrinal correctness, organisational efficiency and the indisputable role of the western proletariat in making the revolution. Its main attempts to rebuild its base of support were centred on the youth organisations of the two largest sections, the Socialist Labour League's Young

Socialists and the French Organisation Communiste Internationale's Alliance of Revolutionary Youth. Its ineffectiveness however was demonstrated in 1968 when the OCI played very little part in the French revolt of May and June, although its hastily formed Federation of Revolutionary Students acquired a reputation as a militant, indeed violent and fanatical, body.[24] Neither was among the most important groups of the revolt. The SLL later said that the OCI and its subsidiaries were 'unable to grasp the revolutionary opportunities which presented themselves. The situation in May-June 1968 caught it [the OCI] by surprise and unprepared'.[25] The main reason for this however had been the neglect of the International Committee Trotskyists of the student movement, and the SLL took no part in any student demonstrations in Britain during the period 1966–69.

It persisted with this chosen course and continued to boost its youth section. This course finally undid the Committee's whole structure. In July 1971 more than 5,000 young people from 32 countries gathered at Essen in West Germany for a rally organised by the International Committee. Not all those present were Trotskyists, and a distinctly Trotskyist motion put forward by the Committee was defeated—with the support of the OCI. A furious argument ensued in which the SLL and the OCI resurrected all their old differences.[26]

By March 1972 the International Committee had fallen apart. The majority section led by the SLL consisted of the Workers' League (USA), the International Workers' League (Greece), League for a Workers' Vanguard (Ireland) the Revolutionary Communist League (Ceylon) and the Socialist Workers' League (Germany). The OCI formed their own 'International Committee for the Reconstruction of the Fourth International', which claimed the membership of the League of Revolutionary Hungarian Socialists, the Bolivian Workers Revolutionary Party and the Marxist Workers League of Mexico. In 1973–74 it entered into talks with the Unified Secretariat with a view to amalgamation. Although it describes itself as 'the only revolutionary tendency in the world',[27] the International Committee is the poor relation of international Trotskyism. Its domestic face is distinctly different, for the SLL (now the Workers Revolutionary Party) possesses a trade union section, the largest Trotskyist youth organisation and one which is mainly working class in composition, and also had its own daily newspaper. These revolutionary conceptions, built on the urban working class, have so far been less internationally infectious than the causes of anti-colonialism and student revolt embraced by the Unified Secretariat. Yet it too has had its divisions.

The realignment of 1963, which set the scene for the decline of the International Committee was dignified by the Secretariat as the

Reunification of Trotskyism. But on the very eve of this auspicious event a blemish disfigured its appearance: in 1962 the Latin American Bureau of the Secretariat broke away to form an independent group under the leadership of an Uruguayan, Juan Posadas. Its main thesis was taken from a Trotskyist doctrine of the immediate post-war period: that capitalism was dangerously unstable and that in its collapse would come a nuclear war, from the ruins of which socialism would emerge. His supporters were depicted as a maniacal fringe desiring nuclear war as a precondition for the revolution and they were, except in South America, very few. In Britain they comprise a 'Revolutionary Workers Party (Trotskyist-Posadist) British Section of the IVth International'. It publishes a monthly newspaper, *Red Flag* and a theoretical journal, the *European Marxist Review* which consist mainly of the statements of Posadas, who finances them, and oscillate between support for the left wing of the Labour Party, wherein is seen a potential leadership, and the Maoist groups whose undaunted dedication it admires.

Although the main strength of the Posadist Fourth International is in South America, small groups do exist in Belgium, France, West Germany, Italy and Spain. South American Trotskyism is a very different animal from its British or European counterpart.[28] In South America, unlike any other part of the world, Trotskyism has meant armed revolutionary warfare. In April 1961 the International met in Buenos Aires to plan political and guerrilla movements across the continent but particularly in Peru, Brazil and Guatemala. It was the desire to emulate the Cuban experience that prompted Posadas to branch out alone and launch a concerted campaign. The activities of the Trotskyist guerrillas spread to Bolivia, Ecuador and Uruguay, from where Posadas still runs his organisation and publishes journals in four languages. Two of the most famous revolutionaries to join the International were Hugo Blanco, a peasant leader who had been fighting a guerrilla campaign in Peru since 1956 and whose imprisonment to a twenty-year sentence seven years later met with protests from Trotskyists throughout the world, and in Guatemala, a former army officer, Yon Sosa, who led a guerrilla group which was affiliated to the Fourth International from 1963 until 1966, when Sosa broke with it over an alleged misappropriation of funds. He was shot dead four years later in Mexico. The campaign ended in defeat and in further dissolution for Trotskyists. It was ironic that the movement should have launched itself into battle among a backward peasantry rather than an urban working class. It illustrated how elastic Trotskyism had become, and how desperate to find fertile ground for its theories, that it could bend basic teaching in the name of doctrinal purity.

Since then, as the centre of conflict has moved increasingly away from the countryside to the cities, the Posadist Trotskyists have acquired their own urban guerrilla force, the ERT (Workers' Revolutionary Army), formed in 1970 by members of the Argentinian Revolutionary Workers' Party. The union which survives in the Posadist International between the guerrillas of Latin America and the English propagandists of the Revolutionary Workers Party, whose office lies a mere hundred yards from Leicester Square, is more mystical than practical. Indeed Michael Pablo himself has questioned the very idea of a Fourth International and has concluded that it is no longer able to further the cause of world revolution, so nebulous and incoherent has it become.

In the early 1960s he set up an African Commission for the International based in Algeria and wished to use it to further revolt in that continent. But as with Posadas, the European section refused to support plans for military action, although it sympathised with the anti-colonialist cause. Preoccupied with events in Algeria and absent from his post, Pablo lost the secretaryship in 1964, and emphasising the new primacy of the Third World in the modern revolutionary process, left the Secretariat altogether in the next year to form his own 'Revolutionary Marxist Tendency of the Fourth International'. It gathered a handful of adherents in Britain by 1970 who published for two years an *International Marxist Review*. Dejected and failed, the Pablo tendency eventually broke altogether with the Fourth International and disbanded. Its few supporters in England who still believed in Trotskyism gravitated towards the International Marxist Group, by that time the representatives of the Unified Secretariat.

During the period that Posadas and Pablo were attempting to chart their own individual courses towards revolution, great changes had occurred in the Secretariat. It waited until the second half of the 1960s before abandoning entryism, after which it emerged as an energetic organisation, willing to amend the holy writ of the Transitional Programme to respond to new forms of activism. To the Secretariat, as well as to many other radicals, it appeared by 1966–67 that the raw material for a world wide revolutionary upsurge lay in student protest and the anti-Vietnam war campaign.

The conjunction between these two movements reached its highest point and developed into a distinct form of revolutionism in France.[29] There the Secretariat organised furiously so that its protégés were in the forefront of the events which culminated in the riots of May and June 1968, the most serious revolutionary challenge to any post-war western government. As early as April 1966 the Revolutionary Communist Youth group, the JCR, was formed, a breakaway from the orthodox Union of Communist Students (UCF) and allied to the Trotskyist Parti Communist International. Later that year the JCR joined the Comité Vietnam National, the equivalent of the British Vietnam Solidarity Campaign established at the same time. These French Trotskyists met their British opposite numbers in 1967 at a conference to discuss the co-ordination of Vietnam demonstrations.[30]

The JCR also struck up contacts with the '22nd of March Movement' of Daniel Cohn-Bendit and together they became the most important political leaders of the May revolt, prominent on the barricades in the Sorbonne and on the Action Committees, as a disciplined, dedicated vanguard, bringing together the disparate forces of revolt. The men who for a quarter of a century had kept the Fourth International alive appeared in support of the students: Pierre Frank, the one time colleague of Trotsky, and Ernest Mandel, a Belgian political scientist and theoretician of student revolt, who has made many speaking visits to Britain since 1968 as the guest of the International Marxists. In June when the revolt had spent its force and the conservative forces rallied, the JCR, CVN and PCI, together with the International Committee Trotskyists were among a dozen organisations declared illegal. The revolutionary euphoria had been dashed but the Unified Secretariat had undergone a radical transformation.

In Britain, the Secretariat's position at first looked less promising. At the beginning of the 1960s the Revolutionary Socialist League dropped its title and its Trotskyist identity in the interests of entryism. The Secretariat floated a number of ephemeral magazines to keep its cause alive, and the main distributor for these was Pat Jordan, a former Communist who had joined the Labour Party in Nottingham, where he ran a bookshop. In 1965, six years after he first became the English agent for the *Fourth International* magazine, Jordan assumed the effective leadership of the International Marxist Group around the journal *The Week*. This began as an entryist body, but after successful exploitation of the Vietnam movement came into the open in 1968 and was recognised in the following year as the British section of the Fourth International.[31]

The next World Congress held by the Unified Secretariat, the ninth since 1938 and third since 1963, took place in Paris in May 1969. One hundred delegates from thirty countries confirmed the impression of the previous year: that the youth and in particular the students constituted a new revolutionary vanguard in common cause with the proponents of black power in America and the anti-colonial guerrillas of the Third World. The western working class, if the French experience offered any guidance, was wrapped in materialism or at best a conservative communism: the young would have to take the lead in revitalising the organs of revolution. At the end of the 1960s this brand of Trotskyism transcended the confines of Fourth International obscurity, for in its internationalism, emphasis on youth and in direct action, it became synonymous also with the current vogue of the New Left.

Within a very short time however this strategy was seen to be erroneous. Youth, and still less the students, could neither make, lead nor even detonate a Marxist revolution: the proletariat remained the decisive class. By 1974 economic crises and inflation had restated this basic truth and the Fourth International was at the time of its next Congress prepared to concede three earlier mistakes. First, there had been 'over-specialisation in applying the entry tactic'[32] which had created difficulties, when the shift to independent activity came, for sections who were unable to make the switch or did it too slowly. Secondly, the International acknowledged that its emphasis on youth had divorced the Trotskyists from the working class, and thirdly it conceded that this had led to a decline into one of unfruitful propagandising as the student vanguard vanished from its hands.

To recover from the effects of these errors and to regain sight of fundamental aims the International set itself new political tasks. These included 'systematic intervention in all agitation among workers in all strikes and campaigns around economic demands'[33] and, through propaganda and education, broadening out these struggles to attack the capitalist system and popularise ideas of workers' control and shop floor organisation through strike and shop-stewards committees. The basic tasks of education should be to instil in the workers a 'non-electoralist and non-parliamentarian view of the question of power' so that workers would be aware of 'the need for armed self-defence against the violence of big capital, both of the extra-legal variety (fascist gangs, private armed forces of the capitalists, secret police forces, strike breakers) and its "legal" variety (police, riot squads and armies) and to undertake a campaign of anti-militarist propaganda including in the army itself'.

The International hoped that by these efforts 'when the next explosion of mass struggle occurs whether it takes the form of mass political strikes, a general strike involving the occupation of factories—there will be a sufficient number of revolutionary worker cadres in the factories, with enough prestige and influence, the revolutionary Marxist organisation will be established in enough places . . . for organs of dual power to spring up in the main factories and regions of the country, for them to federate rapidly into a single system of dual power (a system of the Soviet type even though its name and origins might vary considerably)'. The ultimate aim was restated as a World

Socialist Republic of Workers' and Peasants' Councils governed by 'proletarian democracy'. The Unified Secretariat above any other body had given concrete international expression to an international movement in the form of student revolt. It had glimpsed its dream and did not want to lose its grip but sought to apply the lesson of 1968 to the working class, and to do so returned to the gospel of the Transitional Programme. However the International acknowledges that it has not yet got the means—mass Marxist parties—to carry out this programme, and the political consciousness of the working class is very unevenly developed.

In relation to other Trotskyist bodies the Secretariat is a relatively flourishing organisation. The main burden of work falls however on the national sections, who implement the policies of the International in the context of their own situations, although all of them as a condition of their membership aspire to be a mass revolutionary party. At present, besides the IMG in Britain, the Secretariat's affiliates include the Revolutionary Communist Front in France, the successor to the PCI and JCR and which was for a time known as the Ligue Communiste;[34] an Argentinian section which by the mid 1970s had succeeded the French as the largest group; the Socialist Workers' Party (USA); Revolutionary Workers' Leagues in Belgium, Denmark, Sweden and Switzerland; the Revolutionary Marxist Group in Northern Ireland; the Revolutionary Communist League in Spain, which broke from the Basque separatist movement, the ETA in 1970; with other sections or sympathisers in West Germany, Italy, Japan, Lebanon, Israel, Portugal, India, Ceylon and Canada. These individual sections gather occasionally for tactical discussions on matters of mutual interest, such as student campaigns, or as in 1969 in Turin between workers from Fiat, Pirelli and Renault for planning co-ordinated industrial propaganda in multi-national companies and between every three and five years they come together for major congresses.

The World Congresses of the Fourth International determine its policy and the strategic orientation of the movement. Congress is claimed to be the highest authority of the International and has the power to recognise and discipline national sections. It elects an International Executive Committee of thirty-one members, drawn from as many member countries as possible and which meets every six months to ensure that the policies proposed at congress are being carried out without dissent—once a decision has been democratically discussed the decisions of the congress must be obeyed: this is the principle of 'democratic centralism'. The Executive Committee forms any necessary sub-committees and a Unified Secretariat of six to ten members from its own numbers, although other members of the Executive Committee may attend and vote at the Secretariat's meetings. The Secretariat is responsible for publishing journals and magazines in the International's name, for producing policy documents and press statements and prepares the draft manifestoes which form the basis for discussion at world congresses. It is in day-to-day charge of the running of the organisation from its offices in Brussels and its work is financed by the subscriptions from national sections of one-sixth their regular income. Any section which fails to honour this requirement for longer than six months loses its rights of proportional representation at world congresses.[35]

Demands on individual members, national sections and the international agencies of the International are high in terms of finance and of constant activity. Heretical opinions, though expressed, inevitably lead to a clash with the centralised enforcement of policy. Most sections have remained small and exlusive, but fiercely dedicated. The supporters of this wing of the Fourth International remain preponderantly students rather than workers, for the legacy of 1968 dies hard. It is not surprising perhaps that there are other pseudo-Trotskyist groups who hover on the fringes of the established Fourth International.

One of these peripheral groups is Workers Fight, which from 1968 until December 1971 was a 'Left-Opposition' within the International Socialist group.[36] It was invited in 1972 by the Unified Secretariat to discuss with the IMG the possibility of amalgamation. The talks broke down over differences on doctrine and on the conduct of major propaganda campaigns, but the Workers Fight group declares its qualified support for the Unified Secretariat, remaining critical of the International's inability to build a truly working class party in Britain, which it ascribes to its 'theoretical degeneration'.[37]

Workers Fight does however accept the existence of the International, unlike the newest Trotskyist group to appear in Britain, the Socialist Charter. This is primarily an entryist group which began in 1970 in support of a left wing movement in the Labour Party in pursuit of a charter of socialist policies.[38] At the end of 1973 it declared its Trotskyist sympathies, although it remains in the Labour Party. It maintains that the Fourth International 'no longer exists and that all we have at present is a collection of disparate Trotskyist tendencies completely divergent as to both national and international orientations, varying to an incredible degree in ideological presuppositions, a sad wreckage of a movement'.[39] The Chartists call for the recreation of the International and lean towards the politics of the International Committee, rather than the 'New Leftism' of the Unified Secretariat, but their intention is to continue their own separate course and build on a policy of open entryism in the Labour Party, whose attitude to Marxism is, in the mid-1970s, markedly less hostile than that encountered by Healy's supporters a decade earlier.

For so much of its history, and for so many of its sections, the Fourth International has been little more than the fiction that was described at its foundation congress in 1938. It has seen its introspective pre-occupation with theory lead to friction, and friction to schism. It appears presumptuous, even preposterous, because it has been no more than a distant observer of the events over which it has spent so much energy in debate, and its goal of the world party is as distant now as it was in 1938. Internationally the movement has appeared weak and isolated, an unnatural species forced to find roots outside its natural habitat of Russia without sympathetic governments and sponsors. It is surprising it has survived at all.

Trotskyism's resourcefulness lies in its adaptability in time and place. The primitive Trotskyists of the International Committee, the New Leftists of the Unified Secretariat, the entryists, the party builders, and the guerrillas of South America in illegal organisations—all qualify for membership of the movement: they claim allegiance to a Fourth International, believe in the Transitional Programme and share certain views of the fate of capitalism and on the nature of Soviet socialism, although there is little intrinsic unity between these disparate social groups and political factions. Trotskyism has given them a sense of purpose and solidarity which they would not otherwise hold. It appeals also to those who seek the essence of revolutionary communism unsullied by Stalinism or the realities of power. This idealism and its hope for a genuine Internationalism outside major power blocs enabled Trotskyism to survive in the hands of a few dedicated activists until it was able to attach itself to a movement searching for those principles. Thus the inherent weaknesses of Trotskyism are also the sources of its appeal.

The beliefs and the alignments of British Trotskyists have evolved on the confused and largely ineffectual level of the International, but their domestic performances have however been measurably more effective. They have seen many of their basic ideas gain wide currency: in the discrediting in the eyes of socialists of the Soviet Union's leadership of world socialism, and of the potential of social democracy to change society and in the various expressions of direct action and rank and file discontent. The Trotskyists have gradually been able to dispense with the protective cover of the Labour Party and seize upon the opportunities afforded by change and crisis to reach some new and not unreceptive audiences.

IV

Faces of Trotskyism

I

TOWARDS THE WORKERS' REVOLUTIONARY PARTY

On a Sunday afternoon in November 1973 some 3,000 people gathered in the Odeon, Hammersmith, to celebrate the formation of the Workers' Revolutionary Party. For its national secretary, Gerry Healy, that day marked the climax of forty-five years of ceaseless activity which began in 1928 when at the age of thirteen he joined the Communist Party. Eight years later, disillusioned by the failure of the Communists to win mass support among the working class, he left and joined the Labour Party, where he began his long association with Trotskyism in the form of the entryist group around the journal, *Militant*. Healy parted company with the *Militant* supporters in 1938 to become a member of the Workers' International League, that half of the British Trotskyist movement which refused to support the embryonic Fourth International. From this point on, a direct line of descent passes through a succession of groups to the Workers' Revolutionary Party, the largest-ever Trotskyist organisation in Britain.

Under Healy's leadership these groups have all pursued solitary, not to say sectarian, paths. During the war the Workers' International League was one of the very few political bodies that opposed the general national effort. Four of its members received prison sentences, subsequently quashed on appeal, for encouraging workers to strike against the 'imperialist' war. But the League slowly grew, so that by 1944 it had 250 members and a circulation of approximately 2,000 for its magazine. It was then able to absorb into its ranks, under the title of the Revolutionary Communist Party,[1] the hundred or so members of other Trotskyist groups who had chosen to remain dormant during the war.

After the war the RCP acquired, for what it was worth, recognition as the official British section of the Fourth International and, anticipating a massive upsurge of social unrest, secured the permission of the International to divide itself into two sections: the majority group to continue as an open party, and the rest, led by Healy, to enter the Labour Party and try to move it to the left during the impending, inevitable crisis. But when social democracy, not revolution, emerged from the aftermath of war, Healy switched his justification for entryism to the impossibility of building revolutionary parties in such an unfavourable situation, while the overt RCP lost all appeal and purpose to the extent that by 1949 it chose to disband itself. Of those who continued, one small group followed Tony Cliff into what became International Socialism, another section led by Ted Grant eventually re-formed a Revolutionary Socialist League, while the remainder joined forces with Gerry Healy.

Healy set up a new body, the Socialist Fellowship, with a magazine called *Socialist Outlook*. But by 1951 the Labour Party had banned them both and within two years, after friction between Healy and his colleagues, another Trotskyist enterprise collapsed. Undaunted, Healy redoubled his efforts in the Labour Party; he became chairman of the Streatham Hill Ward branch in South London, cultivated the Bevanites who had been so successful in the 1952 elections to the party's National Executive, and launched another journal, *Labour Review*, to campaign for left-wing policies. At the same time Healy dabbled in industrial agitation, winning some support in the Merseyside docks, among London Transport workers and in the building industry.

During this period, in the middle of the 1950s Healy's organisation had no name, but was known simply as 'The Group'. And like all the earlier ventures had a very small membership: the WIL had at most 250 members, the RCP at its height 500, although only a tenth of that number followed Healy into the Labour Party in 1946, and 'The Group' by 1956 had crawled up into three figures once more.

The first major breakthrough for the Healy-led Trotskyists came after the end of 1956 when some 7,000 Communist Party members resigned. In May 1957 one of them, Peter Fryer, former correspondent of the Communist *Daily Worker* in Hungary became the editor of *The Newsletter*, a new weekly newspaper. It aspired to provide a platform for the ex-Communists discussing whether they should join the Labour Party or form a new political grouping, and claimed that it had no sectional axe to grind but wished to provide a service for all socialists. To extend the debate *The Newsletter* sponsored a Socialist Forum movement that embraced Labour Party supporters, former Communists, Trotskyists, trade unionists and intellectuals, searching together for a 'New Left'.

At first Gerry Healy and 'The Group' were just one interested party in *The Newsletter* and Socialist Forum ventures, but the opportunities presented by this period of flux on the left were quickly seized. In

December 1958 Healy joined the editorial board of *The Newsletter* and three months later became the provisional national secretary of the newly announced Socialist Labour League. Initially it consisted of the kinds of elements involved in the Socialist Forums and declared that it did not seek a position as a new political party in its own right: its aims were to replace Hugh Gaitskell and the 'right-wing' leadership of the Labour Party, to campaign for socialist policies and leaders and to prepare for the beginning of a period of fierce class struggles in which *The Newsletter* would become not merely a discussion sheet but 'an organiser in industrial battles'.[2]

The League's industrial and economic programme for these struggles was based on a Charter of Workers' Demands decided at the end of 1958 by a 500-strong Rank and File Conference, organised by *The Newsletter*. The proposals included the nationalisation of major industries under the control of elected workers' councils, strikes against unemployment, protection of the rights of shop stewards, and the re-organisation of the Labour Party into a vehicle for industrial agitation.

Thus after the succession of unimpressive organisations over the previous quarter of a century, Gerry Healy and British Trotskyism had discovered in the Socialist Labour League an instrument that offered real potential for political and industrial militancy. Over the next fifteen years the SLL advanced steadily. Bursts of growth were punctuated with periodic setbacks until by 1973, when it was larger than any previous Trotskyist Group, Healy was able to proclaim that the Party of Revolution—if not the revolution itself—had arrived. Throughout its life many of the basic aims of the SLL remained constant, such as the ambition to unite the political and industrial wings of the Labour movement into a single entity, and to use this combined strength to banish social democratic policies and leaders from the movement and replace them with Marxist ones. The tactics employed have varied according to the League's confidence in its own strength and its relations with the mainstream of the Labour movement.

One of the SLL's first attempts to mount a concerted campaign to these ends was the National Assembly of Labour in November 1959. The 700 people at its opening conference—a foretaste of the SLL's propensity for mass gatherings—included workers from railways, mines, engineering and building industries, Communists and Labour supporters and many militants associated with the Rank and File Conference a year earlier. Coming a month after Labour's decisive defeat in a general election, the conference drew up a five-point plan to revive the socialist cause. It included the banning of nuclear arms-testing and manufacture—the SLL had participated in the CND's Aldermaston Marches and had advocated strike action to stop the making of weapons; opposition to colonialism and racialism; a forty-hour week, extensive nationalisation and the defence of jobs, wages and shop stewards' influence. The League hoped that local Assemblies of Labour would be formed in constituencies to begin the long task of transforming the party into a Marxist one.

Such designs were doomed to failure before they began for the Labour Party had placed on its list of proscribed organisations both *The Newsletter* and the SLL as early as March 1959, and expulsion of SLL supporters soon followed. Fifty Trotskyists were expelled from party branches in Streatham and Norwood in South London, the heart of Healy's organisation, and similar action was taken against other pockets of his supporters in Leeds, Liverpool, Manchester, Coventry and Glasgow. Healy argued that he and his followers should have the same rights in the Labour Party as Fabians or the *Tribune* group, but their past connections with Trotskyism and Communism ensured that as soon as they openly began to organise they would be swiftly repressed. With the front door firmly shut, the SLL attempted to gain access through a side entrance, the Labour Party Young Socialists. In 1964, when the Trotskyists captured control of the LPYS, the organisation was purged, and, as I shall describe below, the Healyite majority was removed, to become the youth section of the SLL.

At the same time as the League faced the Labour Party campaign against it, Healy and his closest supporters had to deal with their own recalcitrant members. Many of the more energetic socialists who supported the SLL on its foundation either resigned or were expelled within a year or two. Peter Cadogan, later a Secretary of the Committee of 100 and for a short while a supporter of International Socialism, was removed for a 'violation' of the League's constitution and Peter Fryer resigned because of Cadogan's expulsion. Others who parted company with the Socialist Labour League included Martin Grainger (alias Dr Christopher Pallis) who went on to set up the anarcho-syndicalist group, Solidarity; Bob Pennington, who moved to the International Socialists and then to the International Marxist Group; and Brian Behan, brother of playwright Brendan, who was expelled in 1960, ironically, for suggesting that the SLL should become an independent revolutionary party. Both Grainger and Fryer complained of the lack of democracy permitted by Healy and his small band of trusted comrades, and of their unwillingness to allow any dissent from the prevailing doctrine in face of all the external evidence that capitalism was on the point of collapse and revolution imminent.[3]

Stranded between ostracism and desertion, the SLL faltered. During the first four years of its existence it had attempted to create its own organisation, newspapers and policies while enjoying the privileges of

Labour Party membership. Now that Transport House had done its best to purge the SLL from the party, the Trotskyists looked for a drastic reorientation of their effort. After 1963 they began to build an independent organisation outside a Labour Party which they now regarded as an unsuitable agency for the transmission of Marxist revolution.

The first step in the move away from the Labour Party was to declare the SLL's hitherto unmentioned Trotskyist connections. The debate which accompanied the 1963 reorganisation of the Fourth International partly forced this upon the SLL, for *The Newsletter* played an important propaganda role, and the *Labour Review* was wound up and replaced in the spring of 1964 by a new quarterly journal called *Fourth International*. Its editor was Cliff Slaughter, a former Communist and sociology lecturer at Leeds University who joined forces with Healy in 1957. He also became a full-time worker for the SLL co-ordinating work on organisation, recruitment and the 'training of cadres'.[4] Two Ceylonese brothers resident in England, fervent Trotskyists and colleagues of Healy since the days of 'The Group' came to prominence. Tony van der Poorten (usually known as Tony Banda) was appointed Assistant General Secretary for Agitation and Propaganda and Mike Banda, a member of *The Newsletter* editorial board since 1958, became chief editor in January 1964. During that six year period the paper's circulation had increased from 750 copies per issue to 10,300, a rate of advance which prompted the SLL's 1965 annual congress to resolve to launch a daily newspaper in a few years' time.

Politically the SLL was in a weak position. It had failed to win support for its National Assembly of Labour or for its ideas in the Labour Party, save for the Young Socialists. The League had no real power base on which it could build, and, aware of this, tried to keep an open mind about its future attitude to the Labour Party. Its abandonment of 'entryism' was only tactical, because it was, in the words of the SLL's sixth congress in 1964, impossible with a right-wing Labour leadership which eliminated Marxist groups; instead opposition to this leadership had to come from outside the party. Three years later, when the SLL was coming to regard itself not merely as a pressure-group but potentially as a party in its own right, the ninth congress re-affirmed that the development of an independent organisation in no way precluded entryist work in the Labour Party. As an article in *The Newsletter* in April 1967 argued:

'Tomorrow it may be necessary for members of the SLL to infiltrate into the Labour Party to provide leadership for a left-wing moving in a revolutionary direction, but that is not the case today ... What is needed now is the constant struggle to construct an alternative revolutionary leadership to that of the right-wing labour leaders. This task proceeds within the factories, inside the Young Socialists and in demonstrations and other activities designed to rally and organise workers against Wilson.'[5]

While Labour retained the allegiance of the mass of trade unionists, and while it was a party of government, the SLL could hardly ignore it. It consistently urged its supporters to vote for it in general elections not because it had faith in its policies but, rather the opposite, that it believed its performance would 'within a very short space of time expose the pro-capitalist role of Wilson and company to their supporters, thus opening the door to the building of an alternative leadership and a more all-out direct struggle against the Tories'.[6]

The SLL came to depict itself as this alternative leadership, but by 1967 its conception of the nature of this leadership had begun to change. No longer did it see itself in terms of the Labour Party but as a fully fledged rival party in its own right. At the ninth SLL Congress in May 1967 Gerry Healy described his ambition:

'The kind of party which set out to build in Russia is the type of party we are out to build here. We are beginning with the Marxist theory, as developed by Lenin and Trotsky, we are developing this theory as a result of our education and experience of the workers' movement. We are training and educating leaders in the movement who will, as a result of their propaganda and educational work, educate and prepare more cadres and leaders.

'During these experiences we shall continuously engage in all forms of struggle, be it rent strike, a movement or demonstration against the imprisonment of revolutionaries overseas or continuous struggle against the infamous war in Vietnam and the Prices and Incomes Act.

'All of this is a continuous round of activity in the course of building a party. We do not separate our experience in Britain in the fight against the Prices and Incomes Act from our struggle to defend the Vietnamese revolution.'[7]

The support for this new party and leadership would come from the traditional sources of Labour's mass following, and the trade unions in particular. However since 1966 opposition from unions and youth to the policies of the Wilson government had manifested itself in new movements which did not rely on established structures or methods. It was this development which Healy set out to exploit. As he declared at the time of the 1966 seamen's strike:

'We are in the era of the political strike. Although the political strike poses the problems of power that does not mean that the question of political power is on the agenda. Political strikes are necessary for the political education of the working class.'[8]

The road from education to power was the long uphill haul on which Healy wished to embark. To succeed he felt he needed a daily newspaper, a centralised, disciplined party organisation, a mass trade union following under party control, and a vigorous Young Socialists section. Since the end of the 1960s the consolidation of these elements, which comprise the present Workers' Revolutionary Party, has been his all-consuming purpose.

At the heart of this strategy was the harnessing of industrial militancy to the cause of revolution, the constant and unswerving principle of the SLL's politics throughout its life. Without the industrial base all other aspects of the League's programme for its development would be meaningless. The emergence of an SLL-led body of trade unionists did not begin in a massive upsurge of rebelliousness but in the isolation of a relatively small number of militants from the mainstream of union thinking. At the beginning of 1966, 1,500 people had lobbied parliament to protest against incomes legislation but the organisers in Lambeth Trades Council, who were supported by the SLL, were disowned by the TUC. The following New Year the lobby was repeated, led by workers from the CAV/Joseph Lucas factory at Liverpool under the slogan 'Fight the Freeze, Don't Freeze the Fight'. One of their shop stewards, Bill Hunter, a member of the Merseyside Committee for the Defence of Trade Unions, spoke alongside Healy and Slaughter at a meeting after the lobby, which called for the building of a new mass movement of trade unionists.

The Merseyside Committee was an offshoot from the nationwide Liaison Committee for the Defence of Trade Unions, which appeared in 1966 and had attracted increasing attention from the Communist Party. Another group, in the Midlands, had broken away to form an Oxford Liaison Committee, centred on the BMC motor works. In September 1967 this group organised a conference supported by the Merseyside Committee and attended by 394 people, including Alan Thornett, a Transport and General Workers Union shop steward at BMC, Tony Bradley, chairman of the BMC Joint Shop Stewards Committee, Harry Wragg, a TGWU member from Coventry, Peter Ashworth of the National Union of Vehicle Builders and a shop steward at Vauxhall motors, Luton, as well as workers from Birmingham, London, Nottingham and at least eight trade unions, mainly in the engineering and motor industries.

A second conference was held in February 1968 and pledged itself to forming an All Trade Union Alliance, to campaign for nationalisation of basic industries, repeal of incomes legislation and guarantees of full employment and wages. Although this Alliance has never represented the official policy of any trade union and none has ever been affiliated to it, it has provided the Socialist Labour League with the much desired rank and file industrial base, has been a vehicle for the dissemination of SLL propaganda and has acted as a recruiting agent to the League itself. Locally it is intensely active in all the country's major industrial and urban conurbations, holding regular meetings, handing out leaflets at factory gates or wherever disputes are taking place, and engaging in constant agitation in union branches, on shop stewards' committees or in trades councils to press for concerted action for higher wages, to defend jobs or to oppose government policies.

Its largest sections are centred on docks, engineering and mining industries, but, above all the motor industry group has remained the most active, with supporters in the factories of all the country's major manufacturers, and with contacts in Renault and Citroen works through its French counterparts in the international Trotskyist movement, the Alliance Ouvrière. In addition the ATUA has a teachers' section and is supported by a vociferous group in Equity, the actors' union, which includes some of the best-known of SLL/WRP supporters such as Vanessa and Corin Redgrave and Helen Mirren. Connected with the Equity members is a collection of SLL/WRP members from the entertainment world, including Ken Loach, the film director, Roy Battersby, television director and member of the WRP Central Committee, and Colin Welland, the actor and writer.

The propaganda value of these celebrities' support for Trotskyism is an advantage which the SLL/WRP has enjoyed over almost all its rivals and one which it has put to frequent use. On occasion as many as thirty members of the Royal Shakespeare Company, together with a score of celebrated figures from the theatre, television or films, have been persuaded to lend their names to Trotskyist fund-raising ventures, including Young Socialist summer fairs that have realised four figure sums for the organisation or for causes such as the support of strikes at Pilkington's glass factory in St Helens, Lancashire. Large SLL/WRP meetings often include dramatisations of the class struggle portrayed by its theatrical supporters, and reaching a wider audience, in 1974 a BBC television play, 'Leeds United', about a strike in the Yorkshire clothing industry, was produced by Roy Battersby and written by Colin Welland.

Such activities may help to spread the word and lower public resistance to Trotskyist ideas, but they do not materially advance the proletarian revolution. In this decisive task the efforts of the ATUA and its parent body have been less successful. After joining in the protests against the Labour government's proposals for industrial relations reform at the end of the 1960s, it was the election of the Conservative administration in 1970 that set the scene for the ATUA's most active period.

The extent of the Alliance's opposition to Conservative policies and the height of its ambitions was revealed in December 1970 when its second annual conference adopted a Charter of Basic Rights, including the rights to work, to have a high standard of living (despite capitalist crisis), to have decent housing and free welfare services, and above all, the right of workers to organise and to strike. On this crucial point the ATUA wanted total opposition to the Industrial Relations Bill.

'The Tory anti-union Bill', declared the ATUA's Charter, 'aims to destroy the Unions and leave the working class defenceless. It threatens the independent trade unions and political activity of the working class which is basic in this struggle. The working class must never give up these rights, they must not allow the Tories to take the path of Hitler and Mussolini. We must force the trade union leaders and the TUC general council to mobilise the whole movement to defeat the anti-union laws. An Emergency Conference of the TUC must be called immediately to organise a general strike to defeat the laws . . . only the mobilisation of the working class movement in action will bring down the Tories. This movement will demand of the next Labour government that it restore every cut made by the Tories and immediately repeal all anti-union laws. Such a programme can only be carried out by taking the banks and major industries out of the hands of the capitalist owners and nationalising without compensation.'[9]

Supporting this Charter were several dozen trade union branches, particularly from the Transport and General Workers and the engineering union, and Trades Councils at East Ham, Lambeth, Croydon, Lewisham and Jarrow. But their policy was ultimately unenforceable although they did manage to bring out several thousand workers on a one day strike against the Bill. To oppose Conservative policies the ATUA and SLL also organised some of the country's largest political gatherings of the period: 4,000 at a 'Make the Government Resign' rally at Alexandra Palace in 1971, a similar number at an ATUA rally in Manchester in 1972, 8,500 at a Young Socialist meeting the same year, and 3,000 at Alexandra Palace in January 1974 to support the miners.

During this time the ATUA dropped all pretence of being an independent body of workers, official or unofficial, to support the transition from a League to Revolutionary Party and to absorb itself into the party structure as its industrial arm. In this respect the ATUA paralleled the Young Socialists: together they became the principal recruiting agents, propaganda vehicles and agitational weapons of the SLL/WRP leadership. Like the daily *Workers' Press* (which replaced *The Newsletter* in September 1969) they are firmly under the control of the parent organisation's Central Committee. *Workers' Press* was the world's first Trotskyist daily newspaper, with a full-time staff of professional journalists and with £25,000 raised by voluntary subscription to launch its production.

Thus by 1973 all the structural elements of the new party were present. To complete the setting for the transition from League to Party, the leadership needed a situation of economic crisis. The emergence of this crisis is the foundation of the SLL/WRP view of the world, which was summarised by the League's Central Committee in 1967: 'the possibility of the sudden collapse of the post-war boom must be put at the centre of our political work. The capitalist economy is now poised on the edge of a deep world crisis which impels it forward into an onslaught against the working class'.[10] With each fluctuation in currency values, each tremor in the stock market, every strike and every twist and turn in government economic policy, the SLL dramatised the intensification of the crisis. Its rhetoric in the columns of *The Newsletter* and *Workers' Press* grew more frantic, the scale of its demands rose, and its ambitions to exclusive leadership of the 'proletariat' grew also. The General Strike became the standard response to all situations and problems: to bring down a Conservative government's pay policies and replace it with a Labour one, or to demand the release of the Shrewsbury Pickets. During the winter of 1974 the frenetic propaganda of the Healyite Trotskyists reached its peak. On New Year's Day 1974 the *Workers' Press* forecast large-scale unemployment and pay cuts.

'This mass onslaught must be met,' it demanded, 'by the establishment of factory committees to organise the occupation of all plants where employers try to start sackings.

'They (the workers) must remain inside their factories demanding the right to work, then establish impregnable fortresses to defend themselves against the class enemy.

'Alongside the factory occupations Councils of Action must be built in every area to unite all working class organisations in a struggle against the Tory government to bring it down.'[11]

These Councils of Action would form the nucleus of a soviet regime backed up by an ármed workers' militia replacing police and the present armed forces.

In this setting the long-promised declaration of party status was made. Besides the mere propaganda value in the change of title, the transition signified firstly the satisfaction of the leadership at the state of the organisational developments begun in the previous decade. Secondly, it denoted that in the Trotskyists' view the British crisis was moving towards a pre-revolutionary situation in which the prospect of power would present itself to socialists prepared to seize the opportunity, and, thirdly, the seizure did not mean, as it had done during the 1960s, that the Trotskyists would place demands on a Labour government but would capture power in their own right.

Since the two-year period following the forming of the Workers' Revolutionary Party the crisis failed to reach its climax, and as the Labour government offered a less easy target than its predecessor, the WRP has found itself marooned on a plateau of revolutionary expectations, unable to go higher but unwilling to climb down. During the two general elections of 1974 it sought to confirm its new status by putting up its own candidates, standing against right-of-centre Labour politicians like Reg Prentice or in traditionally militant areas such as Glasgow, Merseyside or South Wales. The party fielded eight candidates in February and ten in October; all lost their deposits with less than 4,000 votes between them.

When defining his aims in 1967 Healy spoke of emulating the Russian Bolshevik party. The historian, E. H. Carr, describing the years before 1917 when Lenin was evolving his organisation, noted some of the factors which Healy may also have had in mind, how

'the whole emphasis came to rest upon the need for a small closely-knit party under a strong central leadership to act in the name of the proletariat as the spearhead of revolution. The methods of the revolutionary struggle varied and must be determined empirically from time to time. What remained fixed and consistent was the central plan built up on a sound basis of theory and executed with the support of the masses by a highly organised, disciplined and centrally directed party of professional revolutionaries.'[12]

These qualities of central control, discipline and efficiency are the ones cultivated most assiduously by Healy. An atmosphere of secrecy, particularly regarding party structure and membership figure, pervades all their activities, which are strictly controlled by a central committee. Indeed Healy and his supporters have always been among the most unpopular on the left for these very characteristics: they are frequently attacked as sectarian, fanatical, hysterical and neurotically secretive, and theirs is one of the few organisations for which revolutionary Marxists and Conservatives use the same terminology. Healy has steadfastly refused to take part in united activities with other revolutionaries, whom he regards as Stalinist (the Communist Party), revisionist (the International Marxist Group), or centrist (the International Socialists). However the SLL flirted for a short time in its early days with the Vietnam Solidarity Campaign, but withdrew on an ideological pretext, participated in joint meetings with the IS and IMG during 1973 to protest about police raids on members' homes following bomb explosions in England, and held joint meetings with those same groups on the *cause célèbre* of the Shrewsbury Pickets. The WRP eschews the student movement, black power and the 'alternative society' and stands apart from other Trotskyist groups who lean towards these activities. Its potential violence, implicit in its demands for a workers' militia, is controlled too and SLL/WRP members become less frequently involved in street demonstration brawls than members of some other Trotskyist groups. Similarly terrorism, in the sense of indiscriminate bomb outrages, has no place in its scheme of revolution.

The WRP nonetheless stands aloof from all others, nor will it tolerate dissent in its own ranks. In 1974 one of the most prominent members of the WRP and ATUA, Alan Thornett, lost his position as a shop steward at British Leyland's car plant at Cowley, Oxford, when the management refused to deal with him because of his continual disruptive activities. His work colleagues refused to support him and fell into disagreements with the leadership of the WRP. At the end of the year some 200 party members were expelled or resigned, including branches in Swindon and at Oxford which had been among the most active. Thornett formed his own organisation, the Workers' Socialist League, to fight the alleged dilution of Trotskyist ideals by Healy and the WRP.

Besides a characteristic exchange of propaganda insults between the WRP and the WSL, supporters of the rival organisations competed with each other for trade union support. One of their main battlegrounds was the British Leyland plant at Cowley, the troubled heart of a vulnerable industry, where, at the end of 1975, Thornett recovered some of his lost influence when he was elected, by 77 votes to 64, chairman of a 3,500-member branch of the Transport and General Workers' Union, defeating the WRP's candidate. The limits of his support were clearly demonstrated however in January 1976 when Thornett was decisively beaten for a seat on the Transport Union's Midland regional committee, and in elections for seven senior shop steward posts at Cowley he secured only 526 votes, less than half the number needed to gain a place. Of the 34 candidates in that contest nearly a third were identified with revolutionary groups, but only one, a WRP member, was elected. These defeats came as a particular setback for Thornett and the creation of his own power base, on which the future hopes of the Workers' Socialist League rested.

The absence of the anticipated economic crash, the failure to win massive numbers of workers to its cause, and dissension in the party's ranks, were followed by the bitterest blow of all for the WRP: in February 1976 capitalist crisis exacted retribution when Plough Press Ltd, publishers of the *Workers' Press*, collapsed and forced the paper's closure. The WRP's vision was slipping away, its huge, unrealised ambitions overshadowing its small progress. Its primitive Bolshevism, for so long incongruous, irrelevant and obscure, has in the last eight to ten years been more forcefully expressed and has been able to attract some small degree of support from ambitious, aggrieved trade unionists who have been rejected by Labour or Communist parties, from (ironically) some entertainers indulging in a rather dour Anglo-Saxon version of 'radical chic', washing away their bourgeois guilt complexes by embracing the most bitter, fanatical socialist group they could find, and among some sections of youth—a part of the population whose ethos is supposedly the antithesis of Bolshevik centralism.

2

'LABOUR'S REVOLUTIONARY VOICE':
TROTSKYIST YOUNG SOCIALISTS

'Labour's Revolutionary Voice' is the slogan of the *Chartist*, a newspaper produced by Trotskyist members of the Labour Party Young Socialists. Its declaratory tone announces not merely an editorial policy, but, redolent of all those voices which cry out for the total transformation of society, urges on its audience a profound purpose, suggesting the kind of party they should strive to create. Their aim is to change a party of social democracy based on an alliance of beliefs into one of revolutionary Marxism, and it is a view that has been shared by numerous other groups in the Young Socialists. Most of them have been political lightweights whose presence has not been felt outside the YS but the organisation itself has had a short and turbulent history consisting of a series of running battles between such factions and the hierarchy of Transport House and between the factions themselves. These squabbles have helped periodically to destroy the Young Socialists as a body of any influence within the party or outside, and only the inherent processes of change in any youth organisation, with new members replacing old, have enabled it to be rescued and rebuilt.

If the existence of the Young Socialists has created problems for the Labour Party so too has the absence of any national youth movement. After 1954, when the Labour League of Youth was disbanded, only the National Association of Labour Students' Organisation existed for the specific purpose of putting across the party's message to young people, but to a strictly limited section. In their very different ways the Campaign for Nuclear Disarmament—channelling natural resources of youthful idealism into political action—and the Young Conservatives, a somewhat frivolous but alluring recruiting agent, demonstrated the value of a youth organisation with a broader appeal. In 1959 a working party was set up to look into the problem and in February 1960, just two months after receiving its report recommending a new organisation, and four months after the trouncing in the general election, the Labour Party launched the Young Socialists.

The YS were to be an integral feature of the Labour movement; membership was open to any fifteen to twenty-five year old member of a constituency party, to which the local Young Socialist branches were joined, and nationally the organisation was equipped with a committee, annual conferences, newspaper and written constitution. The growth of the YS was remarkable: from the 262 scattered branches which existed in 1959 there were 578 by the end of 1960, 721 in 1961, 772 in 1962, and 769 in 1963. The beliefs, and in some cases the external political connections, of some of the idealists who flocked to the banner were however to put them on a collision course with their elders. The left-wing domination of the Young Socialists became evident at its first national conference in 1961 when the 381 delegates voted for unilateral disarmament, withdrawal of Britain from NATO, and the ending of all manufacture and testing of nuclear weapons. But more importantly they expressed no confidence in the leadership of Hugh Gaitskell, who had steered the party away from unilateralism, and at conference the next year called for his resignation. The belligerence of the YS was not confined to passing resolutions, for on May Day 1962 their members became involved in violent scenes during demonstrations in London and Glasgow, with the result that the YS federation in the latter city was disbanded.

Through *The Newsletter*, the SLL had made little secret of its intention to infiltrate the ranks of the YS.[13] To promote its interests the League used its own members who remained in the constituency branches, those in CND, and above all the newspaper *Keep Left*, which had begun as a duplicated broadsheet in 1951 among members of the old Labour League of Youth and which by 1958 had achieved a national circulation. Its left-wing policies brought it into contact with Gerry Healy and after the establishment of the Socialist Labour League it quickly became the instrument of the League's agitation and propaganda in the Young Socialists. With this backing *Keep Left* became the most highly organised, most militant and most determined of all the left groups in the YS. Its supporters led the policies attacking the party leadership, who soon became aware of the source of opposition. In 1961 *Keep Left* was proscribed, along with the SLL, but its influence could not be stemmed by this alone. In 1962 four *Keep Left* sympathisers on the National Committee of the Young Socialists were removed, and three of them were subsequently expelled from the party. The editor of the official YS newspaper, *New Advance*, Rogert Protz, resigned because of restrictions on his freedom, and he later became editor of *Keep Left*, after which he was dismissed from his job in the Press and Publicity Department at Labour Party Headquarters.[14]

As it became evident that the *Keep Left* group was increasing its hold over the Young Socialists, the party's officials resorted to more drastic action: just as they had weeded out unacceptable pockets of SLL supporters, so they began on a larger scale to expel the *Keep Left* members, and in 1963–64 they disbanded branches in Leicestershire, Leeds, Bradford and London and the Home Counties. But by 1964 *Keep Left* secured a majority on the eleven-man YS National Committee, including the positions of both chairman and vice-chairman. Criticism of the party policies and tactics during and after the victorious 1964 general election campaign finally broke the patience of Transport House, which refused to recognise the YS national conference planned for the beginning of 1965.

Formal proscriptions of newspapers and organisations, even when accompanied by selective expulsion of individuals and branches and supervisory control carried out by officials at party headquarters, had failed. Armed with an efficient organisation, and policies which expressed the feelings of the rank-and-file, the Trotskyist group had effectively defied the party. It took the outright refusal to allow the YS to continue in its present form, and the reconstituting of the organisation, to force the *Keep Left* group out of the party in its entirety.

Purged of many of its active members the re-formed body, called the Labour Party Young Socialists, has been a smaller organisation. Beginning with 605 branches in 1965 it has developed as follows:[15]

1966	571 branches
1967	576
1968	533
1969	386
1970	437
1971	503
1972	485
1973	350
1974	343
1975	389

Many of these branches are inactive, existing in name only or at most resurrected for canvassing at election times. The considerable drop in the number of branches in 1968–69 occurred in face of the rising chorus of student revolt and the emergence of the International Socialists and International Marxist Group as overt, dynamic revolutionary organisations.

The years after 1973 have seen a consolidation of the Marxists' hold on the LPYS and a continued growth in the new groups. Social democratic youth has thus been deterred from joining the LPYS by the presence of the Marxists, while other revolutionaries prefer the style of organisations emerging outside traditional party structures. The LPYS has been caught between its place in the Labour Party and the revolutionary beliefs of many of its members, uncertain how far it should lean in one direction or the other. One fact is clear however—that although after the removal of the *Keep Left* supporters, the Labour Party hoped for an end to the Trotskyists' 'disruptive activities'[16]—the Young Socialists organisation has continued under the domination of revolutionary Marxist groups.

The first of these to come to prominence were members and sympathisers of the International Socialist movement. In the 1950s when it was known as the *Socialist Review* group, many of its supporters were involved in the Labour League of Youth, and with the establishment of the Young Socialists in 1960 it renewed its interest. They organised around a journal called *Rebel*, published by YS members in London who were also active in CND and who designated themselves 'Socialist Youth Against the Bomb'. In September 1961 *Rebel* merged with *Rally*, the production of YS branches in Liverpool and Nottingham, to become *Young Guard*. As in the case of *Keep Left*, this reflected the political programme of its parent body, which in the case of *Socialist Review* and its protégé meant unilateralism, votes at 18 and nationalisation under workers' control. It drew support from individual Labour Party members outside the Young Socialist ranks and pursued its policy less fanatically than the *Keep Left* programme. *Young Guard* was not placed on the 'Index' of banned publications and, so, to further the image of moderation, its supporters sided against rather than with *Keep Left* during the purges of 1962–64, remaining intact after the restructuring of 1965.

By 1965–66 other IS sympathisers had come to the fore in the LPYS. John Charlton, an IS activist in Yorkshire in the 1970s, became YS chairman, supported by at least one more International Socialist, Mike Caffoor, in 1974 the IS North London organiser. Caffoor also served on the editorial board of a revived version of *Rebel*, which appeared in 1966 at the instigation of seventy LPYS branches in London and the South East. The IS dominated the new *Rebel*—one of the other members of the editorial team was Roger Rosewall who subsequently became an Industrial Organiser for the International Socialists. It attacked what it called Transport House's 'inability to run a democratic Young Socialist organisation' and described the latest official LPYS newspaper, *Focus*, as written 'for unintelligent five-year-olds'.[17]

From 1966 the IS-oriented Young Socialists campaigned on the three issues that were to lead the organisation into open revolutionary politics and out of the Labour Party's orbit: the war in Vietnam and in particular opposition to the Wilson government's support for American involvement; the question of incomes policy to which the IS was resolutely opposed, seeking instead to boost shop stewards' and rank and file movements; and the student revolt in which the IS had been involved since the first rumblings of discontent at the London School of Economics. By 1968 the presence of IS members on demonstrations and in movements outside the Labour Party made it not merely difficult to maintain their 'entryist' front but superfluous.[18]

Since the departure of the IS the 'Militant' has gradually assumed leadership of the LPYS. The group takes its name from its newspaper, which began publication in October 1964, succeeding one called *Socialist Fight*, which ran from 1958 to 1963. Its editor throughout its existence has been Peter Taafe, a member of Walton Young Socialists, and its editorial board includes Ted Grant, a Trotskyist before the Second World War and a member of the Revolutionary Communist Party and the entryist Revolutionary Socialist League.

Patiently, 'Militant' has steered between what it calls the 'lunacy and hooliganism' of the *Keep Left* group and the 'bureaucratic heavy handedness'[19] of Transport House, to become a nationwide body and the dominant tendency in the LPYS. Its main strength lies in north and east London, and in Brighton, Liverpool, the North East, West Yorkshire and Scotland. It has been determined to remain inside the

Labour Party and has resisted the temptation to create its own overt organisation, its supporters being co-ordinated by the Editorial Board, or to become identified with any political grouping outside the Labour Party, Trotskyist or otherwise.

'Militant' has consistently campaigned on a Marxist programme which has been at variance with almost every point of official Labour policy. It proposes a United Socialist States of Europe which it envisages will emerge from the inevitable capitalist crisis; rejects any form of wage restraint or social contract in the context of a crisis for which it regards capitalism not the working class as responsible; and opposes 'creeping' nationalisation as a method of reaching socialism. Instead the 'Militant' antidote to crisis is 'a mighty campaign to turn the unions into fighting instruments of the workers ... to begin an offensive movement of the Workers towards the socialist society'.[20]

The evolution of this society is described by Peter Taafe, who defines its foundation of workers' control as:

'the right of the Working Class and their representatives in the factories to inspect the books of the capitalist industries to check and control all the incomings and outgoings and the actions of management. This is only possible on a mass scale in a pre-revolutionary period just after the conquest of power as in Russia in the aftermath of the October Revolution. Workers' Control comes from below through factory or shop stewards committees. Workers' management comes from above through centralised workers' councils to which the factory committees are subordinated. In a workers' state, unless ultimate management is vested on the workers' councils as a whole, industries would vie against one another, and a national plan could not be operated and consequently society would break up.'[21]

Since 1970 the revolutionary Marxism of the 'Militant' group has been the doctrine of the leading sections of the Labour Party Young Socialists. Its supporters have maintained a majority on the national committee, including the positions of chairman, vice-chairman and secretary, and its nominees have also edited the 'official' LPYS newspaper, Left. Perhaps the campaign which contributed most to its success was that of a Charter for Young Workers in 1970, which drew attention to the alleged exploitation of young people in employment through low wages in long apprenticeships and in leisure pursuits through expensive commercialism, and which attracted wide support in the Labour Party and trade unions.

But 'Militant' sees itself as something more than the representative

of socialist youth. In 1972, while noting 'the ideas of "Militant",
which now more than ever are the ideas of the LPYS', it urged that
these 'must be taken forward into the Labour movement'.[22] This
onward march gained its first victory in that year when the Labour
Party decided to co-opt annually on to its National Executive Committee
a Young Socialist representative, who has always been since then a
'Militant' supporter. The group has also ventured to propose its ideas
at Labour Party conferences.

In 1972 Pat Wall, president of Bradford Trades Council, a local
councillor, member of the Shipley Constituency Labour Party in
Yorkshire, and 'Militant' sympathiser, successfully moved a motion
calling for the re-nationalisation of hived-off sections of industry and
public ownership of land, finance and the building industry, under the
democratic control of the workers. At the same conference Pat Craven,
a 'Militant' supporter in Norwood Labour Party, gained 51,000 votes
in a vain attempt to secure election to the party's National Executive
Committee. 'Militant' has also been keen to take up causes which
run counter to the dictates of the leadership, not only in the context
of industrial disputes but on issues such as the rebel councillors of
Clay Cross, for whom 'Militant' has provided a platform, and Ireland,
where the group produces a 'Militant' Irish monthly, which calls for
the withdrawal of British troops and their replacement by a Trade
Union Defence Force as the custodian of a Workers' Republic.

The rise of 'Militant' is symptomatic of the Labour Party's changing
complexion, the growth of its Marxist wing and the greater toleration
by the party organisation of such views and activities. But a question
mark hangs over 'Militant's' success: whether it is less the product
of a search by sincere Labour supporters for answers to endemic
economic crises and more the result of painstaking entryist work by
committed Trotskyists, who by definition owe no allegiance to the
mainstream of the party.

On a number of occasions 'Militant' has been identified with the
Revolutionary Socialist League—the representatives of the Fourth
International who entered the Labour Party in 1953—either directly
or indirectly. George Thayer considered *Socialist Fight* to have been
an RSL publication; the Communist Party, in a generally factually
accurate pamphlet, equated 'Militant' and the RSL, as did a 'Solidarity'
pamphlet of 1968 and Anthony Sampson in his *New Anatomy of
Britain* in 1971. Most recently a report by the Labour Party National
Agent, Reg Underhill, revealed the whole process of entryism by the
RSL through the 'Militant' group.[23] 'Militant' however resolutely
denies that it is the Revolutionary Socialist League under another
name or even its successor.

The allegations of these outside observers are however supported by some internal evidence. First, it is evident that *Militant's* concepts of the transition to socialism and the workers' state owe a great deal to the basic Trotskyist document *The Death Agony of Capitalism and the Tasks of the Fourth International*, particularly in respect of opening capitalist files, the Trade Union Defence force, the structure of workers' control and the united Socialist Europe. Secondly, some of the leaders of the 'Militant' group have been active Trotskyists and have given no reason to suggest they have changed their beliefs even if they have attempted to bury most of their past connections. Thirdly, one such link they did not hide was that of a firm called 'Workers International Review Publications Limited', which for seven years shared offices with *Militant* and advertised its books and pamphlets through the newspaper's columns. *The Review* had been the title of the RSL's journal until 1958 and the publishing house a distribution centre for Fourth International literature. The company was wound up in 1971 when *Militant* moved to new premises in Bethnal Green and began an association with a new concern called World Books.

Although there are individual links, and others through associated bodies, there is less specific connection between the end of RSL as an organisation and the advent of 'Militant'. By 1963 the League had virtually vanished from sight so deep was its entryism, and its name, journal and meetings were discontinued. 'Militant'—both as groups and journal—emerged over a year later with no apparent connection.

The title Revolutionary Socialist League has been buried and is no longer claimed by any organisation, but it did not cease to exist in 1963. The International Marxist Group was in touch with it up to two years later, and in 1968 when the Fourth International (United Secretariat) recognised the IMG as its British Section it did so because the existing section, the RSL, was incapable of breaking out of entryism and developing as an independent organisation, not because it had folded up entirely. In other words, the RSL, under a different name and trying to cover its Trotskyist tracks, was still in the Labour Party after 1963 and some former RSL members had found their way into the 'Militant' group.

Most of those Labour Party Young Socialists who identify with 'Militant' are oblivious of the possible origins of the group. It has no political or organisational links with the Fourth International or Trotskyism, although it remains ideologically close to the substance of this brand of Marxism. Just how narrow the gap is between 'Militant' and open Trotskyism was demonstrated at the beginning of 1974 when seventeen leading 'Militant' supporters resigned because they regarded as mistaken the group's conception that 'revolutionary activity consists

98

overwhelmingly in a struggle around the programme of a future Labour Government',[24] and some joined instead the International Marxist Group. However reticent the leadership of the 'Militant' group is about the origins of its organisation, there are other Labour Party Young Socialists who are more forthcoming about the provenance of their doctrines.

In 1968, at the instigation of the *Tribune* group and supported by others such as the 'Voice of the Unions' group, an eight-point Socialist Charter was drawn up, setting out a proposed policy for the Labour Party. Its measures included public ownership 'as a real weapon for socialism', redistribution of wealth, full public accountability of private and public institutions, withdrawal from NATO and cuts in military expenditure. It envisaged a 'Socialist and Democratic Labour Party' which must abide by the policy decisions of annual conferences.[25] In less than a year the Charter had acquired the support of 39 Members of Parliament, 65 constituency Labour Parties, four Trade Unions, 24 Young Socialist branches, 30 Trade Union branches and four Trades Councils. A National Committee was formed, a Young Chartist section formed and a Soldiers' Charter drawn up, calling for the democratisation of the armed forces and trade union rights for serving soldiers. 'Militant' was distinctly cool about this exercise, but from 1970 a small group of Trotskyists began organising in the Young Chartists. Within two years, as the attention of their elders turned elsewhere and the movement failed to maintain its initial momentum, the revolutionaries secured control at its annual convention. *Tribune* and official Trade Union support dropped away, leaving the rump of an organisation which has become a 'left opposition' to 'Militant' in the LPYS. It runs its own newspaper, *The Chartist*, with supporters in Young Socialist Branches in Norwood, Streatham, Lambeth, Vauxhall, Woolwich and Brent East in London, and in south east England, Rotherham and Stockport.

At the 1973 Party conference the Chartists circulated a draft programme for the Labour Party which was explicit in its affirmation of faith in Trotskyist teaching and in its desire to 'rebuild' the Fourth International. It predicted that economic crises meant

'a revolutionary situation is approaching. A General Strike is going to come whether we like it or not. But a General Strike is a terrible weapon for those who are not prepared to handle it. Such a strike means that we challenge the constitution and the State. We must be prepared to face the troops being brought in against us. We must know *how* to arm ourselves, *how* to appeal to the troops, how to win them to our side, how to link their desire for democracy within the

99

army to our own movement for democracy in industry and in society.

'A General Strike means either a decisive victory or a serious defeat. It poses the question of power. Either we and the whole Labour movement take hold of the power of the state, or we are crushed, for a whole period ... We will make ourselves clear: if we are not prepared for an armed insurrection, we are not prepared for the coming General Strike.'[26]

In the same document the Chartists outlined the ten measures they would wish a government emerging from such a situation to take:

'1. Emergency joint Labour and TUC conference to act as replacement of "Queen in Parliament" in debating and enacting legislation.

2. Guarantee of trade union rights to soldiers, sailors and airmen, giving powers to arrest officers engaged in anti-government activity. Arming of the working class.

3. Confiscation of ALL major monopolies through trade union mobilisation and occupation of plant.

4. Abolition of Monarchy.

5. Complete re-organisation of Labour Movement on basis of elected workers' councils.

6. Defence of expropriated property with barricades, workers' defence units, etc., as and where needed.

7. Take-over of the mass media through the trade unions concerned.

8. Take-over of key public buildings, communications-points, etc.

9. Seizure of full state power on above basis and implementation of production plan.

10. Appeal for support from European and world working class.'[27]

Such a programme was not taken seriously by the Labour Party. It could afford to tolerate the over-developed fantasies of a small group unable by itself to begin to carry out its ideas and so obviously out of step with the majority of the party. To expel them for preaching undemocratic ideas or running against the principles of the party would have only heightened the Chartists' exaggerated sense of their potential. But a decade earlier excommunication would have been the inevitable course and the fact that this did not happen was as much a reflection of rising Marxist militancy within the party as it was of any forgiving benevolence. Indeed the 'Chartists' have been able to bring on to their platform some leading Labour Marxists, including Joan Maynard, Ernie Roberts and Tony Kelly, who was instrumental in the rejection by Newham Constituency Labour Party of Reg Prentice as its MP.

Between the 'Chartists' and 'Militant' there is only a question of emphasis and tactics not of basic analysis, and together they totally dominate the LPYS to the exclusion of social democratic ideas. They may be in a minority in the party as a whole but are strongly entrenched and have sufficient numbers of prominent sympathisers on the left of the party that any attempt to remove them would create an undue degree of disturbance. Their ideas also run very close to those prevalent in the Labour Party's student organisations, which have also been subjected to much factional in-fighting between Marxist groups.

From the end of the Second World War the National Association of Labour Students Organisations (NALSO) had provided the Labour Party with a steady source of members and since the end of the 1950s it consistently increased its membership. In 1960, 3,000 NALSO members were grouped into fifty clubs and thereafter:

1961	5000 members in 60 clubs	
1962	5500	69
1963	5644	83
1964	6695	92
1965	7000	99
1966	7000	100

At the beginning of the 1960s NALSO held joint conferences with the Marxist intelligentsia of the *New Left Review* and among its members there was a sprinkling of individuals who were, at the same time as their NALSO membership, connected with revolutionary groups. In 1960, for instance, the NALSO executive included two members of the editorial board of International Socialism: Nigel Harris, who edited NALSO magazine, *Clarion*, for two years, and Ken Coates, a former Communist, who was at that time the NALSO secretary. Harris has remained with the IS since, although Coates, after expulsion from 1965–69, returned to Labour's ranks and was a founder member of the Institute for Workers' Control.[28]

After their expulsion from the Young Socialists, the SLL tried to retain contact with Labour through NALSO, and by 1967 there was a four-sided battle emerging, between the IS, SLL, IMG and 'Militant' for control of the organisation. A committee of enquiry into NALSO was set up in 1968 and it reported that:

'increasingly in recent years elements became influential which were in opposition to the party's principles and policies and who wished to alter the purpose for which NALSO was formed.'[29]

The party withdrew its financial support of NALSO and in 1968, after twenty-two years, the organisation was disbanded. Not until 1971 did the Labour Party replace NALSO with a National Organisation of Labour Students, in which the quasi-Trotskyism of 'Militant' became the most prominent stream of thought.

The Labour Party's student section had been undermined by the activities of revolutionary groups who in 1968 proceeded to fill a political vacuum with their own creation, the Revolutionary Socialist Students Federation. At a critical period of unrest in colleges and universities when a new wave of consciousness enveloped the student world, the Labour case went by default. There was no organisation which could have provided a balance to the prevalent revolutionary Marxism and to which non-revolutionary socialists might be attracted. In the absence of this alternative more students than perhaps otherwise might have been the case found themselves sucked into the revolutionary vortex. The under-representation of social-democratic ideas among students at the end of the 1960s clearly connected with the demise of NALSO as a body capable of articulating non-Marxist ideas. Among Young Socialists as well as students there was from the mid-1960s onwards as much, or more, happening outside the Labour Party as in it.

Since their departure from the Labour Party the *Keep Left* group has become the faithful servant of the Socialist Labour League and the Workers' Revolutionary Party. Its aim has been 'to build a revolutionary party to take power out of the hands of the capitalist class', on the assumption that 'young people have an indispensable part to play in building that party'.[30] *Keep Left* has reflected all the shifts in SLL/WRP policy and pursued its own path in its own style, set apart from all other Trotskyist or youth organisation. Indeed it has avoided the temptations of trendy self-indulgence and instead has cultivated an image of working class puritanism. 'The large scale introduction of drugs by Bohemian and middle class elements', stated *Keep Left* in 1967, 'is a great danger to the working class. The Young Socialists oppose it with all their strength. No one connected with drugs will be tolerated in any way.'[31] A greater spirit of self-denial was evident in the winter of 1971–72 when, with unemployment near the million mark, 150 Young Socialists began marches on the theme the 'Right to Work' from Glasgow, Liverpool, Swansea, Southampton and Deal converging on London where at Wembley Stadium on

March 12, 1972, 8,500 YS and SLL members and sympathisers attended a rally. As they had led the column of 53 marchers out of Glasgow five weeks earlier, actor Corin Redgrave and film director Kenneth Loach heaped praise on the Young Socialists. Redgrave said, 'Here on this march we have the material of another New Model Army—the workers' army'.[32]

'Keep Left' does not take all its pleasures so seriously, for one of its attractions to working class youth has been its football tournaments, sports days, discotheques, pop concerts, summer camps—which combine political education with spartan holidaymaking—and fund-raising fairs, at which the SLL/WRP Equity lobby has been invoked on a scale that would be the envy of any village cricket club.

This kind of social activity has undoubtedly contributed to the growth of the Young Socialists into the largest revolutionary youth organisation in Britain. Although because of the Healyite veil of secrecy no membership figures or estimates of turnover are available, the general trend is indicated in a number of ways. First, there is the increased circulation of *Keep Left*, which was able to step up from monthly to weekly production in 1971. Its first issues in 1951 sold 300 copies, by 1964 it had risen to 10,000; 14,000 in 1967; 17,000 in 1968; 19,000 in 1969; 20,000 in 1970; and 21,000 in 1971.

Its sixteen regions throughout the country are able to sustain an unending round of social and political activities, meetings, leaflet campaigns and conferences, and the size of the annual YS conferences is also indicative of the organisation's growth. While the yearly gatherings of LPYS and the declining Young Communist League have totalled no more than 200 people on any one occasion, the 'Keep Left' group has mustered an average of 400 to 500 delegates per conference with another 750–1,200 visitors and observers. In 1972 and '73 the overall total was 1,700 people, in 1974 it reached nearly 2,000 (850 delegates and 1,125 visitors), and in 1975 topped the 2,000 mark with over 1,200 visitors including 200 from West Germany and others from Syria, Greece, Portugal, USA and Ireland.

What kind of young people has it attracted? The appeal and the whole tone of its politics and propaganda is directed towards relatively uneducated working class youth. The masthead of *Keep Left* displays the slogan: 'United all young workers, students, apprentices, un-employed and immigrant youth.' Certainly it has had some success in the latter category. The editor of *Keep Left* in 1972 was Gary Gurmeet, a Kenyan Asian journalist who came to Britain in 1968 at the age of eighteen and joined the Young Socialists the same year. The paper's editorial board has consistently included a number of West Indians, one of whom, Sylvester Smart, contested the Lambeth

Central constituency for the Workers' Revolutionary Party in the general election of October 1974. *Keep Left* has had less influence among students.

After the downfall of NALSO in 1968 and in the light of the SLL's refusal to join any other student co-ordinating body, the League launched Young Socialist Student Societies. They began with groups at Oxford, Manchester, Exeter and Southampton Universities, University College, London, and the London School of Economics. Progress was slow, given the tight discipline in doctrine and activity associated with the SLL. By 1974 only sixteen student societies existed, but the organisation put forward eight candidates for the NUS executive, all of whom were soundly defeated.

The *Keep Left* Young Socialists maintain a very strict regime, loyal to the party and to the International Committee of the Fourth International. The aloofness from solidarity fronts and *ad hoc* campaign committees is a distinct disadvantage to the student societies but it is no problem for the non-student youth who are the primary target.

For every one of the thousand or so Labour Party Young Socialists there are between five and ten supporters for the WRP's group. The *Keep Left* Young Socialists are bigger fish in a smaller pool who, like their Trotskyist elders, anticipate the heady excitement of revolution at any moment. The activities of this group and other Trotskyists left Labour without an effective youth group for much of the 1960s at a time when the contribution of youth to radical politics grew sharply. But by the 1970s a different atmosphere existed in the Labour Party, which meant that Marxists could flourish in the Young Socialists, could cultivate prominent party members sympathetic to their cause, and, provided they did not allow youthful zeal to run away with them, could meet others in the Labour movement on common ground.

Most of the Trotskyist organisations have used the LPYS as a strategically placed barometer to test the favourability or otherwise of the political climate. The *Keep Left* group came to prominence at a time when Trotskyism was anathema to Transport House while the smaller 'Militant' group, ten years later, found that its brand of revolutionary communism led straight to the National Executive Committee. One Trotskyist organisation that has not dipped into the swirling torrents of the Labour Party Young Socialists, even to test the temperature, has been the one most closely associated with student and youth politics, the International Marxist Group.

V

New Lefts and Old

THE ORIGINS OF
THE INTERNATIONAL MARXIST GROUP

During its comparatively short life the International Marxist Group has been associated with a remarkably wide range of ideas and activities in the pursuit of revolution. After four years as an 'entryist' group in the Labour Party, this small but active body moved in 1968 into the realms of student protest, emerged as the British section of a branch of the Trotskyist Fourth International, became one of the leading exponents of the street demonstration and the single issue 'solidarity campaign' in sympathy with revolutionaries in other parts of the world, and proceeded to advance the cause of establishing a new proletarian party at home, to be aided by a Workers' Militia, as the nuclei of a future soviet regime.

Darting from one scheme to another, the IMG's politics have been a rare blend of old and new, embracing in turn the slow march to socialism through the traditional institutions of the British Labour movement, the New Left's experimentations to find alternative roads to revolution and the primitive Trotskyist doctrine of the armed workers' uprising. Of all the groups on the revolutionary left it reflects most extensively all the twists and turns of ideology, and all the fashions and tendencies that have emerged and passed away since the middle of the 1960s.

During this time the IMG has undergone many changes of face, and for an organisation that has spent much of its existence in bitter criticism of the Labour Party, it seems strange to recall that its formation took place within Labour's ranks. The centre of the group's early activity was a magazine called *The Week* which was launched in January 1964 as a 'news analysis for socialists',[1] under the editorship of Ken Coates, the former secretary of the National Association of Labour Students Organisations, one time Communist Party member and lecturer in the extra-mural department of Nottingham University, and Robin Blackburn of the editorial board of the *New Left Review*. Its declared aims were the return of a Labour government with socialist policies, the defence of social democracy against its enemies, the support of colonial movements of national liberation, and the sympathetic reporting of news of opposition struggles in communist countries. In support of these ends *The Week* secured the sponsorship of intellectuals such as Perry Anderson and Tom Nairn, also of the *New Left Review*, Ralph Miliband and Michael Barratt-Brown, trade unionists such as Ernie Roberts of the engineering workers' union, Labour MP's Stephen Swingler and Konni Zilliacus, and Ray Challinor, a former member of the Revolutionary Communist Party and a supporter of both International Socialism and the Labour Party.

The activists involved in the production of the magazine were mainly members of the Nottingham Labour Party, including Ken Coates and Pat Jordan, a bookshop owner who, like Coates, had resigned from the Communist Party in 1956 and had since gravitated towards Labour. In the early 1960s these militants had formed themselves into a loosely organised 'International Group' with the purpose of exploring contacts among socialists at home and abroad to try to organise the revolutionary left into a more cohesive force.

This involved Labour Party membership alongside a covert allegiance to Trotskyism, for despite his profession of loyalty to social democracy Jordan had, since 1959, distributed Fourth International literature through his shop, supporting the old International Secretariat and the Revolutionary Socialist League. Simultaneously with the launching of *The Week*, which marked a big advance for the Labour Party-oriented aspect of this plan, Coates became editor of the *International Socialist Journal* with links to the Unified Secretariat. For the next four years however, Coates and Jordan disclaimed any connections with Trotskyism and sought other allies.[2]

One of the other bodies on the Labour left with which the protogenic IMG became closely involved was the group centred on *The Voice of the Unions* newspaper, which had been published intermittently since before the Second World War. By 1963 its long list of sponsors—including some who also supported *The Week*—included a dozen Labour Members of Parliament, numerous trade union leaders and academics. Like *The Week* it supported the return of a Labour government pledged to a full-blooded socialist programme, and to further its aims launched a series of newspapers in Labour strongholds—*Northern Voice* in Manchester, edited by Frank Allaun, with others on Merseyside, Nottingham and Hull, and papers for individual industries such as *Aviation Voice* for the aircraft industry, *Engineering Voice*, in which Hugh Scanlon was a prime mover, and *Steel-workers' Voice*, which was built around one of the group's major campaigns after the Labour victory of 1964 and called for the nationalisation of the steel industry.

Walter Kendall, writing in the *Voice of the Unions*, regarded this issue as fundamentally important: 'Our aim is clear; we want to wipe out the steel barons as the strongest bastion of the present ruling/ employing class. In their place we want to install representatives of the working class of this country. The struggle to eliminate the steel barons is a struggle to revolutionise the political life of this country'.[3] At this time, the main *Voice of the Unions* newspaper had reached a circulation of nearly 30,000 while the Northern paper sold 4,000 and the Nottingham one 2,000 copies per issue.

In April 1964 *Voice* and *Week* groups combined to promote a conference on workers' control of industry, which attracted a wide range of participants: the left MPs who supported one or other of the journals, including Russell Kerr, Anthony Greenwood, and Bob Edwards; trade unionists such as Frank Cousins, Clive Jenkins, Bernard Dix, Jack Jones and Hugh Scanlon; International Socialists including Paul Foot, Peter Sedgwick and Ray Challinor; anarchists such as Bill Christopher of the Syndicalist Workers Federation, Colin Ward, editor of *Anarchy* magazine and Ken Weller of *Solidarity;* Independent Labour Party members Robin Jenkins and Jenny Morrell and individuals like Pat Jordan, Ken Coates, Tony Topham, who did much of the work organising the conference, Michael Barratt-Brown, Ralph Miliband, Geoffry Ostergaard and John Saville. It was an outstanding success and laid the basis for a series of annual gatherings which were supplemented by local study groups and single industry conferences, particularly for steel, car manufacture, and engineering. The conferences were able to bring together in increasing numbers the widest possible spectrum of opinion on the left, with the exception of the Communist Party and the Socialist Labour League, and they became a focal point of the activity of the two journals that had initiated them. The culmination came in 1968 when, as described below, the conferences were formalised into an Institute for Workers' Control, which, without the International Marxist Group, devoted its efforts to propaganda within the Labour Party.

Thus in just over a year, *The Week* had made such progress that its crypto-Trotskyists decided to consolidate their position by organising themselves more systematically. During 1965, after unsuccessful negotiations with the Revolutionary Socialist League, then undergoing its transformation into the 'Militant' group, *The Week's* Trotskyists— in the words of Tariq Ali—'formally constituted'[4] the International Marxist Group. The fact was to remain a secret, unrecorded and unmentioned until after the IMG's break with the Labour Party in 1968; in the meantime it embarked on a classic exercise of 'entryism', gathering support and exploiting to the full any opportunities to increase its influence that presented themselves.

One such chance arose in September 1965 when Lord Russell, the philosopher and former president of the Committee of 100, became a sponsor of *The Week*, and the financing of the workers' control conferences became inseparably linked with Russell and his Peace Foundation. The Bertrand Russell Peace Foundation was established in 1963, to 'research into matters of peace and war' and was financed by a distinguished array of world leaders, statesmen and personalities.[5]

Within a month of its becoming associated with *The Week*, the Foundation lent its support to the Centre for Socialist Education Campaign, together with *The Week* itself, *The Voice of the Unions*, *New Left Review*, *Militant* and NALSO. Its purpose was to 'promote a grass roots movement which will begin the long and difficult historical process of regrouping the left in the localities. We all agree that this coming together must begin with the trade union militants and the left in the Labour Party'.[6] It established ten branches immediately and another twelve in 1966, organised meetings with the *Humberside Voice* in support of the National Union of Seamen's strike in that year,[7] and sponsored a Workers' Control conference in June 1967. But the ambitious designs of regrouping the left from within the Labour Party and publishing series of pamphlets, papers and books were never realised, for as Charles van Gelderen said: 'Life for socialists inside the Labour Party is frustrating to the point of desperation';[8] within two years some of the key activists on its twenty-one strong committee had moved to other fields, Pat Jordan, Robin Blackburn and Charles van Gelderen in the International Marxist Group, and Peter Sedgwick and John Palmer in the International Socialists.

For *The Week* group the disillusionment with the performance of the Labour government was acute; unlike many left groups it had delighted at the prospect presented in November 1964: 'Mr Wilson,' confidently asserted the magazine, 'has shown his appreciation of the British social structure and his political horse sense in a throne speech which will certainly enthuse Labour's activists and may well create an optimistic mood in hitherto quite lethargic sections of the working class. All the important aspects of Labour's domestic programme are to be carried into effect this session . . . The left can rightly draw encouragement from this'.[9] But in the same month Ernie Roberts, writing in the *Voice of the Unions*, had sounded a warning: 'we cannot accept an incomes policy designed to maintain the present structure of society and keep our present rate of military expenditure at home and abroad'.[10]

Others too in the Socialist Labour League, International Socialism and *New Left Review* had been less sure, and soon *The Week* and its most militant supporters were eating their words. In June 1965 the Third National Workers' Control conference expressed the disenchantment in rejection of George Brown's incomes policy, which it said did not include redistribution of wealth, any provisions for the underpaid, adequate levels of social welfare, or control of property, incomes and prices. By the end of the year Russell had left the party and Coates was expelled for opposing economic and incomes policies, attacking the government's support for the American action in Vietnam at the Labour Party conference in 1965, and for his alleged Trotskyist connections, which he denied. It took him four years to gain re-admission to the party.[11]

But in the story of the International Marxist Group's evolution it was above all the Vietnam issue which acted as the catalyst in bringing about its break with Labour. As early as August 1964 *Week* supporters in Nottingham, including Pat Jordan, had sent a telegram to Harold Wilson demanding he dissociate from United States action. The following year left opposition to the war itself and to the British government's attitude broadened; Vietnam began to supplant the bomb as the primary mobilising issue in the CND; speaking at the London School of Economics in February of that year, Bertrand Russell described the Americans' conduct as 'desperate acts of piratical madness'; and in May 1965 the British Campaign for Peace in Vietnam was launched, with the then Mr Fenner Brockway as chairman, backed by CND, the Movement for Colonial Freedom, church organisations, together with the left wing of the Labour Party and some Liberals.

Not far behind these initiatives, *The Week* launched the Vietnam Solidarity Campaign, the structure of which was planned in the first half of 1966 and which was formally launched in June of that year at a national conference supported by nearly fifty organisations and groups. A council of sixteen members was elected, with Bertrand Russell as President and Ralph Schoenman as Chairman, and including Pat Jordan, Quintin Hoare of the *New Left Review* and later the editor of IMG's *International* magazine, Ken Coates, Tony Topham, John Palmer of the IS and Chris Farley.[12] Its aims were to campaign for an end to American 'aggression' and the withdrawal of its troops from Vietnam, and a reversal of British policy in favour of support for the National Liberation Front in South Vietnam. At first the campaign confined itself to meetings, producing pamphlets, and appeals to the Labour leadership.

From November 1966 the Vietnam Solidarity Campaign worked

closely with the Bertrand Russell Peace Foundation and his International War Crimes Tribunal, which had been set up at the end of the year, with support from such eminent individuals as Jean Paul-Sartre, Isaac Deutscher and Professor Basso, a sociologist at Rome University and editor of the Italian edition of the *International Socialist Journal*. The Foundation, the VSC and the Tribunal shared offices in London, sent a photographic exhibition on tour around the United Kingdom and held joint meetings. Ken Coates became a Director of the Foundation while remaining a member of the VSC council, editor of *The Week* and organiser of the workers' control conferences; Pat Jordan, the effective leader of the International Marxist Group, became organiser of the War Crimes Tribunal's London office and Geoff Coggan, a close ally of Jordan's in the Nottingham Labour Party became the Tribunal's Press Officer. The IMG had thus infiltrated an extensive international organisation, for the Foundation had become a limited company with branches in Argentina, Australia, New Zealand, France, Italy, Japan, the Philippines, India and the United States. Working towards its hearings and final report, the Tribunal sent its teams of observers to Hanoi, including Tariq Ali and Lawrence Daly of the National Union of Mineworkers, who was active in promoting a Scottish Vietnam Solidarity Campaign based on trade union support. The Peace Foundation also despatched what were described as 'fact-finding missions' across the world, including visits made to Havana in 1966 by Ken Coates and Robin Blackburn.

Watching over the world wide operation, the crypto-IMG consolidated its Labour Party base. At the end of 1966 when it became clear that its interests lay in London rather than Nottingham, Jordan moved south, accompanied by his entourage. They installed themselves in North Hammersmith Constituency Labour Party where Jordan and Coggan served on the general management committee; Charles van Gelderen was on its executive and was also a borough councillor. Together they also helped to convert the Fulham and Hammersmith Council for Peace in Vietnam from a relatively moderate body into a pro-Viet Cong Committee of the VSC.

Within eighteen months, however, the united Russell-VSC co-operation had broken down, but by this time the International Marxists had discovered new sources of support and new methods which urged them on to a drastic re-orientation of their whole effort. The first division of opinion came after a demonstration organised by the VSC on October 22, 1967; 5,000 people marched from Trafalgar Square to the American Embassy in Grosvenor Square and became involved in the first of the many violent clashes associated with the anti-Vietnam war movement when some of the crowd attempted to break through police cordons, using sticks and assorted missiles. In the words of a group of sociologists who studied the rise and fall of the Vietnam anti-war movement: 'This event was seen by many of those present as marking a significant break with previous demonstrations both as regards its anti-imperialist political content and the new attitude which some demonstrators displayed towards the police'.[13]

The attitude was one of mutual protection against arrest, and confrontation in a spirit of rebellion. This outburst of revolutionary violence proved too much for some members of the Vietnam Solidarity Campaign: Coates, Topham and Schoenman resigned, leaving the VSC in the control of the IMG, supported by International Socialists. Almost immediately they began planning their next demonstration and in the first two months of 1968 raised £300 to finance the printing of 5,000 posters and 25,000 stickers advertising a demonstration on March 17, 1968. Five times as many people turned out on that day than in the previous October, and the occasion was many more times violent. Unrefined police tactics and the sheer numerical weight of demonstrators produced a bitter confrontation in the grass square in front of the US Embassy. After much missile-throwing and abuse of the police, a mounted charge cleared the area, but 280 people were arrested and 117 police and demonstrators injured. One of the most violent political demonstrations in post-war Britain was described by The Week as 'a big step forward'.[14]

Just two weeks later The Week ceased publication and was replaced in the early summer of 1968 by International, edited for its first four editions by Pat Jordan, after which Mike Martin, a former student of Birmingham University and secretary of the VSC since the end of 1967, took over. This transition from The Week to International marked the break with the Labour Party and the emergence of an open International Marxist Group. It also meant a split between the IMG and VSC on the one hand and the Bertrand Russell Peace Foundation, the Institute for Workers' Control and the Voice of the the Unions on the other, all of whom have remained attached to the Labour Party and have noticeably increased their influence within it.

2

FROM 'ENTRYISM' TO 'NEW LEFT' TROTSKYISM

The Rise and Fall of the Extra-Parliamentary Opposition (1968–70). The IMG's motive for abandoning the Labour Party was first, in the words of The Week prior to the break, that the 'mass left wing opposition to the right wing policies of Labour leaders—which we all expected in 1964 when *The Week* was launched—has not materialised'.[15] This argument has since remained the group's official justification, confirmed by Tariq Ali some years later when he wrote that its early strategy 'premised the emergence of a left current inside the Labour Party which would raise the banners of revolt against the Wilson clique'.[16] And in 1972 a resolution presented by the IMG to a conference merging a youth section, the Spartacus League, with the main group, conceded that there had been 'an incorrect analysis of current within the Labour Party and a failure to break early enough with the practice of entryism'.[17]

In reality entryism had become impossible, since the split in the ranks of *The Week*'s supporters threatened to expose the militant core as revolutionaries and, as the Socialist Labour League had earlier discovered, any suggestion of a Trotskyist cell within the Labour organisation would still not be tolerated.

At first however the IMG was reluctant to reject Labour entirely: Pat Jordan wrote in *International* that 'Marxists should still remain in the Labour Party but doing everything in their power to initiate the most vigorous opposition possible to Wilson'.[18] But by the end of 1968 the continuation of Labour membership was also superfluous, because of the success of the Vietnam protests and the student movement, and all pretence that a revolutionary opposition was possible from within the party was dropped. At that time, in view of the developments outside Labour's orbit, Jordan confidently asserted that 'the objective conditions now exist for building a revolutionary party' which would 're-establish the authority and prestige of Bolshevik norms of organisation', act as the vanguard of the working class generalising its experiences into a corpus of revolutionary theory, and convert the workers to those beliefs and lead them to socialism.[19] Thus in less than a year Jordan and his associates had moved from defenders of social democracy to advocates of Leninist revolution.

Their departure from Labour had however cut them off from the very workers they desired to lead; instead, through the protest of the Vietnam Solidarity Campaign, they had discovered a style of politics that was diametrically opposed to that of the Labour Party and which did not involve the working class. It comprised spontaneous direct action, the student movement and the Extra-Parliamentary Opposition, a concept borrowed from German students and at first it generated much excitement and frenetic activity. This discovery of a 'New Left' accounted for the IMG's optimism that revolutionary methods were a real possibility in Britain, but the attempt to identify it with working class discontent was a delusion.

Setting to work on the heterogeneous forces of the 'New Left' and trying to encase them within the framework of Trotskyist socialism, the International Marxists ranged far and wide. During the summer of 1968, they were hosts of the visit to Britain of Paul Boutelle, the black vice-president of the American Socialist Workers' Party, and sent him on a speaking tour to London, Birmingham, Sheffield, Nottingham, Newcastle and Glasgow. Tariq Ali, the Pakistani Oxford graduate who joined the IMG in the spring of 1968, took the chair and introduced on to the platform British Black Power leaders in groups such as the Universal Coloured Peoples' Association. The International Marxists were highly critical of the reluctance of the Socialist Labour League and the International Socialists to embrace Black Power and asserted that Boutelle's visit and 'his influence on the black community has we are sure, considerably hastened the formation of a Black Power movement in this country with a programme'.[20] That movement, where it had an ideological programme, was however more likely to express it in pro-Chinese than Trotskyist terms, and although the IMG has since taken a close interest in black politics—helping to form Black Defence Committees in London at the beginning of the 1970s for example—its appeal among immigrants has been strictly limited.

During the summer of 1968 Vietnam and student activity shaped the development of the IMG. To plan for a major demonstration against the Vietnam war on October 27, 1968, an *ad hoc* committee was set up, including Tariq Ali, Vanessa Redgrave and Mike Martin, with representatives from a broad sweep of left-wing opinion. As the demonstration approached, rumours of street fighting and great violence, fuelled by the press, built up an atmosphere that was highly charged with emotion. In the event, the vast majority of the 50,000 members were peaceful, although several hundred Maoists and Anarchists attempted to storm Grosvenor Square, in front of the American Embassy, which the main column of marchers had been content to by-pass. October 27 was however more than a mere demonstration. In a special edition to mark the occasion, *Black Dwarf*, unofficial voice of the Extra-Parliamentary Opposition, rejected parliament as irrelevant and the Labour government as conservative. Instead it hoped for a joint committee of all left groups, to create out of the demonstration a new opposition force, based on militant action and the extra-parliamentary New Left. Its dreams were shared by the IMG but they never materialised, and what Mike Martin described as a 'mood of uncertainty and frustration' followed the demonstration of October 27.[21] On that day the 'demo' had reached its zenith, had achieved little and a feeling of anti-climax set in. Attempts to repeat the occasion would have been fruitless since none could have been

113

preceded by such an emotional build-up, and Vietnam's magnetism as a mobilising issue was already beginning to diminish. The lessons learnt in those demonstrations—especially that set-piece confrontation with the police offset any propaganda or recruiting advantages the campaign possessed—would have to be applied in other contexts. Discussion between the rival groups in the VSC on whether it should confine itself to Vietnam or broaden its scope to agitate on domestic social and political issues led to its break-up. Other campaigns modelled on the VSC were launched: a Palestine Solidarity Campaign in 1969 romanticised the Fedayeen, before Black September soured their cause;[22] an Irish Civil Rights Solidarity Campaign in the same year mirrored the pre-terrorist phase of the present Irish conflict, and in 1970 a Ceylon Solidarity Campaign was set up, but with an esoteric appeal for devotees of Trotskyist history. The International Marxists were active in all of these ventures and remained the principal pillar of the Vietnam Solidarity Campaign when all others had deserted it.

Since 1968 the IMG has been firmly convinced of the value of building a domestic revolutionary movement in the 'Solidarity Campaign'. It has scoured the world in search of causes where the issues are clear-cut and where a *cause célèbre* can arouse anti-establishment outrage and moral indignation. Impact and propaganda value are critical since campaigns develop best in a highly-charged climate. The Solidarity Campaigns may reveal something of the passing whims of revolutionaries, their selective moral judgments and their internationalist consciences, but they are more pertinent to revolutionary activism at home than to events in Asia or the Middle East. The basic aim was, in the period 1968–70, to promote the concept of radical politics envisaged in the term Extra-Parliamentary Opposition, an alliance of various schools of thought agreed on their total opposition to established authority and institutions. This amounted to developing a whole new style of activity and a new movement for change, in the context of which campaigning to secure a change in government policy on a specific issue was irrelevant. The Vietnam and other similar campaigns were not, in the minds of the activists who engineered them, mere 'pressure-groups' but were foundations of a new socialist consciousness.

Such ventures were but one half of the total effort: concomitant with them was the student movement, which provided the main source of numerical support and helped finance campaigns with donations from student funds, a practice which has continued since. To Trotskyists of the International Marxists' persuasion students pointed the way to revolution in the west: they were a new vanguard unsullied by the opiate fruits of consumer capitalism that had befuddled the minds of the workers. This argument became the official policy of the Unified Secretariat of the Fourth International, whose leading theorist, Belgian political scientist Ernest Mandel, summarised its view thus: 'The traditional organisations of the workers' movement are profoundly bureaucratised and long since co-opted into the bourgeois society ... However amongst students, a larger minority, precisely because they are in a more privileged social and intellectual situation than the workers, can free themselves'.[23]

Through taking the initiative in direct action, students, it was believed; could revive the tradition of revolution in the west, as events in America and France in particular demonstrated. Trotskyist revolutionaries such as those of the IMG frequently took the lead in student and student-supported campaigns, moulding the inchoate voices of dissent, channelling them into moral protest on issues such as the Vietnam war and then hoping to convert them into conscious revolutionism.

Following their success in the early Vietnam demonstrations, which had galvanised local student discontents into a national movement, the newly emerged IMG took an instrumental role in the formation of Britain's first student body dedicated to the overthrow of the present system, the Revolutionary Socialist Students Federation. The RSSF emerged from a conference held at the LSE on June 15, 1968, and attended by 200 students and revolutionaries from most British universities, together with a number from overseas—among them Fourth International supporters—who were in the country ostensibly for a BBC television programme on student revolt.[24]

The new organisation pledged itself to the revolutionary overthrow of capitalism, support for workers in dispute, and declared itself to be the Extra-Parliamentary Opposition. It grew very rapidly to a strength of several thousand and at its second conference, at the end of 1968, adopted an action programme around the Student Red Base concept: this envisaged the creation of revolutionary cadres in universities and colleges, the mobilising of hundreds of students for militant activity within educational institutions and without, the use of universities and colleges for revolutionary purposes including the rejection of 'bourgeois culture', placing them under the control of the general assembly of students, staff and workers. Within the educational system all selectivity, exams, grading and distinction between forms of higher education were to be abolished and from this secure 'soviet' base the students would go forward to win over the working class.[25]

By the beginning of 1969 however the latent divisions in the RSSF began to appear. Besides the IMG in the Federation were the International Socialists, who despised many of the assumptions of the so-called 'New Left', the *Black Dwarf* and *New Left Review* magazines, the intellectuals of the 'May Day Manifesto Group', the Maoist Communist Party of Britain (Marxist-Leninist) and some anarchists. Above all the others the IMG held high hopes from the RSSF. Pat Jordan wrote that while the VSC had performed a valuable but limited function, the RSSF should be capable of more substantial achievement.[26] It floundered however on the arguments concerning the role of the students in the revolutionary process and their relationship to the working class, which were couched in increasingly dogmatic terms by rival factions. The RSSF's plans for universities failed to materialise, and despite some contacts with workers at Ford's Dagenham plant and with the People's Democracy organisation in Northern Ireland, it was unable to communicate with a wider circle. The IMG accused the IS of poaching the organisation for the benefit of its own membership, the key London branch broke away under Maoist leadership,[27] and the rank and file members not committed to one ideological school or another fell away.

By the end of 1969, the RSSF and with it the Extra-Parliamentary Opposition was dead. The *Black Dwarf* magazine fell under the domination of the International Marxist Group, with Tariq Ali, Robin Blackburn (expelled from his post as a junior lecturer at the London School of Economics for his role in disturbances there) and Peter Gowan as its main representatives on the editorial board. They broke with the magazine in February 1970 to launch the next month, *Red Mole*, a fortnightly newspaper specifically associated with the IMG. Within another six months *Black Dwarf* had folded, and the last symbol of the spirit of 1968—with its demos and student Red Bases—had vanished.

During the last years of the 1960s the Marxist revolutionary groups had converted the student movement to their own ends and attempted to attach to it doctrines of socialist revolution. In the process they at first gave that movement concrete form, but it was too nebulous and wide-ranging to lend itself to encapsulation in Trotskyist doctrine or organisation, the attempt to do which placed it in a strait-jacket that stifled its natural development. The IMG in particular, by the intensity of its commitment, had killed the principal agent of its own designs.

After the Student Vanguard (1970–73). The manifest failure of the basic assumptions of the New Left in the late sixties—revolution in the west spearheaded by students in direct action in association with the oppressed peoples of the Third World—called for a reassessment of the IMG's efforts. First it dropped the ideological arguments identified with the previous phase, restating instead the primacy of the proletariat; and secondly it attended more closely to building its own organisation and less to involvement in general campaigns. Its attempts to shake off the theory and practice of student and 'demo'-based activism met however with mixed success.

Closely behind the establishment of its own newspaper, the International Marxist Group promoted the setting up of Red Circles (in name at least reminiscent of the abandoned Red Bases). They were initially intended to be discussion groups of *Red Mole* readers and eventually local IMG branches. Twenty-four such circles were in existence in March 1970 when the project was launched and the number had increased to thirty-eight by the beginning of the following year. The IMG also formed its own youth section in the middle of 1970, the Spartacus League, under the chairmanship of Peter Gowan. Its aim was to attract the working class youth at whom the Young Communist League, Socialist Labour League Young Socialists and Labour Party Young Socialists also aimed, not merely the narrower category of those in higher education. But the Spartacus League failed abysmally and in 1971 announced its intention to concentrate on activity in the National Union of Students. A year later it was dissolved by the extraordinary means of 'fusing' it with the IMG itself, as though they had been two quite separate bodies. The Fusion Conference—typical of Trotskyists' traditional predilection for grandifying their own internal machinations—admitted the International Marxist Group's earlier mistakes, including the discredited theories of the student vanguard, and took the opportunity to restate its basic policies: the cardinal importance of the Transitional Programme as defined in 1938 by the founders of the Fourth International, the impossibility of 'socialism in one country', the epoch of capitalist crisis and the world-wide proletarian revolt that must follow.[28]

Despite the renewed emphasis on the working class the IMG was unable to escape the legacy of 1968. But henceforth students were designated part of the working class, and the NUS—derided as an establishment bureaucracy in 1968—was depicted as a trade union. Its ideological solidarity with workers in conflict would be translated into the presence of students on picket lines, student funds for strike disputes and the machinery of revolutionary propaganda placed at the disposal of industrial workers. The IMG utilised the literature of the Claimants' Unions, which had been set up in 1970, and in particular the *Claimants' Handbook for Strikers* to service industrial disputes. And in the 1972 miners' strike IMG supporters at Essex University formed a Colchester United Front for the Defence of Miners and supplied a stream of power station pickets and propaganda distributors.

The group's main focus of purely student activity after the failure

117

of the Spartacus League was the Liaison Committee for the Defence of Student Unions, a conscious imitation of the Communist Party-dominated Liaison Committee for the Defence of Trades Unions. A joint venture with the International Socialists at the end of 1971, it proposed a programme of student-worker solidarity, militant action in demonstrations and strikes, especially against interference in student union affairs by college authorities, and against negotiations between the NUS and a Conservative government on issues such as grants. Within the NUS it hoped to unite the revolutionary left against the Broad Left alliance of Communists, Labour and uncommitted socialists, but in less than a year it had collapsed; the IS withdrew leaving the IMG high and dry, and any coherent revolutionary opposition to the Broad Left's domination of the union on a national level was brought to an inglorious conclusion.

Whatever they may have wished, the International Marxists still found their greatest scope for agitation in the single issue campaigns. They supported the Stop the Seventy Tour in 1970, revived the Vietnam Solidarity Campaign during that summer when the American forces invaded Cambodia, and kept interest sufficiently alive to form an Indo-China Solidarity Campaign in September 1972. This was backed at first by the National Union of Students and by Agit-Prop, the now defunct radical news and information service that had premises in East London and included a number of American activists in Britain.[29] The Indo-China Campaign secured the support of the American linguist, Noam Chomsky, and journalist I.F. Stone in December 1972 on the same platform as the North Vietnam's representative in Paris, but its first 'mass' demonstration mustered only 700 people. Politically and emotionally the Indo-Chinese campaign was stillborn: it became lost in a vague generalised 'anti-imperialism' and its propaganda lacked the riveting, compassionate appeal of Vietnam.

The increasingly violent events in Northern Ireland provided the IMG with new issues that demanded attention. A year after the Irish Civil Rights Solidarity Campaign of 1969 came the Irish Solidarity Campaign, with the slogan 'Victory to the IRA' and engaging the IMG, the International Socialists, the republican Clann na h'Eirann, People's Democracy, the Civil Rights Association and the Vietnam Solidarity Campaign. These groups represented some of the most militant British supporters of a thirty-two-county Workers' Republic of Ireland, for whom the renewed conflict in the traditional Achilles heel of British colonialism was a crucial test case and a preliminary to revolt on the mainland. 'Nothing would destroy the credibility of the British ruling class more', declared *Red Mole* in 1972, 'than to be soundly defeated in Ireland. It is . . . in the most immediate interests of the British working class for the British ruling class to be defeated and an understanding of this would immediately raise the revolutionary potential of the British working class.'[30] After the introduction of detention without trial in 1971 the Anti-Internment League was formed with a wider range of support, leaving the IMG as the largest group in the Irish Solidarity Campaign. With it however remained the Workers' Fight, a hard-line breakaway faction from the International Socialists, the Revolutionary Workers' Group, the Irish section of the Fourth International and Saor Eire (meaning Free Ireland) a tiny organisation with Trotskyist connections that had carried out fund-raising bank raids in the republic during the mid-sixties. In the wake of the first bomb attacks by the IRA in England during 1972, the ISC's slogan was changed to 'Solidarity with the IRA', and a rapprochement with the Anti-Internment League was brought about.[31] Bob Purdie, a leading IMG member, became the League's organiser in Glasgow, where he also lost his deposit as a parliamentary candidate in the general election of February 1974.

Although reaction to events in Ireland lent themselves to the promotion of propaganda campaigns, other specialised interests such as the 'women's lib' movement that emerged at the beginning of the 1970s required a less spectacular approach. The IMG set up a women's section in 1970 with its own newspaper, *Socialist Woman*, whose work came to notice the next year when they assisted the progress of a night-cleaners' dispute in London. May Hobbs, who emerged from that strike as the archetypal battling Cockney, thanked the *Socialist Woman* group for its efforts on her behalf and contributed to the campaign to convert the fortnightly *Red Mole* newspaper into an expanded *Red Weekly*, which was launched during 1973.[32] As a counterpart to the women's group, the IMG also has an active Gay Group, similarly arguing that the homosexual condition is the result of exploitation and oppression under capitalism, illustrating once again the group's tendency to try to blend Marxist ideology with the social forces of a 'New Left'.

In general the opening years of the present decade were a period of adjustment for the International Marxists, firstly to make up for ground lost in entryism, and, secondly, to restate their basic beliefs after the erroneous conceptions held in the years devoted to the student movement.

The Crisis of Capitalism? (1974–75): The winter of 1973–74 acted as something of a catalyst for the IMG, as it did for many others on the far left, to present them with what they saw as capitalism's death agonies, demanding their most ambitious statements of policy to date.

The International Marxists believed firstly that their task was to educate the workers into understanding that inflation, unemployment, insecurity and conflict are inherent in capitalism; secondly that they must assist the workers in organising to meet the effects of crisis and to defend their interests, from which position they could, thirdly, lead the workers into the offensive against the capitalists and their supporters.

In language redolent of the 1938 Transitional Programme the IMG freely admitted that violent conflict was inevitable and that the workers must be prepared to organise and resist. A general strike was inevitable, in which situation workers should form local Councils of Action to bring together militants of different persuasions in one body, to take over as a *de facto* authority in factories, housing estates and towns, confront police, and organise transport, essential services and the distribution of food in working class districts. The enforcement of this plan on the streets would be achieved through the 'centralised organisation of picket squads. Thousands of pickets have to be organised not just to stop lorries or scabs going in or out of the factories but to control and patrol the main roads themselves. The defence of these pickets against the police requires the creation of a Workers' Defence Corps. These must be under the control of a central authority, must be mobile and must be able to take on large bodies of police on their own terms'.[33]

This authority would be the Councils of Action, which would become 'foundations of socialist revolution and the backbone of the workers' state'.[34] Looking beyond the revolutionary situation this state would be organised through elected workers' councils to run all aspects of social, political and economic life, culminating in a National Council of Workers' Delegates, backed by a Workers' Militia to oppose reactionaries. Such was the authentic voice of revolutionary Trotskyism at the time of the miners' strike of 1974 and the general election that it prompted. During that strike some IMG-influenced Councils of Action did emerge, as the first stage of the plan, in Oxford, Rotherham and Chesterfield, but ironically it was the election of a Labour government that defused the situation and ensured that the revolutionaries' designs were confined to the pages of *Red Weekly*. The IMG's three candidates in the first general election of 1974 all lost their deposits.[35]

With each twist of the inflationary spiral, each major pay dispute and each failed government policy, the IMG has hardened its attitude to the crisis, repeatedly calling for the general strike that would set its scheme in motion. In support of the Shrewsbury Pickets, miners, railwaymen, or dockers, countless column inches of *Red Weekly* and innumerable meetings up and down the country have hammered the message across, but to little avail.

The truth of the matter is that the IMG has few worker or trade union members. In the middle of 1974 it was reported to have had fifty local branches comprising 1,000 fully paid-up members, with up to 500 serving a candidate membership period of six months.[36] Of these the majority are students, with a few supporters in the National Union of Teachers, the National Association of Local Government Officers, and other white collar professions. Of manual workers the IMG can claim only a scattering of health service workers, some in the mining industry and an active group at British Leyland's Cowley plant. There are some individual members in other unions and industries but the group cannot muster sufficient working class support to organise its own militant trade union body. Its sympathisers have instead tended to become involved in the predominantly International Socialist Rank and File movement or in the Liaison Committee for the Defence of Trades Unions which the IMG officially supported until 1973.

Although the IMG continues to draw its own support from among students, its contribution to national student politics has declined. Attempts to launch an Alternative Left or 'Revolutionary State' in conjunction with other Trotskyists or the IS have not got off the ground and the Broad Left has remained secure at the top of the NUS. In 1974 no IMG representative was elected to the NUS executive and in 1975 only one gained a place. At a local level and particularly in the disruption of meetings and campuses the International Marxists can however still bring pressure to bear. At Essex University in the early part of 1974 the group's supporters were prominent in weeks of occupations, demonstrations and strikes which culminated in one hundred students being arrested when they tried to prevent delivery vehicles from entering the campus. At Kent, Oxford and East Anglia universities—where the IMG disrupted the visit of an RAF recruiting team—the group's sympathisers were sufficiently concentrated and determined to launch into direct action.

On the whole the group's main positive contribution to the revolutionary movement has remained in the single issue campaigns. Events abroad still provide many of the mobilising causes for propaganda campaigns but attention has been increasingly focused on their lessons for socialists in Britain. In the Chile Solidarity Campaign for example, founded at the end of 1973, the IMG and other Trotskyist elements support their exiled counterparts in the militant MIR and argue that the impossibility of a peaceful revolution was indisputably demonstrated in Chile. The orthodox Communists however support the deposed Allende regime for trying the correct strategy, only to be thwarted by fascist militarists. The arguments are not so much about

Chile as about a strategy for Britain, continuing the generations-old dispute whether force is necessary in the revolution. For the IMG, Portugal's experiences re-inforce its view that its cause can only triumph through armed might and the physical elimination of counter-revolutionary interests. The group's campaigns in Portugal are also directed towards boosting the Fourth International sympathisers there, the small International Communist League.

Portugal and Chile are for the IMG living examples of capitalist crisis, where the bourgeoisie has retreated into fascism to defend itself against socialism as the system crumbles about it. And in Britain similar developments have been detected in the growth over the last three to four years of the National Front, the partly fascist, partly populist movement of the far-right. In response, the International Marxists have contributed to an extensive and violent campaign that began early in 1974. Its general election manifesto in February of that year urged that 'wherever the fascists try to appear publicly, the workers' movement must organise to drive them off the streets and force them to seek protection from their natural allies, the bosses' police. "No platform for fascists" must be our slogan'.[37]

The general policy was adopted, among much discussion about the indivisible nature of free speech, at the National Union of Students in April 1974 and numerous National Front and right-wing Tory meetings in colleges and universities were hounded and disrupted. In June, the IMG, with International Socialists and the Communist Party of England (Marxist-Leninist) attended a rally organised by Liberation (formerly the Movement for Colonial Freedom) to prevent the National Front from meeting. A violent clash took place in Red Lion Square, in central London, between police and the left-wingers, during which a student died. A judical enquiry was ordered to investigate the events and it unequivocally blamed the IMG for deliberate premeditated violence.[38] In reply to this verdict the IMG accepted no responsibility for what happened, but blamed instead the Labour government for allowing the National Front meeting to take place, thereby giving offence to immigrants and ignoring the wishes of the workers.[39]

From the middle of 1974 onwards the IMG and other revolutionary groups pursued the National Front across the land. Anti-Fascist Committees soon appeared in South Shields, Basingstoke and Oxford, where 400 Left demonstrators picketed a hundred people at an NF meeting. In Birmingham 500 counter marchers—including local Sinn Fein and Clan nah 'Eireann groups, the Indian Workers Association, Gay Liberation, IS and CPGB, as well as the IMG—outnumbered the Front by five to one. In Kent, at an Anti-Fascist Committee rally,

IMG student president John McGeown shared a platform with Communist Jack Dunn of the National Union of Mineworkers. During the autumn election campaign in 1974 many of the National Front's 92 candidates were harassed and IMG claimed a large share of the credit, although they were more than ably supported by the IS, Communist Party and Labour Party Young Socialists in particular.

Just as the rise of the National Front has been depicted as the reaction of capitalists to their crisis, so too have the policies of the government in relation to the Irish troubles. The IMG election manifesto of 1974 warned that: 'The presence of the British army in Ireland is a direct threat to the British working class, because the techniques being developed there, and many of the soldiers who are learning them will be used by the ruling class to suppress workers' struggles in this country. Already there are reports of crowd control techniques developed by the army in Ireland being used by British police against flying pickets'.[40] Forecasts of military involvement in British politics as a result of economic crisis have become widespread on the revolutionary left and closely linked with the experiences gained by the army in Ireland. By mid-1974, when the Anti-Internment League had long since run out of steam, attention was focused on the army in a Troops Out Movement, which called for the immediate withdrawal of the army from Ireland and the prevention of any further development in its counter-revolutionary warfare tactics. TOM very quickly gained the support of six Labour MPs, and its founding conference in May 1974 was attended by 600 people, including representatives of 14 Trades Councils, 29 trade union branches and 47 students' groups.[41]

The extension of IRA bombing to the British mainland also forced some changes of attitude. At first the IMG declared that it 'unconditionally supports the right of the Irish republican movement to carry on armed action against British imperialism. We do not hold that in principle such armed actions should be confined to the other side of the Irish channel'.[42] The horrors of the Guildford and Birmingham bombings at the end of 1974 persuaded it to condemn attacks on defenceless civilians, but its conscience was only moved to action after the passing of the Prevention of Terrorism Act, when it organised an open letter to the Labour movement calling for the Act's repeal and the withdrawal of troops, drawing the support of several Labour backbench MPs and trade unionists.[43] The IMG's involvement in these anti-military efforts prompted by the course of events in Ireland had indeed met with greater success than most of its earlier campaigns in securing working class support.

Similarly the activities of IMG members in the women's Lib

movement enabled it to strike up many new contacts. The group supported the Working Women's Charter during 1975: at one meeting organised by London Trades Council, the IMG was in the mixed company of the IS and the Communist Party, 46 trade union branches, 26 trades council, and 35 women's groups. The assembly agreed to campaign for equal pay, equal legal and job opportunities and working conditions, increased family allowances, free nurseries and family planning clinics and more women trade union officials.[44] This mainly economic programme was paralleled by the National Abortion Campaign, to press for free abortion on demand, and supported by the IMG, IS and Communist Party, the National Union of Students, miscellaneous women's groups, eleven Labour MPs and numerous Labour Party branches, Young Socialists, and trades councils.[45]

For the hardline Women's Libbers of the IMG the programmes of these initiatives were merely 'transitional demands' that made social and economic sense at a time of crisis. The extent of their ultimate designs were reflected in a document circulated for discussion prior to the IMG's 1975 National Congress:

'The family is a mechanism by which the ruling class throws the responsibility for children on to individual parents rather than on society as a whole. It is a means of passing property ownership from one generation to another and so insuring the inheritance rights of the bourgeoisie. It is a mechanism for the reproduction of human labour power in which women are fundamentally reduced to a reproductive role. It is a mechanism for the exploitation of women as wage workers.'[46]

One fact differentiates the IMG's most recent campaigns from their earlier ventures: the extent to which they have been able to work with members of other organisations, and in particular with the Labour Party, without immediately precipitating ideological schisms. Since 1968 the International Marxists have been contemptuous of Labour's parliamentarianism and savage in their criticism of the party's leadership. In the last two years however they have found many kindred spirits on the left of the Labour Party and in its constituency branches. This is more as a result of the emergence of a revolutionary current in Labour itself—an idea the IMG rejected in 1968—than through the International Marxists' own efforts. By the middle of 1975, as a result of the Left's prominence in the Labour Party and the contacts established during the latest campaigns, the IMG began to revise its opinions, to consider the possibility of supporting sections of the Labour left in its battles against the social democratic wing of the party, with a view to opening up a new relationship between the Labour left and the revolutionary groups. These sentiments were reciprocated by Syd Bidwell MP, former chairman of the *Tribune* group, who, through the columns of *Red Weekly*, urged that its readers 'and young Marxists, including members of the IMG, should forget the romance of other countries—Russia in 1917 and so on—and understand that you can't by-pass the Labour Party . . . I believe all socialists, particularly young socialists, should join the Labour Party and get into the mainstream. I think the various Trotskyist groupings should assess the situation carefully and without romance, and should then help to take hold of the Labour Party locally and nationally for socialist purpose'.[47]

It is yet difficult to discern whether this détente between two bitterly opposed schools of socialist thought is more than just another of the IMG's innumerable tactical switches and the attempt once more to fuse new left and old. In these changes of course, however, it has often found itself at the centre of some well-publicised enterprises, but, involving many other groups for a limited duration, these have not given the IMG any firm foundations on which to build. Participation in any particular campaign has rarely led to increased membership or lasting commitment, and the result has been that the IMG has not grown as quickly as many of its rivals. But its energy and its contacts abroad, through the Fourth International and with other revolutionaries in the Middle East, Chile and Ireland in particular, give it an influence greater than its size would suggest. If the group were to pay closer attention to the Labour left it would find that its former colleagues in the Institute for Workers' Control and Voice of the Unions organisation had made some measurable progress, as evidence of the other side of the revolutionary coin, the growth of Labour far Left.

3

THE MOVEMENT FOR WORKERS' CONTROL

Within six years of its foundation, the Institute for Workers' Control progressed from the obscurity of the Trotskyist-connected fringe to a prominent position on Labour's left wing, supported by government ministers and a dozen backbench Members of Parliament. Its growth reflects both the increasing interest in the subject of workers' participation in the management of industry across the whole of the political spectrum and, more particularly, the steady resurgence of radical socialism in the Labour Party.

The Institute was set up at the sixth national conference on workers' control in June 1968, just a few months after the International Marxist

Group, joint sponsors of the previous five gatherings since 1964, had embarked on their independent course as an open Trotskyist organisation. Supporting the new Institute were the Bertrand Russell Peace Foundation and the Voice of the Unions group with the individual backing of several hundred activists in trade unions, Labour Party and the academic world. Its aims were intellectual and political: 'to act as a research and educational body, to co-ordinate discussion and communication between workers' control groups, and trade unions, to provide lists of speakers and publish important material on the subject of industrial democracy and workers' control',[48] and calling for 'workers everywhere to form workers' control groups, to develop a democratic consciousness, winning support for workers' control in all existing labour organisations, challenging undemocratic actions wherever they occur, and extending workers' control over industry, and the economy itself, thus uniting workers' control groups into a united force in the socialist movement'.[49]

In pursuit of these aims it has produced a prolific output of books, magazines and pamphlets with contributions from trade unionists Hugh Scanlon, Lawrence Daly, Ernie Roberts, assistant general secretary of the engineering union, Walter Greendale, a Hull docker who serves on the Executive Committee of the Transport and General Workers Union, and Brian Nicholson, who works in the London docks. The Institute also publishes a fortnightly bulletin but is best known for its annual conferences, some of which have been attended by over 1,000 delegates. These have extended discussion and debate on the subject of workers' control to an influential circle on the left, including, since 1973, Mr Anthony Wedgwood Benn, who, on being appointed Secretary of State for Industry the following year, invited the Institute to submit its recommendations on industrial democracy.[50]

Closely associated with Mr Benn's ideas has been one of the Institute's Council members, Stuart Holland, who worked in Harold Wilson's Political Office from 1964–68, and was a special adviser to Mrs Judith Hart at the Ministry of Overseas Development in 1974. A year later he published The Socialist Challenge, an analysis of modern multi-national capitalism and a strategy for a peaceful transformation of society to socialism, which was greeted as a major theoretical contribution to the left in Britain. Holland has indeed been closely involved in the evolution of many of Labour's central economic policies during the present decade.[51]

Other prominent supporters include Michael Barratt-Brown of Sheffield University, and Members of Parliament—Stan Newens, Joan Maynard, Audrey Wise, Stanley Orme, Arthur Palmer, Neil Kinnock, Jo Richardson, Harry Selby, Tom Litterick, Eric Heffer,

Michael Meacher and Ron Thomas. Their participation alone is ample evidence of the Institute's tangible advance in the political sphere. One of the most vigorous advocate of workers' control, at the centre of the Institute's activities since its inception has been Ken Coates, who in 1969 regained the Labour Party membership he lost four years previously. Since his reinstatement this former Communist and Trotskyist sympathiser has made several unsuccessful attempts to gain election to the National Executive Committee, polling an average of 50,000 votes.

The Institute's role in more militant activity is less extensive. In October 1970 the 1,300 delegates at the eighth conference on workers' control supported a one-day strike against the Tories' Industrial Relations Bill. 'If the unions were determined,' wrote Coates soon after, 'they could quite certainly stop the Bill. They could by massive action compel the government either to drop the Bill or resign and call a general election. Massive industrial action is justified and necessary.'[52] And in 1973 the Institute became involved in the occupation at Briants' printing works in London, assisting in propaganda and the keeping of accounts. However, although it wishes to centralise industrial and political demands for workers' control into one movement, it generally stops short of creating its own activist groups at local level. It has a few regional institutes in the London area and in the west Midlands and also holds regular gatherings for separate industrial groups, particularly car workers, dockers and miners, attracting many well-known militants. Some otherwise sympathetic groups are critical of its lack of active involvement in industrial disputes. The IMG said the Institute for Workers' Control 'has never clearly defined itself or decided whether it is to be a purely educational organisation or an action-oriented body',[53] and the Voice of the Union has criticised it on similar grounds.

Neither has the Institute stated its own policies or aims precisely, preferring not to tie itself to a dogmatic line and still less to create a pseudo-party organisation. In so far as they have been defined, its goals are for a society of workers' 'self-management', perhaps akin to Yugoslavia, which could be reached only after a phase in which the workers seize control of the present structure and proceed to dismantle it.[54] The Institute's leaders however wish to keep their doors open to many varieties of socialist—Marxist, Trotskyist, guild socialist—and encourage their basic principles to permeate slowly through the consciousness of the Labour Party. Throughout its life, the Institute has been closely linked with the Bertrand Russell Peace Foundation, with which it shares offices. The Foundation takes a broader interest in international affairs and publishes its own series of pamphlets and books, but there is however a clear overlapping of purpose and personnel between the two bodies, and many of its publications have been written by the Institute's supporters.[55]

In recent years the Institute for Workers' Control has moved away from the orbit of The *Voice of the Unions*. But the *Voice* too continues to support the Labour Party as a vehicle for socialism, on the grounds summarised by Ernie Roberts: 'Lenin was right to say that the Labour Party was in effect only an imperfect tool for the workers' use. Nevertheless it has greater potential for the British working class than any other party. Revolutionary tactics within the Labour Party therefore have a much greater chance of getting proletarian backing than the same tactics operated outside the mainstream of working class politics'.[56]

Its scheme of revolution is based not on a single act of the seizure of power but the 'steady erosion of capitalist authority by Revolutionary Reforms within capitalist society'.[57] It is highly critical of independent sectarian parties who try to by-pass the Labour Party, but has stated that 'there is a place waiting in the Labour Party and in the trade unions for all the socialist militants in groups outside'.[58] The *Voice of the Unions* is, however, highly critical of Labour policies in office— it described the Wilson government in 1967 as the 'worst since 1931'.[59] Inside the party the *Voice* has supported many of the ideas associated with the *Tribune* group, the Young Socialists and its campaigns particularly for democracy in the party, which means for Labour leaders rigid adherence and accountability to the decisions of its annual conference.

Its concept of the Labour Party in action is of an organisation that 'must abandon its electoral obsession—both in parliament and local government. We must build up the extra-parliamentary activity of the Labour Party so that it becomes once again the political wing of the organised labour movement. The Party's rank and file must develop real links with shop stewards' organisations, community action groups, student groups and the anti-apartheid movement'.[60]

Extra-parliamentary activity includes factory occupation, not as a symbolic gesture but as a revolutionary act of workers' control.

'The growth of occupation as a form of protest', argues Roberts, 'contains the seeds of workers' control and socialism in that it is a challenge to the private ownership of property.

'That challenge must come from the workers. It must start with the rank and file and express itself in the choice of a militant trade union leadership and ultimately—through the activities of the trade unions—in a revolutionary leadership in the Labour Party.'[61]

Under such a leadership, Roberts foresees the possibility of the transition from a capitalist state to a socialist one: 'The Labour Party should, when it achieves power, set about restructuring the way that representatives are elected. Representatives could be elected directly by the workers from the various industries and services in the country, which of course must be publicly owned, to sit in a new kind of parliament—an Industrial Parliament'.[62]

This is the theory, but like the Institute for Workers' Control, the *Voice of the Unions* group has refrained from creating its own 'party within a party' organisation or from attempting to put its plans into operation with its own limited resources. Its influence is less perceptible than the Institute's, its tone less strident and its immediate political ambitions less obvious. The consolidation of these two revolutionary bodies as left-wing pressure groups on a right-wing leadership is however both a contributory factor towards, and an effect of, the party's general leftward movement. In the mid-1970s, groups such as these, in company with the Young Socialists, have made revolutionary ideas more acceptable to Labour's membership, and the party more attractive to revolutionary activists than at any other time in the post-war era. They have developed strategies of socialism that appear to stand in a non-violent, British tradition of gradualism, and which make full use of existing institutions.

Although many political and temperamental differences exist between Labour's revolutionaries and those in independent groups, the disagreements have often turned on means rather than ends. Some Marxists have indeed begun to feel that the conditions of the 1970s could bring the two strands closer together. One group however has set its face firmly against Labour and embarked upon a separate path, building its own Leninist party, its own trade union movement, propaganda machinery and single issue campaigns—the International Socialists.

VI

'Neither Washington
nor Moscow . . .'

INTERNATIONAL SOCIALISM:
FROM THEORY TO ACTION

For more than a decade and a half the group known today as the
International Socialists languished in obscurity as a tiny faction
attached to the Labour Party, without influence and with no hope of
building the mass revolutionary movement to which its members
aspired. Since then, in half the time of the unproductive period, the
IS has emerged as one of the most active and vigorous groups on the
far left. Like the Workers' Revolutionary Party and the International
Marxist Group it has contemptuously cast off the cloak of Labourism,
but more extensively than either of its Trotskyist cousins has combined
student support and single-issue campaigns with a rank-and-file
industrial network and a nationwide propaganda organisation. As they
enter the second half of the 1970s, the International Socialists
believe themselves to be hovering on the brink of a major breakthrough in their size and appeal, and relish the descriptions of their
group in the conservative press as 'the country's fastest growing and
most professional organisation'.[1]

The State-Capitalist Heresy (1950–66). The origins of this resourceful
body of Marxist revolutionaries were, however, humble and sectarian.
It began as a minority grouping in the Trotskyist Revolutionary
Communist Party during the late 1940s, when it disagreed with the
view of some of the party members that revolution was imminent in
the west. But the forerunners of the International Socialists went
further than this, for they believed that a new revolution was necessary
in the Soviet Union: it was no longer a workers' state, but a 'State
Capitalist' country in which the bureaucracy performed the function
of the capitalists and the members of which had become a new

bourgeoisie. Similarly no revolutions had taken place in the emerging People's Democracies of Eastern Europe or in any other part of the world, and socialism did not, according to this view, exist anywhere.

After the break-up of the RCP in 1949 this group of thirty-three revolutionaries went their own way. The following year they founded a magazine called *Socialist Review* that ran for just over ten years and became known as the Socialist Review Group, the State-Capitalists, or the Cliff Group, after their effective leader, Tony Cliff, an Israeli who came to Britain in 1948 under his real name, Ygael Gluckstein. The isolation of his followers from the rest of the Trotskyist movement was emphasised first during the Korean war when they refused to lend their support to North Korea, and secondly by their criticisms of Yugoslavian socialism as an alternative to Moscow-dominated communism in Europe.

Throughout the 1950s the group could do little except publish propaganda through the *Socialist Review*, and clung to the left of the Labour Party—19 of its original thirty-three members had been in the Labour League of Youth, wound up in 1954.[2] During this period it developed its other characteristic doctrine, that recovery in the west and sustained affluence were made possible by the 'permanent arms-economy' in which military spending and associated industries provided the work that bolstered up the system. For socialists this situation meant adjusting to a long period in the wilderness.

At the end of the 1950s the first opportunities arose for activity rather than discussion. The group seized on the CND as a movement that had great potential for involving workers and young people in an issue that represented in a powerful way the evils of eastern and western blocks: the bomb was 'the supreme symbol of a social system',[3] and the protests did 'today what the slump did between the world wars in the matter of baptising a new generation with political realities'.[4] Although the group argued that a 'blow against the boss is a blow against the bomb',[5] the workers did not respond, but youth did. The group drew some support from the idealistic young who swelled the Aldermaston marches and also through the Labour Party Young Socialists, in which the followers of the Cliff Group were organised around the journals *Rebel*, *Rally* and, from 1961, *Young Guard*.[6]

In 1960 the group had also launched a theoretical magazine, whose title was taken from an American slogan representing the state-capitalist position: 'Neither Washington nor Moscow but International Socialism'. The editorial board of the new journal included Peter Cadogan, former Communist, Socialist Labour League and Labour Party member and a prominent supporter of the Committee of 100; Ken Coates and Nigel Harris, then active in the National Association of Labour Students' Organisations; and two lecturers, Peter Sedgwick and Michael Kidron, a close associate of Cliff and the group's leading theorist of capitalist development. The following year an agitational newspaper, *Industrial Worker* was founded, later to be retitled *Labour Worker*, the *Socialist Review* was wound up, and by 1964 the IS, as the group had become known, could claim for the first time more than 200 followers.

But after the initial surge of activity at the beginning of the decade, the organisation's progress faltered: the bomb ceased to be a magnetic issue, Coates and Cadogan left, with other prominent activists including lecturer Alasdair MacIntyre, and Bob Pennington who went on to the IMG, and its ambivalent relationship with Labour continued its uneasy existence. Although the IS continued to support the party in elections, because it was more likely than any alternative to respond to pressure from below, it distrusted Harold Wilson from the outset— 'as bland and rubberised as his Gannex raincoat' said International Socialism in 1963.[7]

Even before Labour's re-election in the following year the group forecast that the 'white heat of the technological revolution' would force the party to defend and improve capitalism, not to dismantle it, and would necessitate the imposition of a wages freeze and restrictions on the right to strike.[8] Opposed to almost every aspect of Labour policy, the International Socialists came into contact with other revolutionaries who were attempting to create an anti-Wilson movement in the party, *The Week* and the *Voice of the Unions*, whose workers' control conferences, Centre for Socialist Education and Vietnam Solidarity Campaign, they supported.[9] From the middle of the 1960s onwards the IS group was able to bring together its own esoteric theoretical position, some rank and file discontent with the Labour government, and new moods of restlessness stirring outside the party, so that it was able to loosen its dependence on existing political institutions and begin to build its own independent revolutionary organisation.

Into Action (1966–70): From 1966 the International Socialist organisation began in earnest to take shape, founded on the self-perpetuating staple diet of demonstrations and propaganda campaigns, a continual supply of students (with a high turnover of support), and the discrediting of Labour Party and Trade Union leaders as 'handmaidens of capitalism' who would be replaced by a rank and file industrial organisation for the working class, harnessed to a new political leadership—the International Socialists.

In their opposition to the Wilson regime the IS focused on two main economic policies: they rejected any form of wage restraint and supported all unofficial strikes. One of the bulwarks of the workers' defence against the Labour government—who had 'adopted the task of disciplining the working class with a directness the Tories would not have dared to use'[10]—was the shop steward, whose potential power 'derives precisely from the fact that he was elected by the people who know him directly, who work with him and who therefore share a community of interest with him'.[11]

In January 1966 these sentiments found expression in the formation of the London Industrial Shop Stewards' Defence Committee. Of its seven members at least three were IS supporters: Geoff Carlsson, a founder member of the *Socialist Review* group, who was a convenor at the ENV engineering works in North London, where a strike had prompted the setting up of the committee; Jim Higgins of the Post Office Engineering Union, who later became the IS national secretary for a time, and Roger Cox of the Amalgamated Engineering Union, who eight years later went on to become the convenor of the IS National Rank and File Movement. The committee envisaged itself as the embryo of a future shop-floor leadership, opposing government legislation which it foresaw would restrict incomes and the rights of trades unions. The IS supported it in this task and regarded it as 'potentially at any rate, a powerful force and their use of industrial power for political ends a revolutionary one'.[12] The group also provided the committee with propaganda ammunition, notably a pamphlet called *Incomes Policy, Legislation and Shop Stewards*, written by Tony Cliff and Colin Barker of the IS, with an introduction by Reg Birch, the pro-Peking engineering leader who had supported the original ENV strike. But within the year the Communist Party, not to be out-done in matters of industrial agitation, had stepped in to transmute the committee into a vehicle for its own designs, known as the Liaison Committee for the Defence of Trade Unions, and to which the International Socialists lent their reluctant support for the next eight years.

Industry was not the only area that was opening up to revolutionary activity in 1966. In that same year IS members joined the Islington branch of the Campaign Against Racial Discrimination, then a national and broadly-based progressive lobby, and turned to organising immigrant tenants against exploitation by landlords and slum conditions. During the next few years IS groups in many areas—York, Sheffield and Newcastle as well as in North London—pursued the issue of inadequate housing, attempting to demonstrate the detrimental effects of the government's incomes policy on the housing conditions of poor families and calling for the municipalisation of rented property under tenants' control. In 1968 some individual IS members in south-east London joined the squatting campaigns, although the group's national policy was hostile to squatting as a diversionary, reformist activity.[13]

The main source of support during this period, however, was the student movement. Indeed the International Socialists were one of the first revolutionary groups to appear on the scene of student unrest, and the leaders of the earliest troubles at the London School of Economics in 1966 were IS supporters.[14] There the issues had been representation and discipline within the school, but Rhodesia provided an external moral cause, brought into the arguments with the appointment as Director of the late Walter Adams, who had previously worked for the University of Rhodesia.

Vietnam, of course, was the primary mobilising issue and the International Socialists' involvement with the Vietnam Solidarity Campaign and the Revolutionary Socialist Students' Federation paralleled that of the International Marxist Group, but with some important differences of approach. The IS scoffed at the anti-proletarian content of many of the ideas associated with the student movement: they rejected the notion that the workers were no longer capable of bringing about revolution in the west and that students must do the job in conjunction with the peoples of the 'Third World' by spontaneous direct action.[15] Throughout their involvement with students the International Socialists have regarded them as a secondary force to the industrial working class, and argued that their functions were to relate with the workers and propagandise on their behalf. The group's supporters at the LSE in 1969 were able to put this theme into practice by providing strikers at Ford's with 'solidarity' actions in the form of propaganda and fund-raising support.

During 1968 the IS increased its strength from under 500 members at the beginning of the year to more than 1,000 at the end, to become a mainly student organisation. The student branches engaged in a great deal of acrimonious debate with Trotskyist and Maoist groups, which contributed to the rapid break up of the RSSF. They possessed little national influence in the National Union of Students but were able in individual colleges and universities to indulge in the disruptive tactics of breaking up Tory meetings, occupying administrative buildings, and pushing through student unions' declarations of support for overseas revolutionaries or striking workers, all of which has become an endemic feature of higher education in Britain. The IS students also supported the kaleidoscopic succession of 'Solidarity Campaigns' that the IMG in particular launched, although relations between the two were far from cordial. The IS also struck up contacts with the People's Democracy organisation in Northern Ireland, the mainly student organisation founded at Queen's University, Belfast, in October 1968.[16] Two of its most prominent members became closely associated with the International Socialists—Bernadette Devlin, who spoke on their platforms in England, and Eamonn McCann, who later joined the IS and reported Irish affairs for *Socialist Worker*, the weekly newspaper that had been founded in 1968 to succeed *Labour Worker*.

By the end of the 1960s the International Socialists had a nationwide organisation, with 40 branches in 1968 and 66 by the middle of the following year, a quarterly theoretical journal, a weekly newspaper, a publishing company and a printing works. But the student membership fell away substantially at the beginning of the 1970s and the organisation began the crucial task of building an industrial network. The IS was once again to transform its identity as it advanced from one stage of development to another.

2

INTERNATIONAL SOCIALISM: THE RANK AND FILE
AND THE REVOLUTIONARY PARTY

The International Socialists have characterised the present decade as a period in which the deepening crisis of capitalism has forced government and employers to protect their uncertain positions by attacking the working class organisations that threaten them. There has been, first, an 'employer's offensive', manifest through productivity deals, rationalisation and greater unemployment, backed by government policies to limit wages and control the activities of trade unions; secondly there has been an attack by government and the right wing on civil liberties, involving the persecution of non-conformists and minorities, the passing of legislation restricting the freedoms of the working class, and the granting of greater powers to police and bureaucracy, resulting in more official interference in peoples' lives.

Against the attack on civil liberties the IS has campaigned on a number of issues. It joined with immigrant groups, including the Indian Workers' Association, to oppose the 1971 Immigration Act, which tightened up the admission of immigrants in a way that the IS claimed was calculated to divide white and black workers, diverting their attention from the real enemy of capitalism, and was racialist in that it sought to create a second-class citizenry of the black population. At the same time the IS also campaigned fiercely against the removal from the United Kingdom of the German revolutionary, Rudi Dutschke. Although they conceded that he had attended their con-

135

ferences as an observer and had stayed with IS members on several occasions, they maintained he had not actively participated in politics during his stay but was a victim of right-wing prejudice.

Of the same pedigree, in what one Socialist Worker described as a 'growing climate of hysteria and racialism',[17] was the Industrial Relations Act, which according to the IS combined the economic aspects of the capitalists' offensive with the issue of working class liberties. The organisation supported the campaign by the Communist-dominated Liaison Committee for the Defence of Trade Unions against this measure, as it had supported its opposition to the earlier Labour government's proposals *In Place of Strife*. But the IS wanted to go beyond one-day token strikes and marches to build Councils of Action and organise larger strikes, culminating in a national strike that would bring the government down. It was the failure of this campaign under its Communist leadership, combined with the impression that there were emerging untapped sources of rank and file discontent, that persuaded the International Socialists to embark upon the course of building their own organisation for the working class. Their support for the LCDTU lasted, with rapidly diminishing enthusiasm, until 1974, when it was ready to launch its own national industrial body.

For the International Socialists, like all other Marxist groups, conducting propaganda, agitation and organising among industrial workers are tasks of supreme importance, the success of which will determine not only the future of their own organisation but the prospects for turning Britain to socialism. It is work that during the 1970s has combined many kinds of activity: the whole weight of the IS propaganda machine is thrown into campaigns on major issues, such as opposition to wage freezes or in support of large strikes; between these efforts local branches offer support to workers involved in unofficial disputes, offering advice, making printing facilities available or passing on appeals for strike funds through the columns of *Socialist Worker;* the paper itself is the main propaganda medium but is complemented by thousands of copies of leaflets, pamphlets and posters. Translating propaganda into activity, IS members are expected to form Factory Branches, IS Industrial Fractions and Trade Union Fractions to carry their ideas through from the shop floor and local union branch or Trades Councils upwards, and to support the fifteen or so groups in individual industries that comprise the National Rank and File Movement.

Of the National campaigns that draw together these various strands, those conducted during the two miners' strikes of 1972 and 1974 illustrate the nature and extent of IS activity. On January 10, 1972 the Industrial Sub-Committee of the I S issued its one hundred branches throughout the country with instructions: they were to hold public meetings, including street corner gatherings, in support of the miners; to distribute leaflets attacking the Tory government and calling for financial aid for the miners; to leaflet railway stations and coal-fired power stations; to urge the blacking of transport and use of coal. Workers in other industries should be urged into action to help bring the government down.[18]

Leading I S speakers, including John Palmer, then of the Executive Committee, and Wally Preston, secretary of the Manchester and District Electricity Supply Shop Stewards' Combine and editor of a rank and file newspaper called *Advance*, toured the country, particularly mining areas. International Socialist students from Essex University joined power-station picket lines and at Kent University they made arrangements for local miners to travel to Sussex where they were met by I S students at Brighton and provided with food, accommodation and information in order to picket south-coast docks and power stations.[19] During the strike *Socialist Worker* claimed that its sales increased by 50 per cent to reach what was then a record of 27,000 copies for one issue.

After the strike the I S organised a conference in Barnsley which fifty-six N U M members attended and under the guidance of Wally Preston planned a 'Rank and File' miners' newspaper, the *Collier*. At Easter 1972, at the I S annual conference, a member of the Executive Committee, John Charlton from Leeds made the unsubstantiated claim that 'the initiative for the historic picket at Saltley coke depot came from I S members in the Birmingham district'.[20] All reports of activity by International Socialist branches were sent to the organisation's London headquarters on the instructions of the Executive Committee to be collated and studied for revival and adaptation at some future date.

That occasion occurred less than two years later when the I S again prepared for confrontation between miners and the Heath government. This time they hoped to use the strike to win recruits to their own organisation: indeed some favourable auguries were evident, for in one of the most militant mining areas, Yorkshire, I S membership had reputedly increased from 250 to 550 between March and August 1973. I S branches in the South Yorkshire coalfield and in the industrial West Riding did their utmost to capitalise upon this situation— *Socialist Worker* went on sale at thirty-two pitheads, with twelve colleges and universities providing, as they had done before, organisation, funds and willing hands to distribute propaganda material and arrange meetings and leaflet campaigns throughout the region.

Nationally the IS Executive Committee told branches to put support for the miners' overtime ban and strike to 'the top of our priorities' and organise Support the Miners' Committees with other socialist and trade union groups, to provide manpower for picket lines and financial assistance. In addition the Executive asked members to link the miners' dispute with the gaol sentences on the Shrewsbury building workers' pickets.[21] But above all, branches were to channel the militancy into lasting membership of the International Socialists. These plans were over-ambitious: branches in Glasgow, Coventry and Swansea formed District Action Committees on the lines suggested, but recruitment was negligible, with only twenty miners enlisting in December and January. Following the general election and a speedy settlement of the strike by the new Labour government, the IS was denied the cataclysmic struggle, with industrial and social breakdown, for which its leaders had hoped.

Clearly the revolutionary party was not to emerge overnight in a spectacular rush by militant workers to the ranks of the IS. The group, with its national propaganda resources, could service such a dispute—even when it had very few workers in the industry directly concerned—but the growth of its influence among large groups of workers required more long-term and patient work before its involvement could be effective or decisive. For a militant revolutionary organisation such as the International Socialists to plunge openly into industrial and trade union activity is to invite distrust and isolation from non-revolutionary workers, so it has devised a less direct approach to overcome these problems by setting up Rank and File Groups in industries, professions and unions where it has supporters.

The first of these—in the National Union of Teachers—has also been one of the most successful: its journal, *Rank and File Teacher*, began in 1968 with a circulation of 400 copies, reached 2,500 in a year, doubled to 5,000 by 1973, and in 1974 reached a near five figure circulation. Within the NUT it has gathered the support of younger teachers in socially and educationally problematic areas, such as Inner London and Liverpool, has opposed the conservatism of older senior teachers as well as the Communist Party's influence, and in 1974 three of its supporters were elected to the national executive of the union. Nominally the Rank and File Teachers are an independent ginger group in the NUT whose members have, according to *The Times Educational Supplement*, 'gone out of their way to avoid a split with the NUT, even terming their followers "supporters" rather than "members" which would imply a splinter group rather than one working within the union'.[22] Although its appeal is broad it is very much under IS influence: the organisation prints its newspaper and its members include Duncan Hallas, a member of the IS executive and editor of *International Socialism*, and the wife of Tony Cliff, alias Chanie Rosenberg, alias C. Dallas (but rarely Mrs Gluckstein).

In another white-collar union, the National Association of Local Government Officers, the International Socialists are organised in an Action Group with militants of other shades. An anarchist member of the group—one of 50 anarchists—said that the 300 strong group (out of a union of half a million members) includes 30 International Marxists and 165 IS members, seven of whom are on the NALGO national executive of 63.[23] Closely linked with this group are the revolutionary social workers around the journal *Case-Con*, which is subsidised by the International Socialists. They began work in 1973 in London with a particular emphasis on the problems of immigrant youth in areas such as Brixton and, with the NALGO Action Group, formed a London NALGO Social Workers Co-ordinating Committee. One of the aims of *Case-Con* is to forge links between militants in many fields of social work and in local authorities, for, as one contributor to *Case-Con* argued: 'only when such links have been formed, and a large and vociferous group across the field of local government has been formed, can we seriously hope to challenge the right of local worthies elected by 20 per cent of the electorate to know what is best for the community, and question the morality and ability of government to govern'.[24]

Another professional union where the International Socialists have been active is the National Union of Journalists. The group was involved in the Free Communications Group at the beginning of the 1970s, which included a wide range of left-wing journalists and received a grant from the Rowntree Foundation until 1972, after the withdrawal of which it collapsed. The IS subsequently formed their own rank and file group in the NUJ around a newspaper called *Journalists Charter* and by 1975 had forty-eight members.

Most of the Rank and File Groups however are aimed at manual or lower-paid workers. In 1975 there were, in addition to *Rank and File Teacher*, *Nalgo Action News*, *Case-Con* and the *Journalists' Charter*, twelve other newspapers, grouped together in a National Rank and File Movement: *Carworker*, one of the most extensive, involving workers in the West Midlands, Merseyside and Scotland; *Collier*; *Hospital Worker*, mainly for ancillary staff; *Platform* intended for public transport workers; *Textile Worker*; *Redder Tape* for clerical civil servants in the Civil and Public Services Association; *Scots Rank and File*; *Technical Teacher*; *Dockworker*; *GEC Rank and File*; *Building Worker*; and *Electrician Special*.

Circulation of these newspapers ranges from between 1,000 and

10,000 each, and the frequency of their appearance, their quality and the extent of their involvement within the industries or union for which they are intended also vary greatly. One issue of the *Dockworker*, for example, was produced in Southampton, although the group had no dockworker members there.

With the exception of the *Rank and File Teacher* none of these newspapers and the groups associated with them existed before 1970. In 1973, however, the IS national conference declared its intent to organise a National Rank and File Movement, the founding conference of which was held in March 1974. Nearly 500 delegates attended, including members of 51 branches and committees of the Amalgamated Union of Engineering Workers, 37 sections of the Transport and General Workers' Union, 28 NALGO branches, 12 groups of the National Union of Teachers, 9 CPSA branches and 19 Trades Councils.[25] The conference opposed all incomes policies, statutory or voluntary, supported all moves to secure the release of the Shrewsbury Pickets, and pledged itself to oppose 'right-wing' and bureaucratic trade union leaders.

The aim of the movement is to create at shop-floor level what Tony Cliff has described as 'a semi-permanent periphery of sympathisers who will in time be won over to our politics'.[26] The International Socialist organisation itself may take a back seat in the public promotion of Rank and File Groups, for as Cliff has argued: 'often a meeting called under the auspices of the appropriate rank-and-file paper may be more useful than one called directly by the IS. A number of well-known militants who might not be prepared to speak from our platform can then be involved and a larger audience might well result'.[27] Informality and co-operation between small groups of activists are the keynotes of the Rank and File Movement, as Roger Cox, its Convenor, explained: 'There's always been an informal network of militants,' he wrote in *Socialist Worker*. 'During the Perkins lockout in the summer [of 1973] members of the dispute committee stayed with me after we offered to help them through the *Carworker*. I fixed them up to go down to the London Docks through two dock shop stewards I knew who helped produce *Dockworker*'.[28]

Co-existing with the Rank and File Movement is the formal section of the International Socialists' industrial organisation, the Factory Branches, the Industrial Fractions, and the Trade Union Fractions. It was at the IS national conference in March 1973 that the organisation voted for the systematic building of factory branches as 'a basic unit in a revolutionary combat organisation rooted in the working class'.[29] Within four months 27 had been established, 32 by the autumn, 45 by November 1973, a drop to 39 at the beginning of 1974, 40 by March

1974, and down to 38 in October 1974—out of a total of 56 that had at some stage been formed. Tony Cliff has suggested a figure of eight to ten people as the minimum size for a viable branch, which should be properly run with regular meetings, agenda, discussion meetings for 'political education' purposes, act as a cohesive unit in trade union affairs and advance IS policies and the sales of *Socialist Worker* at every opportunity.

The demands of the IS leadership on its members are high and this apart from any other reason may account for the turnover in branches: in addition to the factory activities members are expected to participate in other sections of the IS organisations, including weekend schools and conferences, as well as trade union and trades council affairs. One of the most successful IS factory branches has been at the Chrysler car works in Coventry, where thirty-eight members chose a committee including chairman, secretary, treasurer, *Socialist Worker* seller and *Carworker* seller. During a prolonged strike in the summer of 1973 the branch formed the nucleus of the Ryton Action Committee, organised picket lines and produced a special issue of the *Carworker* which laid all responsibility for the strike on the Chrysler management. Other established IS factory branches include Rowntrees at York; Joseph Lucas, Birmingham; C.A. Parsons, Newcastle; CAV/Lucas, Liverpool, and in plants of British Leyland, British Steel Corporation, GEC, Courtaulds, Guest Keen and Nettlefold, Reed International, Hawker-Siddeley and Rolls-Royce.[30]

The individual branches join with others in the same industry in the Industrial Fractions such as the Automotive Industry Fraction, British Rail Fraction, the Building Workers' section, with branches in Merseyside, at Edinburgh, and the Hospital Workers' Fraction based on groups in Leeds, London, Oxford and South Wales. When the IS has approximately twenty workers in any one union it attempts to organise them into a Trade Union Fraction, of which by mid-1975 it had over twenty.[31]

Until 1970 it was customary to regard IS as a primarily student body led by a core of theoreticians and academics. Then the white-collar professional element, including some of the former students after graduation, became prominent, but still the group lacked the manual or 'blue-collar' industrial base to which it aspired. Although it claimed a majority of manual workers as early as 1971, only in 1973 and 1974 has the balance noticeably begun to change. In July 1973, among some possibly exaggerated claims of large-scale recruiting, 115 AUEW members and 112 members of the TGWU were said to have joined, compared with only 20 teachers, during the first six months of the year. The National Committee of 40 members from 1974–75 was composed of 22 manual workers and only 6 white collar personnel, the others being either students or IS full-time staff and officials.

This extensive network of industrial militants is clearly in its infancy, but through their own branches or under the cover of the Rank and File groups, the International Socialists have been able to contribute locally to some industrial disputes—such as those involving firemen in Glasgow, hospital ancillary workers, ambulancemen and in various strikes and conflicts in the engineering industry. The emphasis on shop stewards' committees, strike committees and unofficial bodies that has always been a hallmark of the International Socialists' industrial agitation is still present, but they do not neglect trade union affairs at shop-floor level. In addition, the IS has shown an interest in Trades Councils, which the organisation aims to re-establish as 'uniting centres of local activity. The Trades Council can become an invaluable channel for IS propaganda, providing opportunities for bringing under our control local trade union branches as well as local shop stewards committees'.[32]

The allegiance of trade unionists is not gained, however, by analyses of state capitalism or exhortations to revolutionary fervour. The IS has its short-term programme, revised according to the prevailing circumstances, which it expects all its industrial groups to pursue and to which it believes ordinary workers will be attracted. During 1975 its immediate economic demands included 30 per cent across the board pay increases with no time limit on re-negotiations, equal pay for women, a minimum wage of £35 a week for a 35-hour week, nationalisation under workers' control without compensation, no victimisation of workers or shop stewards, opposition to all incomes policy or trade union legislation, and wholly enforced closed shops. These items smack of the old Trotskyist tactic of the 'transitional demands', which may appear reasonable to the workers but which cannot be conceded under the present system.

It should not be forgotten that the purpose of all of this work in industry is not to reap the fruits of capitalism for the working class, but to forge the means for its destruction and pave the way for the creation of socialism under the leadership of a revolutionary party.

In company with numerous other organisations on the Marxist left, large and small, the International Socialists aspire to become *the* revolutionary party, a body which, alone, has the dedicated and farsighted leadership, the sound theoretical base, the realistic programme, the efficiency of organisation and the appeal to the masses that will enable it to lead the workers to socialism. The IS concedes that it has not yet reached this degree of all-round perfection, nor are the workers ready, nor the conditions ripe. Building the party involves activity over a wide area, engaging many social interests besides those of industrial workers. The International Socialists run, for example, a monthly women's paper, called *Women's Voice* and a newspaper in Urdu for Asian immigrants entitled *Chingari (The Spark)* which was launched in 1973 with a circulation of 5,000.

Students continue to form an important part of the IS membership. Since the demise of the Liaison Committee for the Defence of Student Unions, the group's position in the NUS against the Communist-backed 'Broad Left' has only weakened. To improve its national position and to co-ordinate the individual groups of IS student supporters, the organisation formed in September 1974 a National Organisation of International Socialist Student Societies, supported by groups in 28 universities, 11 polytechnics, and 12 other colleges of technical and further education. The first test of NOISSS's influence in student politics came in the spring of 1975 when the IS Student Organiser, Terry Povey, contested the presidency of the NUS, only to be soundly beaten by Charles Clarke, a Labour Party Marxist, by 352 votes to 223.

With Trotskyist and other far-left groups, the IS has been successful in disrupting meetings in individual colleges and in particular in enlisting support from among students in its campaign against the National Front. It declared its intentions in this respect at the end of 1973 in a pamphlet which announced IS support for 'physical action against all fascist and racialist marches, demonstrations, campaigns and organisations'.[33] Alongside the IMG and other left-wing groups the IS embarked upon the systematic pursuit of the NF whenever it dared to show its face in public. The Red Lion Square demonstration of June 1974, in which IS members were violently involved, focused public attention on the campaign and helped arouse the latent antipathy that existed between the International Socialists and the police, when the IS produced a poster holding the police Special Patrol Group responsible for the death of student Kevin Gately. The IS campaign against the National Front differed in emphasis from that conducted by the International Marxist Group, in that it did not assume the NF to be the major target, but merely a symptom of the deeper capitalist crisis that was forcing the government, the 'boses', and their agents in the police force to resort to increasingly repressive measures against the working class.

Reaction to events in Ireland has continued throughout the present decade to form an important part of the IS's propaganda activity and has similarly involved hostility between the group and authority. In July 1971, after the introduction of internment, the International

Socialists organised a Labour Committee Against Internment, which gained the support of a handful of Labour MPs, and a score of trade unionists besides leading members of the IS. In two months this committee was transformed into the Anti-Internment League, an umbrella organisation with a distinct revolutionary orientation bringing together IS, IMG and anarchist groups as well as trade unionists and Irish socialist organisations. By the spring of 1972, shortly after the Londonderry 'Bloody Sunday' shootings, the AIL had thirty-six branches throughout the country, organised many marches and meetings, including some demonstrations in London which ended in violent clashes with the police. The IS took an active interest in the League's affairs, printed its newspaper, and IS members served on its committee, the League's Edinburgh organiser, Frank Drain, was a member of both Clann na h'Eireann, the Irish republican organisation and the IS.

At the beginning of 1972 the International Socialists withdrew their allegiance from the People's Democracy organisation, arguing that it did not have any working class membership nor a proper socialist programme. Instead they offered 'unconditional but critical support' to the IRA, an equivocal attitude it has maintained since. The slogan acknowledges the IRA as the principal agent in the struggle against the British army—on whose alleged brutality and repression the IS has spent much vitriol—but disagrees with any programmes either the Official or Provisional wings may have for the reconstruction of Ireland. The IS opposes the use of terrorist bombing against civilian targets in Britain since they 'serve to confuse Irish workers as to the best way to fight British imperialism and to make it easier for the British bourgeoisie to inculcate chauvinistic ideas into British workers'.[34] Its declared support for the IRA, however qualified, has led to some brushes with authority, including the raiding by police of the homes of four IS members in March 1972 after a bomb attack on an officers' mess at Aldershot.[35] Further raids were carried out on the IS and other revolutionary groups a year later after another wave of bombings, and the police action prompted the rare event of a joint IS, IMG and SLL meeting of protest. Politically the International Socialists tried to boost their own supporters in Ireland in the Socialist Workers' Movement, and as the AIL died, moved by mid-1974 on to the Troops Out Movement with the IMG and sections of the Labour Left.

In the anti-NF campaign, the Troops Out Movement, and on other issues such as the Working Women's Charter or the Chile Solidarity Campaign, the International Socialists have continued to join in the unending stream of meetings, demonstrations and protests alongside numerous other groups on the revolutionary left. It has also begun to extend its international contacts.

At the IS's 1974 annual conference were representatives of the French organisation *Lutte Ouvrière*, with which the IS has been in touch for many years, a small American IS group, *Anvanguardia Operaria* from Italy, the Irish Socialist Workers' Movement and groups from Denmark, Sweden and West Germany. After the conference John Deason and Jim Nichol toured Denmark and two IS members attended *Anvanguardia Operaria's* congress in Italy. International Socialists have also travelled to Portugal whose affairs they have watched closely since the overthrow of the right-wing dictatorship, and the organisation has set up Italian and Portuguese Groups to develop contacts in those countries.

All of these activities are channelled at some point through the International Socialists' national organisation, the prospective party machine, partly modelled on the structure of the Communist Party, and run on Marxist-Leninist principles of democratic centralism, with power residing at the top of the hierarchy.[36] The basis of the IS organisation and its day-to-day activities is the district branch. Within the area of a large town or part of a county this unit carries out the bulk of the IS's propaganda, agitation, campaigning and recruiting, and included in it are factory branches, student groups and local branches covering a smaller area. In York for example the district branch contains the town based organisation itself, two student branches, a Rowntree's factory branch and a busworkers' fraction, with joint committees for education and propaganda as well as a general district committee.

Since July 1969, when the International Socialists had 66 district branches, it has grown as follows:

January 1971	84
November 1971	109
April 1972	113
November 1972	130
August 1973	137
October 1974	150

Above the district branches are nine regional units: Scotland, the North East, the North (mainly Yorkshire) the East, South, North West (mainly Lancashire), Wales, the South West, and, the largest of all in number of branches, Greater London and Home Counties region. These co-ordinate the districts in large-scale campaigns and act as the administrative link with the central committees. The largest of these is the National Committee, forty members elected by annual conference and representing the whole country, which meets monthly to discuss policy, plan activity, assess the current political situation in the country and hear regional reports. Until 1975 the National Committee chose from its own ranks a nine-member Executive, but in the wake of considerable strains within the organisation, the rules were changed to allow annual conferences to elect the Executive Committee.[37]

The Executive takes all major policy decisions, directs national activity and campaigns, and has under its control the major propaganda publications, including in its membership the editors of *Socialist Worker* and *International Socialism*, in addition to bringing together the organisation's principal officers, including a membership secretary (who from 1974–75 was Tony Cliff) national secretary (Jim Nichol), treasurer, and at least two full-time industrial organisers. In 1974–75 these were Steve Jeffreys, an engineering shop steward and former I S Scottish Region Organiser, who served on a strike committee at Chrysler's Linwood factory, and John Deason, whose background was similar: an Engineering Union shop steward from Lancashire, he was secretary of a committee co-ordinating factory sit-ins during the 1972 engineering industry pay dispute. The Executive Committee also govern the work of eight specialist sub-committees, for industry, young workers, students, race, women, education, Ireland and international affairs.

The total membership of the IS in 1975 was between 3,300 and 3,500 people. Its fastest periods of growth were during 1968 when the student movement was at its height, in 1971 and 1972 at a time of constant conflict between organised Labour and the Conservative government, and from the middle of 1973 to the middle of 1974, also a period of economic and industrial crisis. The organisation claimed that it increased its strength by two-thirds in 1970, doubled it in 1971, doubled it again in 1972, and doubled it once more in 1973–74. Given a membership figure of 1,000 in 1969 this would have meant a total of approximately 1,600 in 1970; 3,200 in 1971; 6,400 in 1972 and 12,800 by mid-1974. Indeed during 1973 and 1974 the organisation reported some huge intakes of new recruits: 211 from March to May 1973, followed by 281 between mid-May and mid-June 1973, another 315 members in July, with a grand total between mid-March and mid-August of that year of 1,260.[38]

Many of these figures should be treated with considerable reserve, and the International Socialists themselves, always eager to exaggerate their performance, have never claimed more than 3,500 members at any one time. The group has suffered like many on the far left, from an extremely high turnover of members, especially among those who joined as students in 1968 and have now drifted out of active politics. On balance the International Socialists are now probably a mixture of students and young people whose life-style approaches that of the Alternative Society, white-collar workers and manual workers.[39]

The dubious obsession with statistics that the organisation exhibited through the pages of *Socialist Worker* during 1973 and the beginning of 1974 was quickly shelved when its growth stagnated and tensions began to arise between the old guard, many of whom had been active in the group since the 1950s, and some of the newer militants. In April 1974 the divisions within the IS focussed on the future of *Socialist Worker*. Since 1968, when it began with a circulation of 5,000, its sales have been:

October 1971	18,700
February 1972	27,000 (during the miners' strike)
June 1972	60,000 (during the gaoling of Five Dockers)
January 1973	24,000
February 1973	27,000
April 1974	35,000

Its highly professional production and vivid reporting had enabled it to become an extremely profitable venture, and an essential part of the IS's overall work. But in the spring of 1974 the National Committee, by 26 votes to 12, voted to change the character of the newspaper so that it could have closer contacts with the ordinary members, carrying their contributions and identifying with the masses, in this way becoming the paper of a mass party. On the other hand Roger Protz, the editor, wished *Socialist Worker* to continue its role of education and propaganda, combining news, investigative reporting, reviews, and theoretical material with which few new members were familiar. When the issue was referred to the Executive Committee a major split emerged and five executive members resigned, including Protz, Roger Rosewall, a former Midlands regional officer of ASTMS and one-time IS industrial organiser, Andreas Nagliati of the NUR, the then industrial organiser, Nigel Harris, an academic who ran the race sub-committee, and Jim Higgins, the national secretary. A prolonged period of uncertainty for the *Socialist Worker* followed. Paul Foot, son of Lord Caradon and nephew of Michael Foot, became its new editor, with Chris Harman, the former editor of *International Socialism*, taking on the job of political editor of *Socialist Worker* and handing over his previous post to Duncan Hallas. At the beginning of 1975 Foot relinquished the editorship of the newspaper and Chris Harman took over. He told the IS National Committee of the disappointing growth of the organisation since the middle of 1974, and to prepare for renewed efforts to recruit more members the Committee launched a fund-raising drive.[40] Financial support for the *Socialist Worker*, which

147

at various times has been engaged in some costly legal battles, was forthcoming from 28 Trades Councils, 17 sections of the Amalgamated Union of Engineering Workers, 8 NALGO branches, 14 branches of the National Union of Journalists and 4 branches of the National Union of Mineworkers.[41]

As the source of a considerable amount of revolutionary propaganda, the International Socialists have ironically acquired considerable capitalist expertise. Both its two main journals, numerous pamphlets, posters and leaflets and the rank and file newspapers are printed on the IS's own presses, to finance which it raised £30,000 in 1972. Besides its own publications the works have handled many other magazines and newspapers, including *Private Eye*, *Anti-Apartheid News*, *Red Weekly* (the IMG newspaper), *Free Palestine*, *Gay Lib News* and Black Power newspapers. In addition the IS-controlled publishing house, Pluto Press, handles a wide range of theoretical and historical material by International Socialist and other left-wing writers.

Although the International Socialists are prepared to co-operate in certain respects with other organisations to advance the socialist cause, it has become increasingly intolerant of dissent within its own ranks. Yet as the group has grown this has become all the harder to control. In 1968 a small quasi-Trotskyist group called 'Workers Fight' joined the IS, and for three years it existed uneasily within the organisation as a hard-line opposition to the group's leadership, until in December 1971 it was expelled. The main reasons were that it called for the formation of a Workers' Militia in defiance of IS policy at that time, it supported the IRA without qualification, including the right to conduct bombing campaigns against military targets in Britain, and it also regarded the Soviet Union as a 'degenerated workers' state', not as State-Capitalist.

At the beginning of 1972 the group began a separate existence publishing a fortnightly newspaper called *Workers Fight*, edited by an Irishman living in London, Sean Matgamna. It soon formed between 15 and 20 branches, mainly in London, Teesside, Lancashire and the West Midlands and has run two small rank and file newspapers, *Hook* edited by Harold Youd of the Manchester Portworkers' Committee, and *Real Steel News*, edited from Middlesbrough by an AUEW member, Tony Duffy. At its first annual conference in May 1972 it claimed groups in engineering, docks, steel, printing and in the National Health Service where one of its members, Jack Sutton, was the Manchester Branch Secretary of the National Union of Public Employees.

Workers Fight lent conditional support to the Unified Secretariat and had abortive talks with the IMG on amalgamation. It did however work more closely with the International Marxists in Irish campaigns

148

and the anti-NF campaign than with the IS, although it retained some links with its former associates in the Rank and File Movement. During its short but ambitious life—it too hankered after the status of the revolutionary party—it acquired a reputation as one of the most militant smaller organisations, which, ironically, was too unsubtly Bolshevik for the IS. In the middle of 1974 another 'Revolutionary Opposition' group to the IS leadership broke away to form a separate organisation, known as the Revolutionary Communist Group, with some seven branches throughout England, whose members have been active in the Troops Out Movement and the Chile Solidarity Campaign.

During 1975 divisions within the International Socialists intensified. In September three members in the west Midlands were expelled and seventeen resigned after they had campaigned for a Communist candidate in elections for the post of National Organiser of the AUEW. Two months later a faction calling itself the 'IS Opposition' issued a document that drew attention to a crisis in the organisation: falling membership, declining newspaper sales, autocratic leadership. It was signed by thirty-nine IS members including some formerly prominent in the organisation, Roger Protz, John Palmer, Jim Higgins, Granville Williams, former Birmingham organiser, and Harry Wicks, the veteran Trotskyist of the 1930s. At about the same time another group of fifty members was expelled and began publishing its own magazine called *Workers' Power*. In December 1975 this group joined forces with Workers' Fight and a few former members of the Workers' Revolutionary Party to form a new quasi-Trotskyist body, the International Communist League. Thus in less than eighteen months the IS had lost the active support of more than 250 of its members.

The International Socialists seek for themselves exclusive leadership of the working class and the revolutionary movement. They have rejected using the Labour Party to bring about socialism and only support it in general elections to 'show its anti-working class policies in practice and thereby contribute to its downfall'.[42] It scorns also the Communist Party's belief that capitalism can be peacefully transformed or dismantled gradually: violent conflict is inevitable as the workers defend themselves against the capitalists' increasing attacks on their liberties and living standard. As the crisis of capitalism worsens and the conflict deepens, the IS believe the workers will turn to it, to help them build their own revolutionary socialist organisations to 'smash' the system by force.

The post-revolutionary workers' state is described as an 'entirely democratic form of government', run by elected workers' councils. But it 'does not allow capitalist parties or capitalist newspapers. It does not allow former capitalists and their supporters to vote and constantly defends its gains from any attempts to restore the old system of exploitation. The workers' state relies for its defence on the armed power of the working class and, if necessary, its own army ...

'In a workers' state, all workers would be trained to defend their own regime and would serve in a part-time workers' militia. The militia defends the political interests of the working class. It therefore defends the right of strikers, the right to work and the nationalisation of the produce forces. Its officers are elected and subject to political control ... The police and judges are sacked, political prisoners released and all political files made public'.[43]

As they work towards this goal the International Socialist group has been able to create an organisation with some appeal for elements of a discontented proletariat, a radical intelligentsia and an idealistic youth. Its appeal to journalists, social workers and teachers is founded on a thoroughgoing radicalism which exposes social injustice and official hypocrisy, while its attraction for the workers is that it expresses their fears and uncertainties in an insecure, inflationary world and encourages them to use their industrial might.

Since the middle of 1974 it has, however, encountered serious difficulties. The ageing oligarchy that constitutes its central leadership tried to retain absolute control over a growing organisation but found itself challenged, and its intolerance of dissent precipitated the organisation's fragmentation. Its problems stem from its insistence on the revelance to modern Britain of the teachings of Marx, Lenin and Trotsky: the ingredients of imminent economic collapse, social conflict and proletarian dictatorship have proved deficient as an analysis of the nature of the crisis or as a prescription for its cure. Thus while the I S is able in a limited way to reflect the existence of crisis its future growth is limited by the fact that it flies in the face of so many British political traditions and present day experiences.

VII

The Eight Parties
of Anti-Revisionism

I

THE GROWTH OF THE PARTIES

Mao Tse-tung's China has been the inspiration for a new and distinct ideological grouping on the revolutionary left. The formation of numerous pro-Chinese groups throughout the world from the early 1960s was a consequence of extensive debate among communists following the Sino-Soviet split and of the search among revolutionaries in the west and the 'Third World' for new paths to socialism. In Britain the movement's growth has been characterised by an uncompromising sectarianism which has led to its fragmentation into eight independent parties with as many subsidiary bodies; indeed the basic question of how many pro-Chinese organisations exist at any one time is difficult to answer with absolute accuracy, such is their obscurity, small following and instability.

Despite their obvious weaknesses, the followers of Chinese communism have set themselves against all other types of socialist, with each individual group sustained by the conviction that its own particular line carries the certainty of ultimate success in a revolutionary upheaval. Isolation at home is compensated for by the knowledge that each 'Maoist' group has its place in a cosmic scheme of struggle against the common enemies of imperialism and revisionism, under the guiding example of China itself, whose leadership demonstrates absolute and universal truths about the nature of revolution, the forces of history that motivate it, and how in different circumstances socialism should be brought about and sustained. The pro-Chinese movement exhibits many contrasts between the relative insignificance of its British supporters at home and their boundless faith and pretensions as a global force.

In Britain, as in the United States, France, Belgium and Japan between 1961 and 1963, the first separate groups to take a Chinese line were breakaway factions from the established Communist Parties. Their identity did not derive entirely however from the context of Soviet and Chinese divisions. Those in the British Communist Party who identified with Peking rather than Moscow did so to confirm their long-standing opposition to the prevailing—and so called 'revisionist'—doctrines contained in the *British Road to Socialism*. They objected to what they saw as the dilution of revolutionary principles in a long-term electoral programme that dispensed with serious factory agitation and necessitated co-operation with non-communists on a broad 'progressive' front. But the objectors were merely a rump of hard-line Bolshevik and Stalinist traditionalists, mainly intellectuals, a few workers and the impatient young whose views were very much out of favour with the party hierarchy and the majority of ordinary members.

The isolation of the minority became increasingly evident after the Soviet Communist Party's 20th Congress in 1956 at which Khruschev denounced Stalin. It was however the ideological aspects of the Sino-Soviet dispute that crystallised the arguments and reset them in an equation in which the views of the militant traditionalists coincided with Peking's, but their minority position was decisively exposed at the British Communist Party's 28th Congress in 1963, after which disciplinary measures were taken against them.[1] In November 1963, following resignations and expulsions, a fourteen-member Committee to Defeat Revisionism for Communist Unity (CDRCU) was formed, under the leadership of Michael McCreery, an old Etonian and son of a wartime general.[2] He aimed to recreate the Communist Party to lead factory workers to direct action involving 'smashing the capitalist state machine in a Soviet revolution which will be led by the workers' own organisations, Soviets' ultimately to achieve a dictatorship of the proletariat.

McCreery had no doubt that 'there is no escaping the need at some stage of the revolution for armed strength to back the political and industrial strength of the people'.[3] His death in 1965 at the age of 36 robbed dissident British communists of their undisputed leader and foremost ideologist, and his Committee straightaway broke up into rival groups, although it did not finally disappear until 1970. It is easy to dismiss the CDRCU as a total failure, but it successfully implanted the ideas of Chinese communism in Britain through the branches it established in London, Manchester, Scotland and the Thames Valley and South Wales Communist Association.

The Manchester section set up its own Action Centre for Marxist-Leninist Unity in June 1965 and at the end of that year a separate Finsbury Communist Association emerged. The Action Centre launched a newspaper, *Hammer and Anvil*, and with supporters in

London laid the basis for the foundation in September 1967 of the oldest 'anti-revisionist' group in existence, the Marxist-Leninist Organisation of Britain (MLOB). Its aim was to 'rally together the most class-conscious and militant elements from the advanced sections of the industrial working class, working youth and progressive intellectuals; to strive to mould them into a theoretically developed cadre force of disciplined proletarian revolutionaries ... for the establishment of a Marxist-Leninist party at the earliest possible moment; to build a network of cells, groups and fractions in industry, to conduct intensive propaganda'.[4] The élite cadre is regarded as both a necessary preliminary to the formation of a mass party and as a secret militaristic force existing alongside it. The notion confirms the anti-revisionists' view of the seizure of power as a coup under the leadership of the select few.

In January 1968, just three months old, the MLOB repudiated one of its key defining principles by attacking Mao Tse-tung as a 'counter-revolutionary' in favour of Liu Shao-chi, the Chinese party leader disgraced in the Cultural Revolution. In maintaining this position as the only anti-Maoist pro-Chinese group the MLOB is perhaps the most eccentric political organisation in Britain.

Its subsequent history has been of attempts to build bridges to other groups and overcome its isolation. It co-ordinated an Action Council for Anti-Imperialist Solidarity (1968–9), the Socialist Alliance Against Racism (1969–70) and the Black and White Workers' Unity Front (1970–71). Following the collapse of the last of these abortive ventures, the MLOB formed in July 1971 a subsidiary body called the Red Front Movement. This is intended to act as 'the inceptive nucleus of the future revolutionary mass front of the British working class'[5] and to function as a training school for potential members of the MLOB itself. Ever hopeful that it will one day be the vanguard party in a British revolution, it continues to publish, albeit irregularly, two journals, *Class Against Class* and *Red Front*; its membership, once extending to Manchester and Scarborough, is now confined to a handful in south and east London.

Unlike the MLOB, which has long since buried its original connections with the CDRCU, the Working People's Party of England (WPPE) regards itself as the heir of McCreery's Committee. Formed in April 1968 around the London Workers' Committee, publishers since 1966 of the duplicated *Workers' Broadsheet*, the WPPE was for the first three years of its existence, through its work among immigrant groups and its contacts with revolutionaries abroad, one of the most influential of Marxist-Leninist organisations. Its chairman in 1968 was Dr Alexander Tudor-Hart, a Tooting general practitioner then aged 67, and its leading founder members included Paul Noone, a doctor and former member of the CDRCU, and Johnny James, a West Indian accountant who masterminded the extremist take-over of the now defunct Campaign Against Racial Discrimination. The WPPE also emphasises the construction of revolutionary cadres as the prelude to a mass party and the importance for a central party committee in an organisation based on 'democratic centralism'. Its programme is contained in a Five Point Action Programme calling for 'revolution by any means necessary' and self-defence against 'fascist and racialist brutality by the authorities and by thugs in and out of uniform'.[6] Because of what it described as 'the importance of recognising the national question in Britain in relation to Ireland, Scotland and Wales and using this issue to aid the break-up of the bourgeois state'[7] the Workers' Party of Scotland, a sister party of the WPPE, had been formed in 1966. But since 1971 the WPPE's influence has declined. Frequent changes of address, the failure to increase its branches to more than four cadres, in Merton, Brent and Camden in London and in Newcastle, the resignation of Tudor-Hart in 1972 and the publication of its *Workers' Broadsheet* only five times since the beginning of 1972 are all symptoms of its demise.

In contrast is the steady rise of what is now the largest and most important Maoist group, the Communist Party of Britain (Marxist-Leninist)—CPB(M–L). Its founders broke away from the pro-Moscow Communist Party at the end of 1966, quite separately from McCreery's group but as a result of similar arguments about the road to socialism. The CPB(M–L)'s chairman is Reg Birch, a former member of the Communist Party's executive committee, who has served on the Amalgamated Engineering Workers' Union national executive and since 1975 has been a member of the general council of the TUC—its first Maoist member.

After visiting Peking, Birch became converted to Chinese communism and in November 1966 launched a discussion journal *The Marxist* supported by communist militants from the engineering union in north London and the St Pancras branch of the Young Communist League, who renamed themselves the Camden Youth Movement. Promptly suspended from the Communist Party, Birch formed a British Marxist-Leninist Organisation which grew by the spring of 1968 into the CPB(M–L). It has spread its message among engineering workers, students and immigrants and has branches throughout London, in Essex, Sussex, Oxford, Bristol, Liverpool, Manchester and Leeds, with an estimated total following of several hundred. It has the added attraction of being the official pro-Chinese party in Britain, recognised by Peking and Albania: Birch and leading members have visited Tirana on at least eight occasions since 1969 and have been to Peking some six times where they have been greeted by party leaders and officials. Any suggestion that the CPB(M–L) is under any degree of control or influence by the Chinese is resolutely denied. As one returning delegate in 1971 said: 'The Chinese central committee were very interested about political and economic prospects in Britain but they would not dream of any interference, making suggestions or providing any finance.'[8] McCreery had made similar denials in 1964 when he was accused of receiving funds from Albania after a visit there.

International solidarity of a different kind is exhibited in the Communist Party of England (Marxist-Leninist), the British section of a movement called the Internationalists, which was formed in 1963 at the University of British Columbia, Vancouver. Two years later, its founder, Hardial Bains, a French-Canadian journalist, travelled to Ireland to help set up an International branch at Trinity College, Dublin, later to become the Communist Party of Ireland (Marxist-Leninist). After spending two years nurturing this project Bains came to England in August 1967 to found an Internationalist Section at Sussex University and take part in a conference called 'The Necessity for Change' with revolutionaries from Europe, Africa and parts of Asia.[9]

Slowly the Internationalists have built up a network of sympathetic groups in Britain, most of which have operated from 'Progressive Books and Periodicals', a bookshop in the Old Kent Road in south-east London. These have included numerous 'Study Groups' devoted to the affairs of a particular region—India, Pakistan, the Caribbean, the Far East and South East Asia—each with its own newspaper, and an Afro-Asian People's Solidarity Movement formed in January 1970, followed three years later by a subsidiary body, the Afro-Asian Youth and Student Movement, formed in conjunction with the London School of Economics Afro-Asian Society. The same publishing and printing facilities have also been made available to the London, Birmingham and Manchester Student Movements, a Black Workers' Movement, and a 'Necessity for Change Institute for Marxist-Leninist Studies' opened in 1974.

Few of these organisations survive for long or draw any substantial amount of support but are mere propaganda outlets for the Internationalists and their principal representatives in Britain, the CPE(M–L), which itself emerged from the original Internationalist branch at Sussex University. The most strident and fanatical Maoist group of all, the CPE(M–L) makes little attempt to argue its case but prefers to rely largely on selected aphorisms from the Thoughts of Chairman Mao as indisputable proof of the coming revolution. It publishes two journals, the *Workers' England Daily News Release* and

Communist England, and despite its unequivocal distaste for democracy contested several seats in the 1974 general elections, all candidates losing their deposits. Its part in the Internationalist movement was emphasised in 1973 when, during its tenth anniversary celebrations, meetings were held in London, Birmingham, Leicester and Glasgow, where the CPE has branches, in solidarity with Internationalists in Ireland, Canada, the United States, Africa and the Middle East.

In common with all other Maoist groups the CPE(M–L) emphasises the cardinal importance of building a party to lead the proletariat to socialism. Few of them however approach such a status in terms of membership or organisation, and some of the pro-Chinese bodies are more modest about their present achievement. The Communist Federation of Britain (Marxist-Leninist) for example wishes to act as an umbrella for as many anti-revisionist groups as possible, and from there to build up a 'politically advanced cadre force'.[10] It includes a number of former members of the Young Communist League and has worked with other organisations, including the Britain Vietnam Solidarity Front, although most of its attempts to extend its influence have failed. The leader of the Vietnam Solidarity Front was Albert Manchanda, an Indian who came to Britain in 1952 and whose many exploits include membership of a pro-Chinese caucus in the Indian Workers' Association, visiting Peking for an Afro-Asian Journalists' Conference in 1966, a year after which he entered the field of protest against the Vietnam war. An ally of Manchanda during the Vietnam demonstrations was Ed Davoren, who begame the secretary of an Irish National Liberation Solidarity Front, a mainly propagandist organisation which sprang up with the increased violence in Northern Ireland after 1968. Together they organised a breakaway column on the famous march of October 27, 1968 to try to reach the US Embassy. In 1971 Davoren joined forces with a London-based Irish Workers' Group to form the Communist Workers' League of Britain (Marxist-Leninist), yet another contender for the future role of revolutionary vanguard.

Co-operation between different organisations in the pro-Chinese movement is rare, and between any of them and other sections of the left it is virtually non-existent. Their contempt for orthodox communists is inherent but they are equally hostile towards all other varieties of socialist. Reg Birch, the CPB(M–L) leader, has, for example, written that:

'the Labour Movement is staffed today by Social Democrats so that its aims are those of Social Democracy, not revolution; this at this time in spite of the zeal and courage of the workers. The Social

Democrats are the prop of capitalism because they have permeated our class with the idea of "gradualism" and "reformism", evolution, not revolution ... The enemy of the working class in Britain today is of very mixed composition. It includes the ultra-left who sow dismay and division in the revolutionary army.'[11]

Birch's organisation has however received some strong criticism from other Maoists: the CFB(M–L) attacked its rigid centralism, the WPPE its lack of revolutionary socialist zeal, the Association of Communist Workers (a small propagandist group centred on north London and Hertfordshire) criticised it for daring to attribute to their hero, Stalin, the origins of Soviet revisionism, and the Communist Unity Association (Marxist-Leninist), accused it of being a sham, revisionist party. The Communist Unity Association was a product of an amalgamation in 1973 of two tiny groups the Communist Unity Organisation and the Marxist-Leninist Workers' Association. It devotes most of its efforts to attacks upon other anti-revisionists, criticising all forms of united fronts and alliances and describing the Communist Federation of Britain's organisational concepts as un-Marxist.

Except between isolated cells whose survival depends on their finding sympathetic groups elsewhere, any serious attempts to join together rival organisations have been dashed on the rocks of doctrinal purity. Discussion between the CFB and the WPPE in 1972 to work out a plan for closer co-operation broke down when the Federation accused the late Michael McCreery of having failed to understand what was needed to build a correct and proper revolutionary party.

Some less ambitious joint efforts have however been made. During 1973 an Anti-Imperialist Alliance was formed, ostensibly to protest against the then military regime in Greece. It consisted of two London-based exiled organisations, the Organisation of Greek Marxist-Leninists and the Union of Youth from Turkey, together with the London Alliance in Defence of Workers' Rights, the Schools Action Union, the Progressive Student Movement and the Revolutionary Women's Union, from whose address in north London the alliance was co-ordinated. Among these the Women's Union is a subsidiary of the Association of Communist Workers, the other three British groups are connected with each other and the Turkish body is linked with the CPB(M–L). The alliance was in reality a collection of largely fictitious groups who were the subsidiary agents of larger organisations that did not wish to campaign openly together. It illustrates the tendency of the pro-Chinese to create organisations that exist only on paper for the purpose of propaganda and to convey the impression that a particular party or campaign enjoys far greater support than is actually the case. Although the WPPE encouraged its members to work in conjunction with the Labour Party Young Socialists, Young Communist League, and Liberation (formerly the Movement for Colonial Freedom) there is little evidence that it ever succeeded in putting such plans into effect, and its Socialist Federation of August 1970 consisted mainly of its own supporters under other names, such as the Pakistani Workers' Union and some surviving branches of the Campaign Against Racial Discrimination. It has however been virtually alone in even suggesting working with 'revisionist' elements.

Such are the bare bones of the pro-Chinese movement in Britain, the main lines of its structure and development. Of all the ideological groupings on the left it is the most bewildering in its complexity, the most esoteric, the most fervent in the pursuit of its faith, but the least successful in the execution of its designs. The questions present themselves of what motivates the imitators of an asiatic peasant guerrilla war and revolution in a western urban society, how they go about the business of bringing this revolution nearer, what goals they seek, and indeed why their movement should exist at all.

2

THE APPEAL OF MAOISM

All the 'anti-revisionists' stress the basic importance of ideological correctness as the key to success, but there is little agreement among them on what in practice is correct. All are united however in the identification with the People's Republic of China, which separates them from the rest of the revolutionary left. They emphasise the continuity of Chinese socialism and the thinking of Mao Tse-tung with the traditions of Marx and Lenin and not any divergent strains. Reg Birch, chairman of the Communist Party of Britain (Marxist-Leninist) has described the implications of this framework:

'We must see the great developments of Marxism-Leninism through the teachings of Mao Tse-tung which led the great Chinese people to victory and to develop socialism. These developments of that great teacher are not for the Chinese alone, they are part of the universal truth of Marxism-Leninism; adapted they apply everywhere in the world...'[12]

To emphasise their claim to ideological purity, the followers of Mao prefer to call themselves, not 'Maoists', but 'Marxist-Leninists', a label which they frequently attach to their organisations to denote their own superior vintage, clearly distinguishable from diluted revisionist imitations. In reality they are not the doctrinal puritans they would have the rest of us believe nor are they notable for their profundity in arguing socialist theory. Indeed they give very little independent thought to the many problems contained in the application of their beliefs to a country such as contemporary Britain. Rather it is an article of faith to accept without question the 'principles of scientific socialism' on all essential matters to the extent that there is no requirement for independent reasoning. Like the practitioners of Ingsoc in Orwell's *1984* all inconvenient facts and intellectual means to oppose are obliterated so that all that remains are slogans against which there can be no opposition. The 'Marxist-Leninism' of the pro-Chinese consists basically of a simplistic analysis of class structure, a Bolshevik concept of the seizure of power, a Stalinist view of its retention combined with selected quotations from the 'Little Red Book', the Thoughts of Chairman Mao Tse-tung.

Basic tenets and assumptions are treated with a naivety which emphasises the essential fanaticism of Marxist-Leninism. The nature of the present order of society and the need for its overthrow is abundantly clear, for 'under the capitalist dictatorship in Britain, there is fear, insecurity, a lack of peace of mind and almost constant worry . . . Physically and culturally there is widespread poverty imposed by the system'.[13] This system is monolithic and all pervasive:

'The [working] class enemy who runs the shops, fixes rates of pay and fines is easy to recognise. But it is necessary to recognise and expose his stooges and henchmen as well. Labour and Tory governments pretend to run the country in the interests of the majority of the people who voted for them. They serve only the interests of the class enemy. In the interests of the class enemy they control the police and army which are the ultimate guarantee of the continued exploitation of the worker.'[14]

The 'Marxist-Leninists' depict an intensifying crisis whose outcome is revolution by the oppressed masses:

'Capitalism is now developing towards fascism—the Corporate State. The Industrial Relations Act, the Immigration Acts, the Wage Freeze and the numbers of civil liberties that are going out of the window are all evidence of this . . . The choice is clear— fascism or revolution. There is no longer a middle course of class struggle conducted within the safe limits prescribed by social democracy. It is all-out class war. War to the death between the two great camps, workers and capitalists. The death knell of capital is tolling. Revolution is truly the main trend.'[15]

Acceptance of violence as an inevitable part of the revolution is a corollary of the rejection of the parliamentary road to socialism. Without exception all the pro-Chinese groups are agreed on this point. As the Working People's Party of England put it:

'We must have no illusions as to the road to working class power in this or any other country. Political power grows out of the barrel of a gun. The Ruling Class have guns and will not hesitate to use them when pushed to it. The masses must be prepared to meet counter-revolutionary violence with revolutionary violence. This is the price we must pay for workers' power.'[16]

No 'Marxist-Leninist' would wish to be accused of welcoming this violence, for as the Communist Party of Britain (Marxist-Leninist) states: 'We will all take up the gun, not with the relish of shedding blood, but with the conviction there is no other way to achieve our emancipation'.[17]

The morality of violence does not arise: the criteria are what is necessary to carry through the revolution. Any problems about its use concern tactical and political considerations in the advancement of the cause, and because they are counter-productive and lose support among the masses, individual acts of terrorism or isolated incidents of violence are considered deviationist. This has not however prevented some of the more impatient 'Marxist-Leninists' from disregarding the rigours of their ideology. In 1972 the chairman of the Workers' Party of Scotland was jailed with his party treasurer and two other members for offences in connection with a series of armed bank robberies intended to raise funds for the party.[18] And in January 1974 four members of the Communist Party of England (M–L) were found guilty of possessing petrol bombs and assaulting police.[19] Shortly after their arrest a year earlier the CPE(M–L) defiantly stated its position:

'When we use arms to fight the enemy we shall be the last to deny such a charge, it will be no secret and we shall proclaim it from the roof tops that the armed struggle of the working people of England has begun. We say to the enemy, rest assured that the people of England, Ireland, Scotland and Wales will surely take up arms against you in the not too distant future.'[20]

It is doubtful however that Chairman Mao would approve of these forays into urban guerrilla warfare, for they appear to ignore his guiding principles for the revolutionary guerrilla: first, build a base of support among the masses, and from there launch carefully calculated military raids to undermine or destroy enemy targets while one's own strength is preserved. And to this he would doubtless add—don't get caught. The Working People's Party of England recognised the heretical sources of inspiration for their Scottish comrades' efforts when they disowned their 'undisciplined and incorrect Tupamaros-style raids'.[21] Blind faith and impetuosity has however led the Maoists into such acts of violence and their 'guerrilla fighter' image attracts violent or potentially violent elements who are not prepared to concede, as many Marxist-Leninists do, that the moment for the use of force has not arrived. The problem which they have to face is that with such slender resources they cannot hope to achieve their huge ambition; and in a situation where violence is not appropriate other methods must come to the fore.

In this respect 'struggle' is a key word in the Marxist-Leninist vocabulary. It denotes all the many forms and phases of all the propaganda, agitation and organising that are necessary to bring about revolution. Reg Birch has applied the notion of a long-term guerrilla struggle to his propaganda on industrial conflict: strikes should be launched on a limited scale only where the workers are strong enough to push back weak employers and in situations where the relative strengths are reversed they should hold back, and in particular, refrain from encouraging any premature general strike that would invite total defeat. The level of struggle, political and industrial is however constantly intensified, proceeding 'from guerrilla struggle to protracted struggle from protracted struggle to guerrilla war, from guerrilla war to People's War, armed Struggle'.[22] To be successful, struggle has to combine what is described as a 'mass line' and the leadership of the party. In Birch's words:

'Whether the struggle is in factory, trade union, school, university or wherever the ruling class or its agents are challenged, we cannot be effective unless we are involved. Such involvement entails a proper understanding of the role of the party in relation to the mass. The party line must be a mass line ... Our party, founded by industrial workers, must be a part of our class and must in every sense belong to our class.'[23]

The relationship between the party and the mass of workers is that the former must mobilise the latter on basic economic issues of wages and conditions, gradually increasing their political awareness until the needs of the masses and the aims of the party are united under party leadership. The identity of the 'mass' is, as Birch suggests, variable, to include immigrants, students or workers, for example, and the method of struggle may differ accordingly. Maoist revolution is a process of total transformation made up of many diverse and local tasks, but so long as the overall purpose is maintained there is no inconsistency between the various aspects of activity. Keeping in mind the ultimate goal, the Communist Party of England has most clearly described what is entailed in the realisation of its plans:

'We want to abolish parliament and the monarchy, destroy the state and its instruments of repression, overthrow monopoly capital, expropriate the property of the bourgeoisie, and establish the political authority of the working class as the ruling class creating an entirely new state, the Socialist Republic of England. Such socialist revolution can never be achieved without struggle.'[24]

The boundaries of revolution are not drawn at national states, for the Marxist-Leninists consider it their duty:

'to promote active international solidarity with the allies of the British working class ... to build that firm organisational unity between the working masses of imperialist Britain, and the worker/peasant masses of the colonial countries ... and to cultivate and propagate proletarian internationalism in the struggle against imperialism and revisionism.'[25]

Successful struggles in one area aid the cause in another as the balance of political and economic power is constantly tilted further against the interests of the common enemies. The revolutionaries of each country and region must however act in a manner appropriate to their particular local circumstances. Nationally and internationally, Maoist revolution is a matter of strategic consistency and tactical flexibility.

Similarly the maintenance of revolutionary ardour after the seizure of power can only be assured by combining many varied tasks, embracing not only facets of the economic and political structure but in overcoming deeply engrained social and intellectual traditions. In the trials and errors of the Hundred Flowers Campaign, the Great Leap Forward, and in particular the Great Proletarian Cultural Revolution, western Maoists admire the triumph of revolutionary purity and zeal over bureaucratic conservatism. In China constant criticism and self-criticism, ceaseless study of the main theoretical works, and the breaking down of social and functional distinction between workers, peasants, intellectuals and officials, and the purging of all cultural remnants of the old order have constituted the essential aspects of the total revolutionary transformation of China and the Chinese people. Cultural revolution and, moreover, international cultural revolution of this kind offers to some western revolutionary idealists a profound purpose and an appreciation of the extent of their mission.

Enveloping the whole is the figure of Mao Tse-tung. He is the immediately identifiable symbol of the revolution in all its aspects. To his admirers he is all things: agitator, party leader, army commander, national leader, poet and philosopher. His writings are a freely translatable common language through which Mao demonstrates his supreme command of revolutionary theory and practice and through which his far-flung followers can communicate with each other. Paradoxically, the very qualities in the character of Mao, and the presentation of his thoughts that lend a sense of unity to his supporters, also enable them to pursue their own particular lines. As an International Socialist writer observed: 'the very generality and abstraction of "Mao Tse-tung thought" along with its repertoire of homespun adages involving the priority of local experience, has made it easier for its followers to strike out a modestly independent path'.[26]

Maoist teaching, whose 'Biblical' qualities are able to sustain a number of conflicting interpretations, can be put to use to justify the needs of alienated minorities, dignify the rivalries of petty faction, satisfy the wants of frustrated individual would-be revolutionaries and erect an edifice of philosophy on a wasteland of sterile dogma. In the name of international revolution and scientific socialism, Maoism has fulfilled all of these functions for the tiny pockets of its supporters in Britain, each burrowing away in his own fashion with varying degrees of success.

The core of the struggle is the urban working class, the most important component of the masses. In this context only the Communist Party of Britain (Marxist-Leninist) has made any impression, on the foundations laid by Reg Birch and his supporters in the north London branches of the engineering union. The CPB(M–L)'s newspaper, *The Worker*, constantly hammers out the guerrilla struggle theme, reporting plant by plant disputes in engineering and motor industries in particular. It enthusiastically greeted the flying pickets of the miners' and builders' strikes in 1972 as a new guerrilla tactic which provides 'detachments of mobile militant workers who can be thrown into the struggle anywhere and achieve local superiority over employers and any blacklegs or police in their pay'.[27] Prominent members of the CPB(M–L) such as John Hannington, an engineering shop stewards' convenor, and Ken Didsbury, an AUEW member who works for British Rail in north London, have at various times attempted to drum up support from students to forge an alliance between them and the workers.

The appeal of Maoism among students has been greater than for the more pragmatic trade unionists. On the campuses of America and Europe in the later 1960s Chairman Mao's portrait had a decorative as much as a political function but he did symbolise one of the rebellious students' essential points—the total rejection of western society and its values. The novelty and sheer audacity of Maoist revolution appealed to a sensationalist vein in the students' inchoate political awareness and expressed their desire to overturn all existing assumptions of radical revolt. The connection between Maoism and students was however a nebulous one which rarely resulted in a lasting commitment, although it gave to Maoism during the second half of the 1960s a considerable boost in the west, extending its appeal beyond the existing circle of diehard Stalinists to a new and in some ways more energetic group.

In France and Italy in particular, Maoist groups have made a violent contribution to student riots and disturbances. In the United States the radical SDS (Students for a Democratic Society) contained a militant Maoist element whose bid to gain control of the movement in 1969 led to its division into rival factions, and a similar fate befell the British Revolutionary Socialist Students' Federation, the *ad hoc* creation of midsummer revolt in 1968. From the outset doctrinal disputes between International Socialists and International Marxists plagued its progress and within a year Maoist students supported by the CPB(M–L) had gained control of the vital London RSSF branch. Under Maoist leadership this branch continued its activities long after the rest of the organisation had effectively folded, providing platforms for CPB speakers and joining forces with the Schools Action Union, which had also fallen to a group of London Maoists, and taking part in demonstrations with the Maoist-influenced Black People's Alliance. The CPB(M–L)'s work among students has continued beyond the heyday of the 1960s into the present decade when they have preached not the students' role as a new vanguard but their place alongside the workers. Its representatives have become a small but active section of NUS conferences, opposing the tendencies of orthodox Communists and the Broad Left.

The Communist Party of England (M–L) has approached student politics with its customary virulence. The CPE(M–L) together with its subsidiaries, the Birmingham and London Student Movements and the sympathetic London School of Economics Afro-Asian Society, claimed a large part of the responsibility for the physical attack on psychologist Professor Hans Eysenck and the disruption of his lecture at the LSE in May, 1973. The London Student Movement's newspaper admitted in its first issue, published soon after the incident, that a CPE(M–L) member led the disruption of the lecture and started what it described as 'a mass democratic discussion on the principle that fascists have no right to speak. Several members of the broad masses . . . addressed the students'.[28] In a subsequent issue it proudly declared: 'We the anti-fascist students representing the interests of the people and the proletarian ideology of Marxist-Leninism—Mao Tse-tung Thought resolutely denied fascist Eysenck the right to speak. And the whole world knows now that the banner of the October Revolution has triumphed over the evil forces of fascism at the L S E'.[29]

At the same time as Maoism began to find support among the student population it was also striking a chord among another group with quite different problems. Immigrant politics is governed by many factors: the immigrants' varied ethnic and religious traditions, the political life of their own countries, their relations with each other, and above all the attitude of the host community. In the 1960s, as immigration and race relations became issues in British politics, the immigrant's sense of identity and his militancy increased, combining socialist traditions with the younger and more strident tones of revolutionary Black Power. Maoism, with its appeal to the unity of the peoples of the Third World, provided an ideological framework for the expression of this awakening consciousness.

One of the first, and in the short-term one of the most successful, Maoist incursions into this sphere was the coup at the end of 1967 which secured control of the Campaign Against Racial Discrimination. Formed in December 1964, CARD combined white liberal opinion with Asian and West Indian bodies into a pressure group to secure legislation preventing discrimination in areas such as employment and housing. After the passage of the 1965 Race Relations Act it turned to community action politics and the building of a more widely based movement. By 1967, beset by political and ethnic differences it was in 'a state of limbo detached from the political structure and from the immigrant communities'[30] and had become an easy prey for militants who knew exactly in what direction they wanted the organisation to develop.

The co-ordinator of the take-over was Johnny James, a member of the CARD executive and organiser of the small Caribbean Workers' Movement, a propagandist group based in London and with distinct Maoist leanings. His allies in ousting CARD moderates from their executive positions at the organisation's third annual conference where Paul Noone and Alex Tudor-Hart of the then London Workers' Committee, who had set up CARD branches in Brent and Camden together with the Maoist organisers of the Universal Coloured Peoples' Association, formed earlier in 1967, Obi Egbuna, a Biafran writer, and a Guyanan, Ajoy Ghose. The coup was executed after some dubious manoeuvres by James to obtain voting credentials for his supporters, who included 'black Maoists, mainly West Indians, concerned not just about change in Britain but revolution in the home countries; Black Power advocates mainly Africans and West Indians who were relatively well versed in the rhetoric of Black liberation as espoused by

Fanon and Carmichael; white Marxists; and a number of West Indians who were simply angry at the course of events in Britain and within CARD'.[31]

The CARD organisation never recovered from this event. The coup did however enhance the position of the London Workers' Committee which five months later reformed itself into the WPPE, with James, Noone and Hart on its central committee. The new party pressed on with other activities in the Pakistani population in north London, where it formed a Camden Working People's Defence Organisation to forestall attacks on Pakistanis. Street patrols were set up by the Camden CARD branch (run by Paul Noone) as the only means of self-defence because, as it later alleged, 'the Metropolitan Police in Camden and Islington have been allowing and will continue to allow robbery with violence, window breaking and petrol bombing, so long as the victims are coloured'.[32] In reaction to these events the WPPE also helped launch a Pakistani Workers' Union which published newspapers in Urdu and Bengali.

Maoist rhetoric also established a point of contact with the Indian community. The Indian Workers' Association, established in 1930 and with over 25,000 members in Britain, exercises significant influence, but it is also deeply divided ideologically between groups which include pro-Chinese and pro-Soviet viewpoints. One Maoist, Jagmohan Joshi, was general secretary of the IWA in the mid-1960s though his position was hotly disputed by his rivals. Reg Birch opened the IWA's 1967 congress, and a CPB(M–L) speaker in October 1971 told an audience of 500 at a meeting organised by the Greenwich District of the IWA that 'Indian workers in this country must fight capitalism along with the rest of the British working class'.[33] In other words the particular problems of immigrants in Britain were part of a wider class struggle which transcended racial barriers.

This point has been forcibly expressed also by Marxist-Leninists in the Black Power movement. At first the slogan 'Black Power' encapsulated in the starkest racial terms the awakening consciousness and the new militancy of Africans, American negroes and West Indians. But the phrase has many shades of meaning and the political movements associated with it are extremely wide-ranging, encompassing ideas of racial separatism, nationalism, the Muslim faith, the cultivation of an 'Afro' culture, and anti-imperialist revolution. It is in the latter context that Maoism has made its impact on the Black Power movement.

The first Black Power group with a discernible Marxist-Leninist strain was the Universal Coloured Peoples' Association formed in June 1967. It became a notorious propaganda agency, fiercely spreading the message of black liberation in immigrant communities in London where it claimed as many as 700 members within three months of its foundation. It succumbed to the intense rivalries between groups and personalities and had faded within three years, although many of its leaders have emerged in other organisations.

A Goan who came to England in 1963, Tony Soares was a committed Marxist-Leninist and a member of the Working People's Party of England. He became active in the UCPA and in the Notting Hill section of the Vietnam Solidarity Campaign, his activities in which earned him a year gaol sentence in 1969 for distributing pamphlets prior to the Vietnam Demonstration of October 27, 1968, inciting people to acts of violence. Three years later, as editor of a Black Panther oriented newspaper, *Grass Roots*, run by the Black Liberation Front, he found himself in trouble with the law once again: this time, for publishing detailed instructions on how to manufacture Molotov cocktails, he received the then unusual sentence of a period of compulsory community work. The magazine was forced to close down for a period but was subsequently revived as a community newspaper for blacks in London. Serving the same interests from 1969 has been the magazine *Tri-Continental Outpost*, which has supported Chinese-backed movements in Africa and Asia and whose founding editor was Ajoy Ghose, a leading figure in the UCPA.

Another original member of the UCPA, Roy Sawh, soon broke away to form his own Universal Coloured and Arab People's Association, succeeded by a Free University of Black Studies in London (at which members of the Marxist-Leninist Organisation of Britain spoke) and then in 1971 by a Black Workers' Defence League to oppose Conservative legislation on immigration. The League included the Indian Marxist Leninist Association, a fragment from the orthodox Communist Party which had also been a part of the MLOB's Black and White Unity Front.

Following Enoch Powell's famous 'rivers of blood' speech on immigration in 1968 and in opposition to a tightening of immigration policy, the most ambitious organisation of all was founded, the Black People's Alliance. The convenor of its founding conference in Birmingham was the IWA Maoist, Jagmohan Joshi, who enlisted the support of some twenty varied ethnic and political groups. For two years, supported by white revolutionaries, it participated in a number of street demonstrations, mustering up to 5,000 people, but it did not have a sufficiently firm base to progress beyond this or to consolidate itself into a more coherent body, and it too collapsed.

Its place was taken in 1971 by the Black Unity and Freedom Party, which combines a revolutionary view of the world with the Maoist awareness of the need for immediate social work locally in fields such as education and housing. Although it emphasises its own role as a specifically black organisation, it works with sympathetic white groups such as the Irish National Liberation Solidarity Front in particular, to oppose and draw attention to alleged police brutality and harassment, has branches in south and east London and Manchester, and publishes a newspaper, *Black Voice*. Its growth has been unspectacular but the BUFP has been one of the more stable black Marxist-Leninist organisations and has maintained the extensive Maoist influence that has existed in the crowded field of immigrant politics since the mid-1960s.[34]

Much of that influence has been felt in London and in particular in the less prosperous parts in an arc from Camden in the north going eastwards around to Brixton in the south. The concentration of Maoist activities in these areas applies not only to the black groups for the CDRCU, the CPB, CPE, MLOB among others have their offices and many of their supporters there, and some Trotskyist and anarchist groups have similarly established themselves in those parts. The decaying Victorian surroundings, the depressed environment, the mixture of peoples and the hostility to authority encourage a spirit of radicalism and provides the revolutionary with a relatively favourable social milieu and a base for the development of an urban revolutionary movement.

In that same setting, the faded heart of a former empire, numerous bodies furthering the cause of 'liberation' in Africa and Asia have set up home. They have found a natural affinity with immigrants in this country and with the white revolutionaries engaged in the struggles of 'proletarian internationalism'. The Kwame Nkrumah Institute for Writers and Journalists, for example, is run from a basement flat in north London; it produces *Liberation Struggle*, a newspaper whose editor, Chenhamo Chimutungwende, a former member of the International Marxist Group, describes it as: 'an anti-imperialist monthly forum for and by militants in the overseas communities in Britain and Europe covering the direction of events in Asia, the Caribbean, Latin America, the Middle East and with a special focus on Africa'.[35] It supports the Black Unity and Freedom Party for its Maoist ideology and has links with other pro-Chinese organisations in this country such as an 'All-Africa Revolutionary Marxist-Leninist Movement', the Organisation for All Progressive People from Africa, and the 'Afro-Asian People's Liberation Movement'. Other groups have their own contacts: Tony Soares and *Grass Roots* contributed to the Revolutionary People's Communications Network run by exiled American Black Panthers in Algiers, and the CPB(M–L) is in touch with the Zimbabwe African National Union, the pro-Chinese wing of the Rhodesia black nationalist movement and, as we have seen, the CPE(M–L) through the Internationalists has its own chain of kindred spirits across the world.

Of all the international contacts established by the British Maoists, perhaps the most interesting have been those of the Working People's Party of England. In 1968 it invited the readers of its *Workers' Broadsheet* to get in touch, through it, with the Canadian revolutionary group, the Front for the Liberation of Quebec (FLQ), who, it said, were 'preparing to fight to defend workers' power from the boss class and other Yankee lackeys'.[36] The FLQ had been engaged in sporadic terrorist operations since 1963 and by the end of the decade acquired international notoriety for the kidnapping of government figures in Canada and a British diplomat, James Cross, after which Canadian Prime Minister Pierre Trudeau took action to eliminate the group. It is impossible to discern the extent of the WPPE's links with the FIQ, but it claimed to have been in touch with the Canadian terrorists since 1966 and two unnamed Quebec revolutionaries attended the WPPE inaugural conference in 1968.

The British Maoists' attempts to create the international dimension that is such an essential part of their creed have been as patchy and haphazard as the rest of their activities. At first it seems surprising that they have so few links with their counterparts in western countries, among, for example, the fifty or so separate Marxist-Leninist groups that existed in western Europe in 1970.[37] Indeed throughout the west Marxist-Leninism has emerged in a broadly similar pattern—in Europe, North America and in countries of such varied traditions and situations as Iceland, Japan and Australia. It has been located on the fringes of student movements and in small circles of intensely dogmatic Communist theoreticians, with little support among the working class. The WPPE was in touch with Swedish Maoists, and the MLOB, always the exception, has been closely linked with a small Free Socialist Party of Germany which includes members from east and west Germany and whose leader, Gunter Ackermann, addressed the MLOB's opening congress, emphasising the need for co-operation between his party and sympathisers in the USA and Austria.

Why, then, have most of the British Maoists looked to the very different African and Asian movements for sympathy and co-operation? This is because of the black presence in Britain, the former imperial connections, and the place of the third world in the Maoist scheme of revolution. The 'storm centres' lie not in the 'heartlands of imperialism' but in those parts of the world where the people are engaged in colonial or national liberation, principally in South America, Africa and Asia. Only when the imperialists and revisionists are defeated overseas will the balance of global power be so poised as to raise the possibility of revolution in the west itself. It is therefore ideologically, indeed spiritually, important, for the western Maoists to bridge the gulf that exists between themselves, as products of urban democratic societies, and the new vanguard of peasant guerrillas.

Some similarities between the development of Marxist-Leninist movements in western and Third World regions have however been detected. The French writer, Regis Debray, wrote of the pro-Chinese groups in Latin America: 'At the first stages of organisation they are able to attract honest and resolute militants, thanks to their programmes and their promises. Very soon, however, their method of work, the noisy opportunism of their political line, the hypocritical sabotage of their own official line on the armed struggle lead the revolutionary strata, principally the youth to abandon them. Then they find themselves grappling with the hostility of yet another organisation'.[38] He concluded that as a result of this: 'the "storm centres" and their revolutionary vanguards seem to move increasingly away from the forms of organisation and agitation inspired by the Chinese comrades, whereas they gain ground among the European militants and in politically becalmed regions'.[39]

Debray was writing in 1967 on the eve of the student revolts that pushed Marxist-Leninism to the fore in Europe, and at the same time as there was evidence of 'inspiration by the Chinese comrades' of a more direct sort. An investigation by *The Times* News Team in 1966 discovered what it called the 'behind-the-scenes influence of Chinese diplomats'[40] in encouraging those who were prepared to put China's case against the Soviet Union's. In particular, contacts were made through Afro-Asian and black organisations and through using European marxists, such as Jacques Grippa, a Belgian Maoist leader and the focal point for the dissemination of literature and the building up of a pro-Chinese revolutionary network in Europe. One of the Chinese roving agitators, Gora Ehrahim, a South African resident in Peking, visited Britain where he met many of the active Marxist-Leninists, including Johnny James, Albert Manchanda and Ajoy Ghose, and also attended the Internationalists' 'Necessity for Change' conference in 1967. In this context Maoism is an instrument in the competitive subversion between the Soviet Union and China, but since the end of the 1960s when, after the Cultural Revolution had subsided, China adopted a more open policy towards the west, her active involvement has declined. But in the visits of British Maoists to Peking and in the torrent of propaganda supplied by the Foreign Language Publishing House in Peking to selected bookshops in Britain, the influence can still be detected.

In Britain the pro-Chinese groups have emerged as neither text book Marxist-Leninists nor as pure Maoists. They are however the puritans of the revolutionary movement in their moral and intellectual absolutism which permits no argument and which demands total and rigorous devotion to the cause. Such intolerance inevitably leads to fragmentation, fragmentation to weakness, and weakness to a retreat into a still more resolute and unshakeable faith. Their emergence tells us more about the psychology of revolt than its theory. Indeed their attempts to apply the conspiratorial techniques of Leninism and Stalinism and their efforts to adapt the guerrilla struggle of China to modern Britain must so far be judged a failure.

Maoism has appealed to those individuals and groups who can find no conventional outlet for their frustrations or grievances, among alienated minorities, the young in search of sensation, and obsessive rebels who relish the prospect of conflict and violence. For them Maoism provides a refuge, an identity and a vehicle. Perhaps mindful of their localism, their failure to organise effectively and the evident streak of violence, Peter Sedgwick described the Maoists as 'uncompleted anarchists'; when Manchanda and Davoren led their supporters into Grosvenor Square on October 27, 1968 it was perhaps no coincidence that they were accompanied not by the red flags of Marxism but by the black flags of anarchy.

VIII

The Libertarian Alternative

I

THE ANARCHIST TRADITION

In 1872 the majority group of the First International, led by Karl Marx, excluded from its Hague Congress the Russian revolutionary Michael Bakunin and his supporters. Shortly afterwards, in a letter to a Belgian newspaper, Bakunin set out his view of the differences that had split the International into two irreconcilable camps, spelling its effective end. He attacked his opponents as worshippers of state power who would deny the masses those very liberties they claimed to seek. 'Between the Marxists and ourselves,' he wrote, 'there is a chasm. They are for government, we for our part are anarchists.'[1] Since that parting of the ways the chasm has only widened, and anarchism has drawn on many schools of thought and many modes of action to progress along a separate but devious path as the mainstream of anti-authoritarian, individualistic socialism.

The popular image of the anarchist as a mad sinister bomb-thrower bent on destruction and chaos, without a constructive thought in his head, is a distorted view. As a set of ideas and as a political movement anarchism is more substantial and constructive than that familiar picture of unbridled nihilism suggests, but it is also less easily defined. George Woodcock, the Canadian anarchist and historian, captured its elusive and nebulous qualities when he wrote that:

'To describe the essential theory of anarchism, is rather like trying to grapple with Proteus, for the very nature of the libertarian attitude—its rejection of dogma, its deliberate avoidance of rigidly systematic theory, and above all, its stress on extreme freedom of choice and on the primacy of the individual judgement, creates immediately the possibility of a variety of viewpoints inconceivable in a closely dogmatic system. Anarchism, indeed, is both variable and mutable and in the historical perspective it presents the appearance not of a swelling stream flowing on to its sea of destiny (an image that might well be appropriate to Marxism), but rather of water percolating through porous ground—here forming for a time a strong underground current, there gathering into a swirling pool, trickling through crevices, disappearing from sight and then re-emerging where the cracks in the social structure may offer it a course to run. As a doctrine it changes constantly; as a movement it grows and disintegrates, in constant fluctuation, but it never vanishes.'[2]

The history of the anarchist movement in Britain exemplifies this imagery. The 1880s saw its emergence in London political clubs of European emigré groups, followed in the subsequent two decades by an upsurge of anarchist ideas in numerous political and literary journals, in Jewish communities and in the burgeoning labour movement. In the years immediately preceding the First World War, the anarchist influence manifested itself in syndicalism, but in the post-war era the movement declined, growing irrevocably apart from the working class and continuing only as a vague strain in literary Utopianism. The 1930s and 1940s saw a revival in anarchist fortunes when anti-fascism, the Spanish Civil War and undercurrents of pacifism gave an immediate relevance to some essential anarchist ideas. The momentum did not survive into the 1950s, when a period of relative domestic tranquillity and social conformity becalmed the anarchist impulse. Its influence was confined to a small core of activists and pamphleteers, mainly in London and around the newspaper *Freedom*, who, like so many of their predecessors were but 'a chorus of voices crying in the wilderness'.[3]

An unforseen recrudescence of anarchist ideas and activities, beginning in the early 1960s, opened up a fresh era for the movement. Anarchism's influence by the end of the decade was more widely extended than during any other period. Its activities embraced anti-nuclear weapons campaigns and squatting, industrial syndicalism and rural communism, pacifism and terrorism, opposition to the Vietnam war and 'Free Schools'. Modern anarchism is a blend of old and new, of concepts first formulated in the 19th century, recast in a changing social climate, and of a new libertarianism, whose values coincide with those of traditional anarchism.

The doctrine of anarchism is based on a faith in the essential goodness of man: that he is capable of organising his affairs in voluntary and peaceful co-operation with his neighbours without the need of a coercive authority and without economic exploitation. As socialists, anarchists oppose capitalism and the private ownership of property as fundamental sources of inequality. But their beliefs stem also from a

173

liberalism which sets the interests of the individual above those of government, whose authority is for the anarchists the power of manipulation, coercion and repression: all governments, whether in representative parliaments or in dictatorships of junta or central committee, serve only the interests of their own élite group and deny to the majority of the population their liberty and identity.

The State, 'a parasite upon Society',[4] maintains an apparatus of repression in police forces, the army, legal system, bureaucracy and monarchy, and through education, the press. and the churches, the machinery of indoctrination works for the State to preserve the status quo. In particular anarchists oppose the organised violence of war, which they see as the supreme expression of State power and the ultimate denial of human freedom.

In place of this repressive hierarchy, and its attendant, exploitative institutions of big business and finance, the anarchists would substitute a form of direct democracy. With the removal of all central authority and the destruction of all institutions, men would, so anarchists believe, come together spontaneously to co-operate in fulfilling their basic requirements through small communities in which each individual had a part to play in decision-making and exercised control over his own destiny. Nicolas Walter, a prominent figure in the modern British anarchist movement, has described one vision of a society of free communities working together in the common interest:

'There would be work associations, from the workshop or small-holding up to the largest industrial or agricultural complex, to handle the production and transport of goods, decide conditions of work and run the economy. There would be area associations from neighbourhood or village up to the largest residential unit, to handle the life of the community—housing, streets, refuse, amenities. There would be associations to handle the social aspects of such activities as communications, culture, research, health and education'.[5]

Thus anarchist society does not mean a state of disruptive chaos, but it is a highly-organised entity, concerned with the identity of the individual and the quality of life.

Not all anarchists would agree with the details of Walter's picture, for like so many radicals they are in more general agreement about what they oppose than in the precise nature of any new order. Beyond the shared view that the inherent authoritarianism of all governments is an evil and a burden on all men, there are many varieties of opinion on how society can be otherwise organised. The individualists argue that the sanctity and uniqueness of the individual should not be compromised, even in observing the rules of behaviour which any society demands: the individual is real but society is artificial and abstract. Similarly other anarchists adopt a contemplative or religious stance and tend to withhold from organised or political activity, but both philosophic and individualistic schools are important strands in the psychology of anarchism, relevant to an understanding of the British movement, which has always had a strong individualist element.

Anarchist-communism proposes a decentralised society of small communities. The members of each commune own jointly all wealth and the means of production, and participate in decision-making to promote the welfare of the community. The commune, equivalent to a small village, is intended to be an economically self-sufficient and politically autonomous unit subject to no external constraints. Anarcho-federalism develops the principles of co-operation between the basic units of the communes where there cannot be complete individual self-sufficiency. Beginning with the smallest groups, from neighbourhoods to towns, to districts, to regions and nations, federations of elected delegates would plan common services and joint co-operation, but no commune or federation would have the right to impose its will on a smaller group. The spirit of voluntarism and individuality stands alongside an instinctive human interdependence as the foundations of the anarchist order, which necessitates a simpler way of life than modern industrial urbanism.

Anarchism has its industrial face however in syndicalism, from the French word meaning trade union. The anarcho-syndicalist concept of a federal society is founded not on geographical communities but on factories and industries. The syndicate—the organisation of the people at their place of work—is both the means to overthrow capitalist domination and the basis of the new society. It firstly organises the methods to achieve its end, the full range of direct industrial action, including economic and political strikes, boycotts, sabotage and occupation of factories, culminating in the social general strike to paralyse and destroy the present system in all its aspects. The economic goals are the abolition of wage labour and the establishment of workers' control of the means of production through the syndicate; the political aims are the organisation of society in syndicalist federations, factories joining with factories, industries with industries in a network of committees working from the bottom upwards so that the workers retain responsibility and control.

In preparing for anarchism in a fully industrialised society, in accepting the framework of class struggle, and in the dangers of authoritarianism contained in the larger federations, syndicalist philosophy is unacceptable to many pure anarchists. But the syndicalist concept of workers' control is, in the words of Colin Ward—a former editor of

Anarchy magazine, who has described himself as 'an anarcho-communist in the Kropotkin tradition'—'a manifestation of the struggle for personal and social autonomy which is the aim of every school of anarchist thought'.[6] Christie and Meltzer, the Anarchist Black Cross group, have distinguished between the revolutionary syndicalism of rule by committees that stops short of anarchism and full-blooded anarcho-syndicalism which means 'the full participation of all within a free communistic society'[7] and the strict accountability of committee delegates to the rank and file. Syndicalism remains very much a part of the main anarchist movement and not a half-way home between anarchism and Marxism.

All these varieties of anarchist belief originated in the 19th and early 20th centuries in the works of Godwin, Proudhon, Stirner, Bakunin, Tolstoy, Kropotkin and Malatesta, among others, whose ideas still exercise great influence over the anarchist movement.[8] As a measure of the potency of this tradition, a survey of British anarchists in 1961 discovered 149 individualists, 112 philosophic anarchists, 91 pacifist anarchists, 81 anarchist communists, and 68 anarcho-syndicalists.[9]

Modern anarchism has however become increasingly diffuse. Writers such as Sir Herbert Read, Paul Goodman and Dr Alex Comfort have added to fundamental ideas, while present-day social and political conditions have suggested many other new concepts. For every generalisation there must be a paragraph of qualification about the movement today. Only the syndicalists tend to form their exclusive organisations and the rest of the classic schools are spread throughout the movement in groups that belong to no one particular branch but are mixtures of them all. Indeed many activists who could in all essential respects be designated anarchists prefer, in view of the term's antiquity and its associations with violence, to call themselves 'libertarians'. This title is found as a general description of any non-Marxist, anti-authoritarian socialist, but in particular to describe those militants of the Committee of 100, who were anarchists in all but name, and, ten years later, the politically-engaged wing of the Alternative Society.

The foundations of anarchist philosophy concern the nature of the ideal society, but they also govern the means to that end. A pacifist anarchist will hardly engage in violence, for example, nor will an individualist occupy himself in trade union work. All except a few extreme individualist or philosophic anarchists would agree that some kind of revolution is required to remove the capitalist state. On what is to be done to bring about this revolution and so create the conditions for anarchy there is deep disagreement. But, just as all anarchists, syndicalists and libertarians share an aim that is the antithesis of conventional politics—the destruction of power not its seizure—they also share some general rules concerning organisation, methods and activity that are the negation of all accepted forms of political behaviour. These rules demand that to achieve the desired state all organisations must be small, voluntary, temporary, functional and autonomous. Anarchists do not seek to build hierarchical party machines as the vanguards of revolution. 'Freedom', as one modern anarchist has declared, 'cannot be brought about "for the masses" by a "politically conscious" minority or élite . . . A free society cannot be established by political parties and leaders however sincere . . . If we really want freedom we must do it ourselves.'[10]

The classic (that is 19th century) anarchist concepts of political activity are 'the propaganda of the word'—writing, discussion, arguing— and 'the propaganda of the deed', the path of direct action. This second aspect has caused the movement much trouble, largely as a result of its lasting identification, since the end of the 19th century, with individual terrorism and assassination. In the last twenty years however the nature of the 'deed' has undergone great modification.

Direct action remains the anarchists' principal political technique. Its functions are first, actively to create the framework and the style of an anarchist society in the shell of the old, and secondly to use the anarchist structure as a base from which to mount attacks on the present order. From a syndicalist viewpoint the process is seen as follows:

'Workers' councils, united with others, industry by industry and locality by locality, are the basis of a revolutionary movement and also of a change-over in the system. It is possible now "to build the new society within the framework of the old", by the creation of units in industry; localised associations for mutual aid and protection; co-operative endeavours and even clubs of common interest. A living commune can by-pass the state and ignore laws imposed upon it that it does not wish to observe unless the authorities use force. And a commune active in co-ordinating workers' councils, tenants' associations and many other action groups would be the fall-back unit in any creation of a free society. It circumvents the need for the state and thus negates authority. It makes it possible for the state to be abolished.'[11]

Similarly the Alternative Society libertarianism, through its communes, free schools, or the underground press, employs the basically anarchist notions of a structure that by-passes existing organisations and points the way ahead to a new society.

In moving on to the offensive against the *ancien regime* the problems of conflict and violence are raised. Confrontation with the forces of the

177

State through direct action may take many forms, in acts of civil disobedience and passive resistance, in demonstrations, squatting, or sabotage, and may result equally through violent or non-violent acts. Direct action is used in some way no matter what the circumstances—in a general strike on the eve of revolution itself or in situations where there is no potential for the creation of a protogenic anarchist society nor for a mass assault on the State. Then anarchists may adjust themselves to 'permanent protest', in small guerrilla raids, to prick society's conscience, probe its weak points, and seek what small gains they can with whatever allies they can.

The problem of using violence against authority is constantly debated by anarchists but there is no one attitude among them. Some, as much as Maoists or Trotskyists, consider violence an inevitable part of revolution, but others reject it entirely as itself a form of coercion, morally unjustifiable. An overriding impression conveyed by many anarchists on the subject is, however, one of ambiguity. They maintain that a definition of violence in physical terms alone is meaningless since there are many other forms of violence, cultural, psychological and social, which emanate largely from the State, itself an institutionalisation of violence. Resistance against a State that is by definition innately violent, will inescapably be drawn into violence itself as the only means of self-defence. But this can be justified, as 'anarchist violence is the destruction of authority',[12] a Marcusian argument that makes a philosophical distinction between revolutionary and counter-revolutionary action. With this in mind the group known as 'Solidarity' has given itself a *carte blanche*: 'We are not pacifists. We have no illusions about what we are up against. In all class societies, institutional violence weighs heavily and constantly on the oppressed. Moreover the rulers of such societies have always resorted to more explicit physical repression when their power and privileges were really threatened. Against repression by the ruling class we endorse the people's right to self-defence, by whatever means may be appropriate'.[13]

The morality of violence is not discussed, and likewise, an article in *Freedom* after one of the Angry Brigade explosions obscured the ethical issues by refusing to repudiate all violence. It rejected what it called 'deliberate terrorism' but accepted the inevitability of sabotage and assassination in certain cases, and accepted violence in destroying the present system, but not in building a new one. It also argued that:

'As anarchists, we will not condemn any person who feels impelled by a passionate hatred of the present system to use its own weapons against it. When a social and political system is maintained by violence, it is tempting to try and destroy it by violence. And when normal methods of action are ineffective, it is tempting to lose patience and strike what is hoped to be a more effective blow. We understand such feelings and sympathise with them . . . But we do not believe this is the way to establish anarchism. This does not mean we are against the use of force, any more than we are necessarily in favour of it. There are circumstances in which it is the only possible method of action.'[14]

The anarchists' attitude to violence is so often equivocal and subjective, varying according to beliefs and situations. Despite the desire of many modern libertarians to bury the violent part of their movement, it is just one of the many aspects of the anarchist tradition that remains very much alive. The movement and the ideal have proved again sufficiently flexible to accommodate their many conflicting tendencies in the modern revival of anarchism.

2

ANARCHISTS IN ACTION

One of the clearest facts about the many developments in the revolutionary movement during the 1960s is the rapid growth of its anarchist wing. At the beginning of the decade libertarian ideas spread in the 'ban-the-bomb' movement and in particular through the militant activities of the Committee of 100. The radicalising effect of those campaigns paved the way for the formation in 1964 of an Anarchist Federation of Britain to co-ordinate activity over a wider field. In the second half of the 1960s anarchism enjoyed an unprecedented degree of influence, mainly among students and young people, not merely in Britain but throughout much of the western world. Since 1971 however the movement has encountered many problems of direction and purpose: the individualists traditionally so prominent in British anarchism have been unable to withstand the pressures from new groups demanding more effective national organisation on one side and, on the other, the fragmentation of activity into localised libertarianism of the Alternative Society. The story of the evolution of contemporary anarchism must begin however with the protests that swelled up in the 1950s against Britain's possession of nuclear arms.

Anarchism Revived (1958-67). When the Campaign for Nuclear Disarmament was formed at the beginning of 1958, the total number of anarchists in Britain was no more than a few hundred, of whom only a minority were active in pursuing their beliefs. The movement comprised the Syndicalist Workers' Federation, which had been established in 1946 out of a collapsed Anarchist Federation of Britain, a small group of activists centred on London, and *Freedom*, the newspaper which has represented the movement's one constant feature since its foundation in 1886 by the Russian exile, Prince Peter Kropotkin.

It was natural that the small circle of existing anarchists should find their way into the CND. The movement has always had a strong pacifist strain and is vehemently anti-military (although the two elements should not be regarded as synonymous). In the early and mid-1950s, anarchist sympathisers had participated in some small-scale protests against atomic weapons, including the Direct Action Committee, with supporters of the Peace Pledge Union, then still associated with the magazine *Peace News*, and assorted militant pacifists. The CND provided these activists with a much wider forum, whose history is told elsewhere.[15] One of its effects, quite unintended by many of the well-known figures who supported it, was to introduce thousands of young people to a style of radical politics beyond that of the conventional, parliamentary system: the Young Communist League, Young Socialists, International Socialists and the anarchists all increased their following as a result of involvement in the campaign. The former, Marxist, organisations emphasised the way in which the bomb was symbolic of the evils of capitalism, while the anarchists concentrated less on theology and more on the possibilities for direct action and instant democracy that the campaign had opened up.

The anarchist contribution, and indeed their gains, exceeded those of other revolutionary groups. By the middle of 1960, militant supporters of the campaign had become tired of its orientation as an establishment lobby, on which they blamed its lack of results. Under the aegis of Bertrand Russell and through the energetic work of one of his associates, Ralph Schoenman, an American whose political views were close to anarchism, the Committee of 100 was formed in October 1960, backed by more than a hundred leading figures from the arts. Its rank and file supporters included those militants associated with the Direct Action Committee, but few at the outset were anarchists in any formal sense, although the activists included what have been called 'emotional' or 'unconscious' anarchists[16]—anarchists in all but name. It was the latter group in particular who led the Committee into open hostilities against the State and some of its supporters towards the conclusion of conscious, formal anarchism.

This alliance of assorted militants took hold of the Committee's activities during the summer of 1961. Until then its activities were peaceful enough, and as ineffectual as the conventional tactics of passive marches and lobbying. The activists however pushed through plans for a demonstration in Trafalgar Square in September 1961, and despite a government ban and the imprisonment of four committee members, including Bertrand Russell, for conspiracy to incite a riot, it went ahead, with fighting between demonstrators and police, and over 1,300 of the estimated 6,000 protesters arrested. Driven on by the developing conflict, the militants attempted to organise mass demonstrations of civil disobedience at eight nuclear bases throughout the country. Less than a tenth of the expected 50,000 people turned out, and the authorities' response was unremitting—in February 1962 six of the organisers were imprisoned for periods of twelve and eighteen months under the Official Secrets Act.

From that point onwards the Committee of 100 and the wider CND movement went into decline. Russell himself resigned the Committee's presidency, public sympathy for unilateralism waned and the celebrities deserted the cause. Where the constitutional protests of CND had failed the Committee resorted to more militant tactics. To try to counter the ever more damaging effects of militancy, the activists' response was yet greater militancy, accelerating the decline they had precipitated. CND itself suffered irreversibly from these developments, and although it has remained in existence, it is a shadow of its former self.

The anarchists, however, concentrated on the Committee of 100, to which their greatest contribution was its utter destruction save as a vehicle for direct revolutionary action. Indeed the anarchists' part in the 'ban-the-bomb' movement as a whole was to help convert a legal, peaceful, mass campaign to one dominated by small, clandestine groups of militants.

By the end of 1961 however the anarchist movement had noticeably grown. The circulation of *Freedom* topped the 2,000 mark for the first time since the war and in 1961 the newspaper had helped launch a new monthly magazine, *Anarchy*, edited by architect Colin Ward. While *Freedom* concentrated on news and traditional forms of agitation, *Anarchy* devoted its pages to cultural, social and intellectual issues, and in education, ecology and the environment, for example, its concern preceded by years any wider public interest. This partly reflected the non-violent anarchists' concern for the quality of life and partly the coincidence between anarchist values and those of the 'New Left', whose search for a humanistic ethos of socialism that emphasised the fulfilment of the individual's identity and creativity provided a unique opportunity for the airing of anarchist ideas. And on the economic and industrial level, the anarchist movement tried to take advantage of a less unfavourable climate, when in 1961, the Syndicalist Workers' Federation and the London Anarchist Group formed a short-lived National Rank and File Movement, to promote the idea of workers' control and the aim of the 'International General Strike Against War', a slogan that brings together all the basic ingredients of classic anarchist activism.[17]

Those aspirations might well have been applied also to the group that became known as 'Solidarity' and which emerged in 1961 under the title of 'Socialism Reaffirmed'.[18] Its first members included some of those who were expelled from the Socialist Labour League, including Dr Christopher Pallis, alias Martin Grainger, who became the group's effective leader. Although the 'Solidarity' group has never had more than a few hundred members and has a very loose organisational structure, its supporters have been consistently active in a wide range of issues, beginning with the Committee of 100.

During the winter of 1962–63, the anarchists, conscious and unconscious, syndicalists and 'Solidarists' combined to steer the Committee in a truly subversive direction. At a conference, held in February 1963 to discuss 'The Way Ahead' two militant lines emerged. One wished to extend the Committee's activities to other areas such as industry, housing or to external issues such as Greece or South Africa. A second current of opinion also wanted to move away from merely symbolic demonstrations, not to build a mass movement on other issues, but rather physically to attack civil defence locations and expose State secrets. These distinctly anarchist views were summarised in a pamphlet called *Beyond Counting Arses*, later reprinted as a 'Solidarity' pamphlet.

One of the first targets for the group that wished to broaden the scope of the campaign were industrial workers. Ken Weller, an engineering union member and supporter of 'Solidarity', convened an Industrial Sub-Committee of the Committee of 100 to 'enlist the support of hundreds of thousands of workers'.[19] Docks and Engineering Liaison Committees were set up, Pat Arrowsmith and Bertrand Russell, among others, addressed factory gate meetings, and 130,000 copies of an *Appeal to Trade Unionists* were printed, calling for mass civil disobedience and resistance by workers against the manufacture of weapons of mass destruction. Such propaganda had been an integral part of the Marxists' efforts to turn the CND and the Committee of 100 to revolutionary ends, but all these appeals, from whatever source, were ignored by the workers.

Given the failure of this approach, libertarians looked elsewhere for issues. Some 'Solidarity' members turned to activity on the problem of of housing, while other anarchists tried to internationalise the cause through Anti-War International conferences held on the continent under the auspices of the War Resisters' International, the pacifist body founded in the 1930s. And in 1963, all of the libertarian groups— the Syndicalist Workers' Federation, the 'Freedom' Group, London

Anarchist Group and 'Solidarity'—joined with the Communist Party to try to wreck the visit of Queen Frederika of Greece to Britain; a total of forty-three people were arrested in demonstrations.

It was in clandestine activities against the State however that the libertarians were able to develop most fully their new determination. The arguments of *Beyond Counting Arses*, urging a campaign of active resistance against the State, strongly influenced a group of Scottish members of the Committee of 100, including some 'Solidarity' supporters and anarchists. In 1963 these militants organised themselves into the Scots Against War group and for the next three years conducted a fierce propaganda campaign with pamphlets such as *How to Obstruct the Warfare State*, in support of a series of raids, arson and robbery at civil defence and military establishments. They broke into defence premises at Rosyth, Portlethen and Glasgow, attempting to obtain secrets; set off explosions in Glasgow in May 1966, and blew up a Royal Observer Corps post at Aberdeen in the same year. The Scots Against War literature also encouraged attacks against US Servicemen and they were reported to have conceived, but abandoned, a plan to rob the payroll of a Scottish newspaper group. But when some members had been arrested the group eventually faded away in search of other issues.[20]

Beginning at the same time, a more notorious but less violent series of events revolved around a group known as the 'Spies for Peace', which originated among libertarian supporters of the Committee of 100. Their campaign to put into practice their beliefs in active resistance against the Establishment began with the fortuitous discovery in February 1963 of the location, in an underground bunker near Reading, of a secret Regional Seat of Government (RSG), intended for use in a nuclear war or other extreme emergency. The discoverers themselves went underground, took on the title 'Spies for Peace' and circulated their findings in a pamphlet *Danger! Official Secret*. This was first distributed on the CND Easter March in 1963 when anarchists led a small demonstration to the site of the exposed RSG. An outcry was raised in the press for the arrest of the 'Spies for Peace' but widespread support was forthcoming from the libertarian left. Numerous reports and summaries of the original pamphlet were circulated, including one at the 1963 annual conference of the National Union of Students, and in June of that year a number of libertarian groups, including the London Anarchists, 'Solidarity', the SWF, and members of the London Committee of 100 together with the Independent Labour Party, combined to report the events of spring 1963 in a pamphlet called *Resistance Shall Grow*.

More break-ins and discoveries of classified civil defence material followed, which led to demonstrations at other suspected RSG locations, including Dover, Preston, Brecon and Edinburgh, at which anarchists, SWF and 'Solidarity' members, encouraged by *Freedom* newspaper, were prominent. The work of the 'Spies for Peace' was taken up by others, including the members of the Ilford Libertarians and Essex Committee of 100, who broke into Ilford Civil Defence Headquarters, but with the forces of law and order hot on its heels the 'Spies for Peace' broke up and moved to other activities. The group had applied some of the cardinal principles of the anarchist 'propaganda of the deed' to attack the State and, by example, point the way to others. Nicolas Walter described their work as a perfect example of anarchist activity, although he said 'not all those involved in it were anarchist'.[21] It showed, in the words of the *Resistance Shall Grow* pamphlet, 'the advantage of an *ad hoc* organisation coming readily into being and if necessary disappearing with the same speed'.[22]

The identity of the Spies for Peace and their importance in the development of the anarchist movement in the last decade, was emphasised in two articles published in 1973 in a magazine called 'Inside Story', edited by Wynford Hicks, of the Syndicalist Workers' Federation, with Nicolas Walter as features editor, and which purported to print the stories Fleet Street refused to handle. The articles described the composition of the Spies for Peace—eight people in their twenties, all of whom were brought together in the Committee of 100 from a variety of political backgrounds and who had all been arrested for their earlier political activities—how they carried out the 'Spies for Peace' campaign, and what they did after the initial events of 1963. Some became involved in a Pirate Radio station which broadcast against the 1964 General Election and which intended to broadcast civil defence secrets but subsequently collapsed. Their later activities were varied:

'Some helped produce the fake American dollars bearing slogans against the Vietnam war during 1966 and 1967. Several took part in the Brighton Church demonstration in October 1966. A few were involved in the springing of George Blake from Wormwood Scrubs in October 1966. Several took part in the Greek embassy demonstration in April 1967. Some joined the Committee of 100 demonstration at the Corsham complex in May 1967.

'At a late stage tenuous connections were made with a new tendency on the libertarian left. One of the contacts of the Spies for Peace, who had been prominent in the Radio Pirates was involved in an attempt to fire a harmless rocket at the Greek Embassy in 1967. None of the groups was in fact involved in the developments culminating in the Angry Brigade but those connections were not entirely tenuous.'[23]

The group was also in touch with the Scots Against War, the Ilford Libertarian Group, and the First of May Group. Its connections with the latter, when members of both bodies were involved in the production and circulation of the bogus dollar bills, help explain the tantalising ambiguity at the end of the quotation from *Inside Story*, for after 1967 the First of May Group went on to carry out a campaign of terrorism in Britain and Europe, and was directly involved with the emergence of the Angry Brigade, as I shall recount below.

In relation to some of the other activities to which the articles in *Inside Story* referred, a certain pattern is discernible, in which the supporters of a number of separate anarchist and libertarian organisations are prominent. A reference to the 'Brighton church demonstration' was the attempt to shout down the then Prime Minister, Harold Wilson, as he was addressing a service held on the eve of the Labour Party conference in 1966, the year of his second general election victory. Involved in this widely publicised incident were individual anarchists, supporters of the Committee of 100, the 'Solidarity' group and the tiny but extremely active Ilford Libertarian group.[24] Some members of the latter organisation had been reported to the Director of Public Prosecutions earlier that year after they had distributed leaflets urging voters to spoil their ballot papers as a gesture of opposition to representative democracy. The occupation of the Greek Embassy in London the following spring similarly involved a wide range of libertarian activists, among whom were formal anarchists, supporters of 'Solidarity', and the Scots Against War group. Distinct lines between these bodies cannot be drawn, for individual members of one group were often on close personal terms with members of another, and the organisations' membership also overlapped.

All of these events illustrate the nebulous but interlocking development of modern anarchism, its sometimes spectacular activities on the fringes of wider movements, and the dedication of its protagonists. Like the imagery invoked by Woodcock, the movement ebbs and flows, disappears from view occasionally but never quite dies. In the activities that grew out of the Committee of 100's attempts to oppose nuclear arms, numerous contacts were established and events set in train that laid the basis for the creation of an endemic guerrilla opposition to the British Establishment. Although the whole truth is inaccessible, this current flows through the very heart of the revolutionary movement, threatening at its will to burst its bank and flood an unsuspecting country with its audacity.

At the same time as these underground activities were taking place, the public face of anarchism was advancing. In 1964 the Anarchist Federation of Britain (AFB) was formed, reviving the name of a body that had existed from 1936–46. The first proposals for a national federation came at the end of 1963 at a time when the focal points of the CND and Committee of 100 were beginning to lose their wider appeal. London, the centre of anarchist activity, took the lead in January 1964 forming a London Anarchist Federation embracing a separate London Group, Enfield, Notting Hill and Woolwich Anarchist Groups, and an Iberian Federation of Libertarian Youth in exile in London. Three months later this was followed up with a national conference in Bristol attended by between seventy and eighty people. It brought together twelve groups, whose personnel 'constituted mainly anti-bomb militants disillusioned with the political slant of CND, who realised that the logical development of the practice of direct action was the acceptance of the philosophy that went with it'.[25] In other words, the conference, and the Federation it set up, included those converted 'unconscious' anarchists, as well as the majority of existing anarchist groups, including *Freedom, Anarchy* and the SWF.

The AFB decided against a formal membership system and demanded only agreement on a general policy document that stated basic anarchist principles. It did however appoint a six-strong secretariat to co-ordinate activities and convene annual conferences, half of whom were concerned with international liaison. One of the AFB's first activities was the abortive promotion of an anti-general election campaign to encourage mass abstention at the polls. Its progress was at first slow but steady: organised into regional federations, the total number of affiliated groups was 14 by May 1965; 17 in December 1965; 20 in June 1966; 28 in December 1966 and 30 by December 1968.

Yet, as if to emphasise the contradictory tendencies inherent in anarchism, while the Federation was growing the established Syndicalist Workers' Federation was in decline. Its fifty or so members included some who were very active in libertarian politics: Bill Christopher, its secretary, who also contributed a column on industrial news to the *Freedom* newspaper; Stuart Christie, a former member of the Labour Party Young Socialists and the Scottish Committee of 100, who acquired some notoriety when he was imprisoned by the Franco regime from 1964–67 for smuggling explosives into Spain and who later founded the Anarchist Black Cross group; Laurens Otter, who has organised anarchist groups in Oxford, Croydon and Shropshire and has been a regular contributor to *Freedom*; John Lawrence, a member of the printworkers' union SOGAT and an industrial militant of long standing;[26] and Wynford Hicks, who founded the first modern Oxford University anarchist newspaper as a twenty-year-old undergraduate in 1963, was a member of the Oxford Committee of 100, became one of the three-man International Secretariat of the Anarchist Federation in 1964, represented the SWF at the 12th Congress of the International Working Men's Association in Paris during that year and later edited the magazine *Inside Story*. With the evident revival of anarchism the SWF activists hoped to reap some benefit. They supported the first workers' control conference sponsored by *The Week* and *Voice of the Unions* in 1964, when they also formed an Industrial Sub-Committee to propagate the idea of workers' control, to develop contacts among shop stewards and to make printing facilities available for workers in dispute. But like the National Rank and File Movement three years earlier this enterprise led nowhere, confirming once again the difficulties experienced by libertarian revolutionaries in trying to put their views across to trade unionists and industrial workers. The SWF's failure in this area was compounded by the activities of its leading members in other aspects of the libertarian movement, which, ironically, drew support away from the SWF itself to the AFB and local anarchist groups. The consequences were the decline in circulation of *Direct Action*, which was wound up at the beginning of 1968, and the effective end of the SWF, devoid of a role at a time when events seemed so uniquely propitious for anarchists.

This lack of results in industry was shared also by a London-based group of anarchists and syndicalists who in the 1966 seamen's strike produced four issues of a broadsheet called *Ludd*, which urged that the 'duty of every trade unionist and militant member of the rank and file [is] to ensure the complete success of the seamen's strike'.[27] This would be achieved, it maintained, by spreading the strike to other industries, particularly the docks, and the setting up of joint councils and action committees to organise the workers. But with no members among the seamen in the docks or any related trade unions the 'Luddites' were powerless to effect their designs. Members of the 'Solidarity' group in Aberdeen did however manage to strike up some contacts among unionists at the same time, when, aided by the Young Communist League, members of SOGAT and the Amalgamated Engineering Union, they produced a magazine called *The Paperworker* which was circulated among the 5,000 printworkers in the city.

So many of the libertarians' activities during this period fell into that category of 'permanent protest' and implicitly conceded the impossibility of realising ultimate aims. Despite the growth of their movement they could only embarrass the State, not destroy it, and had to accept that only gestures of revolutionary intent were realistic, not revolution itself. It is perhaps because of this apparent hopelessness, flying in the face even of a democratic system, that the public's awareness of the renaissance of libertarianism was blunted and led the writer of an article in *New Society* during the middle of 1965 to observe that 'The anarchists no longer figure in the popular imagination except perhaps as figures from the past, planning the assassination of statesmen and the abolition of government'.[28] Three years later no one could maintain that view of the libertarian movement.

'Raising the Black Flag' (*1967–71*). The newspaper *Freedom* itself caught the prevalent mood of the period when it declared that: 'During 1968 the black flag of anarchy has been raised in Paris and Mexico City, in Columbia University and Brussels, in London and in Rome. From Peking to the Pentagon via the Vatican the spiritual and temporal rulers of the world know that they are faced with a crisis of authority which will not be resolved until mankind is free from deceit and coercion—the means of government everywhere ... today it is only anarchism that meets the situation'.[29]

The source of this new confidence, unmatched even when the Committee of 100 was at its height, was the appeal of anarchism among students. The educated and the youthful have traditionally comprised most of those who identify with the Utopian goals of anarchism. The *Freedom* survey in 1961 showed that 253 out of the 358 British respondents had received some form of higher education. Students, teachers, lecturers and writers provided the highest occupational categories and 293 were under forty years old. By the end of the decade the proportion of younger people was appreciably higher. The rapid growth of the Anarchist Federation of Britain in 1968 and 1969 was due mostly to the influx of students: in August 1968 the Federation had 53 affiliated groups, in October 1968 62, in May 1969 85, and in October 1969 there were 100 sections, the majority of which were student groups, and most of those at universities.

It was not only the idealism that attracted students but also the justification of spontaneous direct action, the promise of instant democracy and the vision of an alternative society to the present centralised, bureaucratic, materialistic and hierarchical system. Traditional anarchist concepts were also fused with 'Situationism', a creed of total opposition to all forms of order, in culture and in the organisation of society, that originated in France. For a brief period the combination of Anarchism and Situationism provided an explosive philosophy that rationalised many of the more sensational theatrical outbursts of direct action in universities such as the daubing of walls with paint, or the occupation of buildings to create alternative 'free' universities.[30] The student anarchists of the late 60s were active also in the anti-Vietnam war campaign and on the largest demonstration, on October 27, 1968, the anarchists, according to the *New Society* survey, comprised nearly a quarter of the marchers.[31] For this occasion the anarchists formed themselves into a United Libertarian Group to dissociate themselves from the pro-Viet Cong stance of the Vietnam Solidarity and to emphasise their opposition to war and government as such.

Besides the growth of the AFB, the rising fortunes of anarchism were reflected in the sales of *Freedom*, up to 4,000 in 1968, those of *Anarchy*, which reached 3,500 in 1969, and the number of subscribers to *Solidarity* magazine, up from 200 earlier in the decade to 1,400 in 1969.

In this situation the 'Solidarity' group attempted to reform its informal structure: in 1967 its supporters in London instituted a membership system to replace the existing loose association of sympathisers and two years later attempted to extend this on a national scale among 'Solidarity' groups in South Wales, Lancashire and in Scotland.[32] These moves towards greater cohesion were, however, inconsistent with the kind of organisation 'Solidarity' basically wished to be. It stands on a vaguely defined border between Marxism, anarchism and syndicalism, and its ideas have been much influenced by a French group called 'Socialisme ou Barbarie', whose leading theorist, Paul Cardan, regards revolution as 'the autonomous and self-conscious activity of the masses',[33] leading to a society run by elected workers' councils in which all social relationships would be transformed. 'Solidarity' eschews any ambitions to be a party that will lead the revolution. It has described its purpose as not 'yet another leadership, but merely as an instrument of working class action. The function of Solidarity is to help all those who are in conflict with the present authoritarian social structure, both in industry and in society at large, to generalise their experience to make it a total critique of their condition and its cause and to develop the mass revolutionary consciousness if society is to be totally transformed'.[34]

Autonomy is the keynote of its character, to the extent that each separate group produces its own magazine with its own views and it is virtually impossible therefore to distil a precise 'Solidarity' policy on any issue. The activities of the various 'Solidarity' groups are wide-ranging and its output of literature prolific, on subjects as diverse as the Kronstadt Mutiny in Russia in 1921, Hungarian Workers' Councils in 1956, or industrial disputes at Pilkington's glass factory in Lancashire or at Ford Motors at Dagenham, where it has had some sympathisers. The Solidarists have also acquired some notoriety for their discussion of sabotage as a weapon in industrial struggle.[35] Their pamphlets have been translated into a number of languages by foreign groups with whom they share some basic principles, in France, Sweden, Belgium and Holland. Because of its self-imposed limitations as an organisation 'Solidarity' has, however, been unable to fulfil the potential its energetic supporters have so often displayed, and new organisations have emerged to meet the demands of a growing interest in libertarianism.

Prominent among the more recently established groups is the Anarchist Black Cross, whose best-known member is Stuart Christie, who joined after leaving the moribund Syndicalist Workers' Federation. The primary aims of the Black Cross are to help political prisoners, who are coincidentally usually anarchists in Spanish gaols, with cash, gifts and propaganda, and its international secretary is a Spaniard, Manuel Garcia Garcia. In London the Black Cross shares premises with exiled Spanish anarchists at the 'Centro Iberico', and with the International Libertarian Centre. This centre is used for many social events—including film shows and an 'Anarchist Cabaret'—apart from being an important meeting place for European and British anarchists.

The Black Cross is however something more than a welfare and social organisation. Similar groups exist in Berlin, Cologne, Hanover, Brussels, Dublin, Milan and Chicago, and at least three Black Cross members have met with violent death: Karl von Rauche and Tomas Wiesbecher were shot by police in Germany during 1972 as suspected members of the Baader-Meinhof terrorist group, and Guiseppe Pinelli, an Italian, was killed in Milan in December 1970 in mysterious circumstances when he fell from the window of the police headquarters where he was being interrogated about terrorist acts. Indeed Christie himself was accused of conspiring to cause explosions for which the Angry Brigade claimed responsibility, but he was acquitted. In reaction to these events, *Black Flag*, the British organisation's newspaper, has declared that 'Interpol has in the struggle against libertarian revolution (and against us in particular) been acting as a unified political body',[36] and on another occasion it described the Special Branch as 'the armed wing of the Tory Party'.[37]

Theoretically the Black Cross organisation is syndicalist and coined a slogan 'Form Fives' to urge the creation of a 'framework of militants all over the country, all believing in workers' councils and all believing in militant action'.[38] Most of its contacts have however not been among the workers but among students, including at various times University College, London, the City of London University, London School of Economics, Cambridge University, and in Bristol, Oldham, Liverpool, Derby, Sheffield, Cardiff and Leicester.

The internationalism implicit in an organisation like the Black Cross is an important part of the anarchist movement. It expresses itself through participation in demonstration of protest against militaristic anti-socialist regimes, of which Spain is the prime target, in typically anarchist gestures such as the breaking of windows at Iberia Airline's London offices—for which two SWF members were gaoled for two months in 1964—and in money-raising campaigns, such as Freedom's 'Spanish Resistance Fund'. International activities stem from contacts between affiliated groups in different countries, but depend greatly on personal contacts, which may be established at formal gatherings, such as the international anarchist congress Stuart Christie attended in Italy in 1968, or the journey to England made by Dutch Provos in 1966 to help set up a Notting Hill Provo Group, in return for the earlier participation of fifteen British anarchists in a demonstration in Holland. Another example of this kind of joint activity came in 1972 when Albert Meltzer, a leading figure in the Black Cross group and a one-time member of the London Anarchist Group, visited Germany to discuss with German anarchists the co-ordination of propaganda between Ford motor factories in Germany and Britain in the event of further disputes in the company's British plants.[39]

On the international scene, however, it has been the rising tide of terrorism that has attracted most attention. In Italy, West Germany and Spain anarchist terrorism has reached more serious proportions than in Britain, where the major responsibility for terrorist acts during the present decade has been that of the IRA. For five years, before their attacks on the British mainland began in earnest in 1972, numerous relatively small explosions and fires that were set off in Britain were the work of libertarian groups, with an international flavour or implication. Besides the efforts of the Scots Against War against American installations, incidents have included those at the Greek and American embassies in 1968 in which the Spies for Peace Group may have been directly or indirectly concerned; the bombing of the Bilbao Bank in Covent Garden in July 1969 for which an English member of a self-styled Sidney Street Appreciation Society of Anarchists was gaoled for twelve months; the machine gunning of the Spanish Embassy in London in December 1970 for which, among other explosions, the Angry Brigade claimed responsibility; the short-lived campaign by the anarchists calling themselves 'Freedom Fighters for All', who during 1973 placed small explosive devices outside the Portuguese Consulate in Cardiff and an officers club at Aldershot, and, above all, the activities of the First of May Group.

One of the most consistently active libertarian terrorist groups, the Movement of Revolutionary Solidarity, more usually known as the First of May group, emerged during 1966 in Italy. Its roots were in the

European anarchist movement, in France and among exiled Spaniards, but also in Britain. In March 1968 it placed notices in *Freedom* and *Direct Action* claiming responsibility for a bomb placed at the Spanish Embassy in London. Over the next three years the First of May Group lent its name to an extensive bombing campaign on the continent, including in May 1971 bombs at three British owned offices in Paris; in addition a further twelve explosive devices were planted in the United Kingdom mainly at the offices of foreign governments and financial interests. It is however doubtful whether there is one First of May Group but rather a number of loosely related cells. In January 1974 the group's name was used by terrorists who threw a petrol bomb at the Spanish Cultural Institute in Dublin. Several members of the Irish 'New Earth' anarchist group were arrested, a relatively recent formation with no apparent connection with the First of May Group's previous activities.

Among others with whom the First of May Group came into contact in Britain was the Notting Hill branch of Lotta Continua (Fight On), an Italian based group that in turn was in touch with 'Big Flame', a libertarian socialist organisation that originated on Merseyside but which has spread in the present decade in the Midlands and London. Most significant of all was the First of May Group's direct connections with the Angry Brigade, which claimed responsibility for at least twelve explosions in the London area in 1970 and 1971, and for which many of the materials were obtained from the Group's European sections. Indeed in the eyes of the authorities the two groups were synonymous, for four of the five people who were imprisoned in connection with the Angry Brigade's explosions were at the same time held responsible for the deeds of the First of May Group in Britain.

So far as is known, none of the Angry Brigade's members belonged to any formal anarchist or other political organisation but, as their own supporters explained, although the majority of the Left rejected their politics they 'also recognise that the Angry Brigade identify themselves as members of the libertarian Left and repudiate orthodox or straight socialist politics'.[40] They rejected Marxist-Leninist doctrines that warned against the counter-productiveness of individual terrorism not related to a broader movement and that advised instead patient work among the proletariat and the building of the party. Their sources of inspiration were traditional anarchism of the attack on the state through the 'propaganda of the deed', the Guevarist strategy of the guerrilla fighter who leads the way for lesser spirits, the symbolic revolutionism of the student movement, the dramatic nihilism of the Situationist philosophy, and the creation of the new order in the libertarianism of the Alternative Society.

Their radicalism began in the student movement—Hilary Creek and Anna Mendelson were at Essex University, and James Greenfield and John Barker were together at Cambridge, and progressed to local libertarian activities. As their supporters stated they were all 'active in different sections of the movement—their involvement covers such things as diverse as Claimants' Unions, Women's Liberation, Gay Liberation, tenants and squatters' campaigns, radical student politics, experiments in communal living'.[41] They also joined in protests against the Conservatives' Industrial Relations Bill, and met those revolutionaries on the continent, including the terrorists of the First of May Group, who encouraged them to adopt the violent course of action that marked the climax to the libertarian left's attacks on the state, only to be broken by concerted police and legal action.

Their supporters have analysed the kinds of targets they chose and the reasons for the attacks. First were those connected with the industrial struggle—the Department of Employment and Productivity bombed in December 1970, and the home of its then Secretary of State, Robert Carr, the following month; second were the attacks on symbols of the 'repressive apparatus'—the home of Sir John Waldron, the Commissioner of the Metropolitan Police, the Police National Computer Centre at Tintagel House in London, and a Territorial Army Recruitment Centre in Holloway. Third was what the Angry Brigade's supporters called the

'yet less developed area of struggle concerning in the main the women's movement, that around the spectacle, the leisure merchants, the institutions that create and manipulate our desires. The bombing of the BBC van the night before the Miss World Contest and the night before the women's collective action against the contest. The bombing at Biba's, the high boutique which sells off the peg trends, images and roles to women and men'.[42]

As acts of revolutionary terrorism, their purpose was not necessarily to arouse the masses, or to provoke 'fascist' repression, or even to break the will and the nerve of government and people, for they were examples of armed propaganda, carried out as symbolic gestures. The bombings were the means of ensuring that the revolutionary message was heard by the general public.

The propaganda element was contained in the communiqués that were sent to the press after the explosions. The sixth of these nine bulletins summarised the Brigade's view of the need for revolutionary change and the form it must take:

'We have sat quietly and suffered the violence of the system for too long. We are being attacked daily. Violence does not only exist in the army, the police and the prisons. It exists in the shoddy alienating culture, pushed out by TV films and magazines, it exists in the ugly sterility of urban life.

'The question is not whether the revolution will be violent. . . No revolution was ever won without violence . . . organised violence must accompany every point of the struggle, until armed, the revolutionary working class overthrow the capitalist system.'[43]

This was not, however, the voice of an oppressed proletariat but that of educated members of the bourgeoisie, bored with the society for which they had been prepared and disillusioned with the achievements of their own student movement. Like the Baader-Meinhof Red Army Fraction in West Germany, and the Weathermen in the United States, the Angry Brigade resorted to the most extreme form of political action they could devise, to carry on in desperation a struggle that had failed or had been abandoned. Violence, as the antithesis of the 'shoddy and alienating culture' they so despised, had a cathartic value that offered through publicity and excitement an immediate sensationalised reward, and relieved their individual frustrations. The Angry Brigade as tacticians of revolutionary violence were not sophisticated urban guerrillas but were cast rather in the mould of the traditional anarchist bomber engaged in an isolated struggle against society. More significant was the social context of the Brigade, the framework of the alternative society that it used as the base from which to mount its attacks on the State.

The campaign conducted by the Angry Brigade coincided with, and was indeed a dramatisation of, a growing crisis in the libertarian movement. During the present decade it has become increasingly divided within itself, torn between pacifism and violence, between systematic national organisation and purely local activity, between industrial agitation and the *ad hoc* creation of alternative ways of life. The Angry Brigade represented just one of many permutations of these conflicting elements in the libertarian crisis.

Anarchists in Crisis (1971–75). As the wheels of fashion turned, the anarchist movement found itself within a very short space of time in a state of utter confusion. Many of the groups that had contributed so much to the heady days of 1968 and 1969 declined rapidly. The sales of *Freedom* slumped to 1,000 and in 1972 a £2,000 loss nearly forced its closure, although it has been able to remain in production as a fortnightly instead of a weekly newspaper. In 1971 Colin Ward relinquished the editorship of *Anarchy* and control of the magazine fell to a 'collective' in north London, who transformed it into a provocative underground journal, discussing drugs, sexual revolution and urban guerrilla warfare. Like many other anarchists (including Stuart Christie and the Black Cross) the new editors of *Anarchy* were highly critical of the pacifist tendencies of the editor of *Freedom*, Jack Robinson, and broke away from the parent newspaper. Its appearance became increasingly irregular and in 1973 it finally collapsed, only to be relaunched the following year by another 'collective' who have tried to create once again the seriousness that characterised the editorship of Colin Ward.

Perhaps the most spectacular decline of all was that of the Anarchist Federation of Britain. Even when its following was at its height there were rumblings of discontent: during 1969 differences arose between the London regional federation on one side and the federations in the North West and in Yorkshire on the other; the latter two groupings held a 'Northern Conference' to work out a common platform, but failed to agree on where they disagreed with London. The roots of the libertarian movement were altogether too diverse to be united in one national federation and as the student support fell away, and the movement's internal conflicts became sharper, the Federation withered. By 1971 it had lost 30 per cent of its membership and by 1973 had ceased to function at all. During that year attempts were made to form a new federation; 'Freedom', which had fallen out with the old organisation, called for a new co-ordinating body, and Nicolas Walter offered to convene one in London. Only in 1974 did any signs of renewed unity among anarchists show themselves with the appearance of *Wildcat*, a newspaper containing information drawn from all sections of the libertarian movement.

As a direct consequence of the failure of the AFB, a new national group appeared in 1971 called the Organisation of Revolutionary Anarchists (ORA). Inspired by a French group of the same name, the ORA included many of the groups of the former Yorkshire Anarchist Federation in the Universities of Hull, Leeds, York and Sheffield and soon acquired contacts in approximately twenty cities including London, Birmingham, Manchester, Lancaster, Nottingham, Leicester and Glasgow. Its monthly newspaper *Libertarian Struggle* has been produced by groups in rotation, although the Leeds and York groups provide the necessary administrative backing. The two people most directly concerned in the foundation of the ORA, who issued its first pamphlets in May 1971 and helped arrange its first conference in November 1971, were then York University students, Keith Edwards-Nathan and Ro Atkins. Edwards-Nathan was formerly active in Harlow Anarchist Group and in the AFB, and has since worked as an economist at the

Cuban Embassy. Ro Atkins has worked on the underground Christian newspaper *Catonville Roadrunner* and ran a Libertarian Women's network from a Walthamstow address which has been used by the local anarchist group and the Portuguese Organisation of Revolutionary Anarchists.

ORA saw its role as to counter the effects of individualism and the prejudice against organisation that existed in the AFB, and to develop a coherent theory and structure for what it described as its 'libertarian communism'. In 1974, however, divisions arose in the movement between those who believed anarchism was inherently incapable of providing an effective national organisation and those who wished to continue along the existing path. The former group, including Edwards-Nathan, turned to Trotskyism and the Organisation of Revolutionary Anarchists came to a virtual standstill. It was revived at the end of 1974 and redesignated the Anarchist Workers Association (AWA), with a formal structure and membership, to pursue five aims:

1. the 'preparation of the working class for their seizure of power'.
2. offering 'a lead within the working class movement by example and explanation'.
3. to 'develop and support working class organisations that are the forerunners of workers' councils and to develop them in revolutionary consciousness'.
4. to 'establish international links with libertarian revolutionary organisations and groups'.
5. to 'combat attitudes of sexism, racism and national chauvinism as attitudes that help maintain class society'.[44]

The AWA, like its predecessor the ORA, contains few workers and consists mainly of students engaged in the staple diet of contemporary libertarianism—activities among claimants, tenants and squatters.

At the same time as the Organisation of Revolutionary Anarchists appeared, another national group was founded, called the Anarchist-Syndicalist Alliance (ASA) campaigning on the general principles of industrial libertarianism. Its most active centre is in Lancashire where it is supported by many groups who previously identified with the North-West Area Federation of the AFB. Branches have also been formed in eight cities, supported by an industrial network covering contacts—but not necessarily groups—in another four centres for road transport, building workers, engineers, shipbuilding, social services, urban planning and education. The alliance, however, is minute—only twelve people attended an Industrial Conference in March 1973.[45] To improve its position it has discussed possibilities of joint activity with other syndicalist-oriented groups such as 'Solidarity', or the ORA.

The Anarchist Syndicalist Alliance's contact in Poole has also formed a South-West Regional Committee of the Syndicalist Workers' Federation which he is engaged in attempting to revive. A new version of *Direct Action* appeared in May 1974 and a national provisional secretary of the SWF was appointed. The 'Solidarity' groups have also made some further attempts to organise into one national body, and in 1973, after three conferences to tackle the issue, set up a national membership system but re-affirmed the cardinal principle of local autonomy.[46]

Despite the vigour exhibited by the syndicalist wing of libertarianism, the movement lacks appeal for industrial workers and offers little competition for the more highly disciplined Marxist groups. Indeed in 1974 *Freedom*, never popular with the collectivist wing, went so far as to say that 'anarchists are today the laughing stock of the authoritarian left, completely ignored by militant workers'.[47]

For those not engaged in industrial agitation, or in talking about it, the present decade has offered some new variation on the traditional libertarian themes of pacifism and anti-militarism. The Irish conflict has focused attention on the counter-revolutionary role of the army. In 1971 Keith Edwards-Nathan through the then Organisation of Revolutionary Anarchists attempted to organise a campaign to incite disaffection among British troops.[48] The idea was taken up two years later by the British Withdrawal from Northern Ireland Campaign (BWNIC), the libertarian counterpart to the Troops Out Movement.[49] Its prominent supporters included Nicolas Walter, Bernard Miles and other former Committee of 100 activists including Pat Arrowsmith, who was sentenced to eighteen months' imprisonment in 1974 for incitement to disaffection. Fourteen other members of BWNIC were also arrested in 1974 after leaflets entitled *Some Information for Discontented Soldiers* were found in their possession but were acquitted in the following year of charges under the 1934 Incitement to Disaffection Act.

BWNIC's efforts have been largely confined to distributing such leaflets at barracks and military displays, taking part in non-violent demonstrations and in enlisting support through organisations on the continent such as War Resisters' International and the International Fellowship of Reconciliation, a Christian organisation. It also assists soldiers who wish to desert from the British Army in seeking political asylum in Sweden, although no more than a handful have taken up the offer.

Nationally and internationally the very essence of the anarchist philosophy prevents its organisational development beyond a certain level. Structurally the movement is in a constant state of flux as groups rise to a natural peak and then collapse. The anarchists themselves are generally careless of the need to build their organisations, and there is much movement between groups and overlapping support—few have a formal system of paying members. Organisation is secondary to the need for activity on particular issues or in specialised areas. The success of anarchism depends on the social and political environment and its ability to identify and exploit those issues and areas where there are favourable general developments. While one part of the movement may be dormant or ineffective, the adaptability and breadth of anarchist interests may enable another section to flourish.

It is, ironically, because there are so many possible areas of activity today that anarchists are so divided about the direction of their movement. The collectivists and syndicalists are very active but appear to have made little impact nationally or in industry; the local activists of the Alternative Society convey a quite different picture, an appreciation of which is necessary for a full understanding of contemporary libertarianism.

3

THE ROAD TO HARMONY NATION

Since the middle of the 1960s, the rejection of the western way of life by an increasing number of young and mainly well-educated people has provided anarchism with a new and extensive forum for the application of its philosophy. The elements of this nascent revolutionary movement derive from disillusion in four main areas in western society: first, there is a rebellion against the economic factors of the competitiveness and inequality of capitalism, and against consumer materialism; secondly there is disenchantment with the institutions of government, the lack of democracy they permit, their increasing centralisation and ever expanding bureaucracies; thirdly there is a rejection of conventional social values and an uprooting of all established patterns of behaviour and relationships; and fourthly there is total rejection of western culture, embracing institutionalised religion, the style of urban life, and mass commercialism. This movement of rebellion expresses in many different ways and is in many respects a personal and reflective one, centring on the individual's own life style. A great deal of this is beyond the scope of this study, but what concerns us here is the extent to which the various experiments to find new values and ways of life, collectively called either the counter-culture or the Alternative Society, indicate the emergence of a post-Marxist revolutionary ethos, and the extent to which they contribute actively to direct radical challenges to the existing order.

In America, where the counter-culture is more highly developed than in Britain, numerous writers have detected just such a process and believe that it points the way to a post-industrial future.[50] And many have pointed out the favourability of these developments to anarchism: 'a new historical concept ... for anarchist principles ... new problems have arisen to which an ecological approach offers a more meaningful arena of discussion than the older syndicalist approach. Life itself compels the anarchist to concern himself increasingly with the quality of urban life'.[51] George Woodcock has argued that modern anarchists are indeed not so much concerned with apocalyptic revolution in the old manner, but take a broader, more pacific, view of social change and how a free society could be created out of experimental communes, free schools, workers' control, neighbourhood groups and ecology.[52] Anarchism and the Alternative Society do have much in common: neither offers a systematic ideology, both oppose authoritarianism of the left as well as of the right, they both emphasise the identity of the individual, and, consequently, stress the need for simplicity and smallness in social and political organisation, and both are at once experimental and Utopian.

The Alternative Society is only partly concerned, actively and consciously, with changing the rest of society, and many of its activities are apolitical and egocentric. Gradually, since the end of the 1960s, its outward looking activist wing has advanced to arrive at many of the same conclusions as anarchists. This has given rise to new forms of 'unconscious' anarchism, which indulge in the same kinds of activities as parts of the formal anarchist movement, but without the label; this convergence has created a blending of anarchism and the counter-culture so that in some situations neither party is distinguishable from the other, but has added to the existing stock of formal anarchist groups and activities. This process has been a mutual exchange of ideas, actions and personnel in which anarchism has politicised the counter-culture and the counter-culture has socialised anarchism.

The resultant movement for social and political change, an integral part of both anarchism and the Alternative Society, calls itself the libertarian left and consists of 'small groups based on friendship and political activities, and a rather larger collection of rarely active sympathisers who are drawn mainly from the ranks of middle class, i.e. student drop-outs'.[53] Libertarianism focuses its efforts on a wide range of mainly local issues—squatting, the underground press, communes, claimants, free schools, information and aid centres, sexual liberation and ecology—each of which it pursues in piecemeal fashion varying in emphasis from area to area and depending on the energies of the small groups of activists.

The breadth of libertarianism and its connections with anarchism are epitomised in the history of one militant, Bill Dwyer. A contributor to *Freedom* and reporter on the Irish situation at the end of the 1960s, this clerical civil servant is perhaps best known for the Windsor Free 'Pop' Festivals which he helped organise from 1972 to 1974, firstly with Paul Pawlowski, head of the 'Church of Aphrodite', and then with Sid Rawle, communitarian and one-time publisher of the *International Times*. The last of these occasions ended in scenes of fighting between adherents of the counter-culture and police, and led to an official enquiry. Dwyer, also a commune dweller, was subsequently sentenced for his part in the Festival, including inciting people to commit a public nuisance, using threatening behaviour, assault and criminal damage. He has also been active in the squatting movement with, among others, members of the then Organisation of Revolutionary Anarchists and the East London Squatters' Association. In 1972 Dwyer received a two-year suspended prison sentence for possessing 1,400 tablets of the drug LSD. Shortly before his trial he justified his position through the newspaper of the West London Chapter of the Yippie White Panther Party: 'I shall be fighting the case on a basis of a not guilty intent, that this is a matter of conscience in which I believe acid is a holy sacrament which greatly assists the individual in cleansing himself of selfishness and the various million inhibitions bestowed upon him by an authoritatian moralistic society'.[54]

The White Panther Party, modelled on the American Yippies (politically active hippies), were one of the more exotic local libertarian groups. They were engaged in a Free Food Distribution Project in the Portobello Road, have been involved in squatting and helped form a Street Theatre Guerrilla Group to perform spontaneous revolutionary playlets wherever they found an audience. Barely a city or urban community in Britain has been without this kind of group at some time since 1968, supporting existing local activities, creating its own propaganda enterprises and publishing a newspaper. Hundreds of ephemeral, informal and cheaply-printed publications have appeared with titles such as *Muther Grumble* in the North-East, and *Ned Gate* in west London. Among those more closely connected with formal anarchism have been *Speedfreak* and *Black Mass* (East London), *Grass Eye* (Manchester), *Alarm* (Swansea), *One and All* (Cornwall), *Black Pudding* and *Anarquista* (Yorkshire) with others circulating more widely for special interests, such as *Minus One* for individualists and *Glob*, a humorous magazine. They have each continued a style and tradition begun first on a national level by *IT*, *Oz*, *Ink*, *Fapto* and *Frendz*. Some continuing magazines still circulate nationally such as *Peace News*, which since its break with the Peace Pledge Union has become increasingly committed to non-violent libertarian revolution with distinct anarchist leanings, and *Catonville Roadrunner* which has combined Christian and anarchist philosophies.

Education is a topic in which libertarians have traditionally taken a close interest and one which has been very much alive in the last decade. Many alternatives to compulsory state education, examinations, streaming and selectivity have been discussed through groups such as the Libertarian Teachers' Association, formed in 1966, and the Movement for the Educative Society and the Abolition of Schooling, sponsored by *Anarchy* during its hippy phase in 1971. On a more serious level anarchists have discussed a range of possibilities including the experiences of A. S. Neill's Risinghill and Michael Duane, the London headmaster and supporter of children's rights, who has spoken at Anarchist meetings. The libertarian educationalists have, however, been divided between those who wish to work within the present system and those who wish to opt out—a division which has reduced the Libertarian Teachers' Association to ineffectiveness.

The supporters of Alternative Schooling have developed the concept of the Free School. One of the first experiments of this nature was the London Free School, modelled on the Free University of New York, which attracted fifty people to its opening in Notting Hill in 1967. Its purpose was not to serve merely as an educational agent but to provide the framework for solving the shortcomings of local authorities in meeting the needs of poor children of all ages. The following year an Anti-University was established in London, again following American examples and with a distinct anarchist basis. It was supported by a number of leading academics in psychology and the social sciences and ran courses for some 200 students on guerrilla warfare, workers' control, religion, Black Power, and art, among other subjects.[55] This was itself a short-lived experiment, but by the mid-1970s more than a dozen Free Schools, running on libertarian principles, existed throughout the country.

One of the central features of local libertarianism has been squatting. It has engaged the energies of anarchists, who regard it as a classic illustration of direct action and direct democracy, by-passing established channels, Trotskyists, Young Liberals, radicals in the field of 'community action', and the rootless hippy young. It is not, however, a coherent movement and has become increasingly divided between the reformists in what is now accepted by some London boroughs as legitimate squatting in aid of homeless families and the revolutionaries whose illegal squats have resulted in violent clashes with bailiffs and the police.

Anarchists have influenced both wings of the movement, which began in 1968 with the formation of the London Squatting Campaign. The inspiration for this came from Ron Bailey, who with Jim Radford, a close colleague in the Ilford Libertarian group, gathered together an assorted collection of radicals, including two other anarchists, three 'Solidarity' members and two Young Liberals, to launch the campaign in November 1968.[56] Its aims were to use direct action to secure the housing of homeless families and the rehousing of families in slum and hostels, but also to pursue the wider aims of conducting an all-out attack on local authorities and to radicalise existing movements in the housing field, such as tenants' associations and community project groups.

It was these broader political aspects which Bailey regarded as the main purpose of the Campaign and which he hoped would create a mass movement like that of 1946 when nearly 40,000 people were squatting in more than 1,000 disused military camps throughout the country. In the following year the London Squatters' Campaign mushroomed with a number of successful family squats, particularly in south-east London. In 1969 the Lewisham Family Squatters' Association, one of the LSC's offshoots emerged and gained the recognition and cooperation of Lewisham Council. As a result of this, Bailey became at the end of 1970 the first field officer of Shelter's Family Squatting Advisory Service. Squatting had become respectable, acknowledged as a short-term means of tackling the growing housing problem, but this new-found status also continued the division from the squatters' Movement.

The more militant wing came to the fore in 1969 during the occupation of 144 Piccadilly and other empty properties in central London by the hippy-based London Street Commune. Bailey dissociated himself from this group, but *Freedom* offered the Street Commune the refuge of its Whitechapel offices following the removal of the hippies from all other premises, and Jack Robinson criticised Bailey's approach to squatting as a 'reformist' not a revolutionary activity.

At the beginning of the 1970s militant political squatting faded, but with much property left empty by speculators at a time of growing shortages of housing, the anarchists, libertarians and some supporters of the International Marxist Group joined forces to form in 1973 an All-London Squatters' Group to develop illegal squats as a challenge to local authorities and to highlight the scandalous speculation in property. Since then squatting has spread quickly throughout London to become the means of survival for tens of thousands of people, families as well as the rootless young and encouraged by revolutionaries and liberal protest groups alike. Libertarian activists have played a prominent part in the explosion of squatting, although the leader of the All-London Squatters is Piers Corbyn, a member of the IMG, the only Marxist group to retain an interest in the activity since the International Socialists discarded it in 1968.

Like squatting, the commune movement has become an integral part of the new libertarianism. Some examples of specifically anarchist colonies and communes existed at the end of the last century,[57] but today's experiments range much more widely in their sources of inspiration, composition, structure and purpose. Andrew Rigby, who has made an extensive study of British communes, has noted six types: self-actualising communes where a contribution towards a new social order is made by providing the individual with an environment in which he can develop his potential; communes for the mutual support and brotherhood of their members; activist communes which are used as a base for political activity; practical communes formed for economic reasons; therapeutic communes for the social, spiritual care of the individuals in them, and religious communes held together by a shared faith.[58]

Rigby recognises also the anarchist influence and the revolutionary potential of the commune. Many of these types reject western social convention but could hardly be described as revolutionary, such as the Zen Buddhist or Sufi Muslim communes in Gloucestershire. Indeed some anarchists, Stuart Christie of the Black Cross and the 'Solidarity' groups for example, are contemptuous of quietist, mystical communes which they believe have little to do with revolutionary activity. Those that are consciously concerned with promoting change in the society around them may however be said to employ the classic principles of anarchist organisation—they are alternative structures containing the nucleus of a new order in the shell of the old and are a base for attacks on the present order. In his survey Rigby found not only anarchists and former anarchists in activist communes but International Socialists, members of the Student Christian Movement, Young Liberals, and former members of the CND, Committee of 100, Socialist Labour League and Socialist Party of Great Britain.

Many communes of all types are affiliated to the Commune Movement, which emerged in the middle of the 1960s.[59] Its secretary has been Nicholas Albery, who also ran the advice centre called BIT which has supported many kinds of alternative projects and which Rigby described as 'the linchpin of the London underground scene'.[60] Since 1974 BIT, with *Peace News* magazine, has supported CLAP, the Community Levy for Alternative Projects, a scheme to raise support for ventures that are too 'unusual, imaginative, alternative or revolutionary to get money from the regular sources'.[61] Projects as diverse as the Maoist-oriented Black Liberation Front, Dundee

Arts and Crafts Centre, Bill Dwyer's Windsor Free Festival and the Swananda Yoga Centre have appealed for money through CLAP.

The confusion of varied interests that make up the Alternative Society tend to come together through the columns of the underground press and in centres that offer information and advice. In Leeds, for example, 153 Woodhouse Lane has housed at one and the same time an information centre, a branch of Release, the drug advisory service, women's lib, gay lib and claimants' branches and the Leeds Anarchist Group. Occasionally a single organisation can attempt to forge a more coherent approach, such as that attempted by 'The Dwarfs', who existed from 1972 to 1973. They wished to create 'Harmony Nation', which they envisage as 'a loose federation of organic libertarian communities' practising a simple life style in small rural groups. The earth's natural resources would be left untouched—the only source of energy would be the power of water mills—and industrial production would be confined to basic manual crafts.[62] Towards these ends the Dwarfs supported various kinds of communal experiment, set up their own first commune, called 'Harmony Village', and ran vegetarian food shops.

Before they split up as a national group to concentrate on local concerns they tried to move towards co-ordinated political activity. In Plymouth, one of the forty or so cities and towns that acquired a Dwarf contact, the local group worked with anarchists and claimants to form a Housing Action Group in aid of squatters. Elsewhere the Dwarfs joined with anarchists and libertarians in community action, free schools and information services. In 1971 Dwarf groups blocked Oxford Street with bicycles, a publicity exercise organised by Vic Anderson, an Oxford graduate, a former member of 'Solidarity' and an editor of *Resurgence*, the magazine for non-violent ecological radicalism.

'Resurgence' is one of a number of groups and magazines which have been active in exploring the possibilities of peaceful revolution in a post-industrial society with the emphasis on ecology. Others include the former Peace Pledge Union magazine *Peace News*, the Non-Violent Action Groups, twenty of which have been formed since 1971 and the inspiration for which is a mixture of Quaker pacifism, community libertarianism, anarchism and ecology; *Undercurrents*, an alternative technology magazine; *Street Farmer*, which is concerned with the decentralisation of cities and industry, and *Commitment*, which took part in the blocking of Oxford Street with the Dwarfs and which ran an anti-census campaign in 1971. At the beginning of the 1970s some libertarians expected ecological radicalism to produce a great upsurge of activity. 'What next for the underground then?' asked *Resurgence*. Its answer was that:

'Ecology is an issue which can attract the militants who want to block roads and the quietists who want to grow food by hydroponics. Ecology has all the emotionalism and opportunity for moral indignation which Banning the Bomb, Vietnam and apartheid once provided foci for. But it also has the advantage of being nearer home, in the sense of involving people in a much more direct way, in housing and transport for example, which because of their immediacy are more likely to attract "ordinary" people and are also more open to effective direct action.'[63]

So far ecological revolutionism has failed to make this degree of impact and to some extent it has been defused by the much wider interest in recent years in the conservation of the earth's resources and pollution. This is a debate to which anarchism has a particular contribution to make for, as Woodcock has described, anarchists at the turn of the century—including Kropotkin—were very much concerned with the problems of industrial waste, centralisation and over-population that occupy today's radical ecologists.[64]

Although the British counter-culture appears engrossed in parochial activities it does not forget the fact that in the United States and in parts of western Europe its counterparts have reached a more highly developed state and some of its supporters also try to put into practice the principles of universal humanitarianism that underlie it. The International Fellowship of Reconciliation, for example, supported a number of prominent British churchmen, formed a European Workgroup for an Alternative Society to study ways of bringing about non-violent revolution and a democratic socialist alternative society. It has provided a 'retreat' in West Germany for revolutionaries, runs courses and a European School for Non-Violence, with supporters from six western European countries.[65]

The new libertarianism of the Alternative Society looks both backwards and forwards, back to a mystical pre-industrial golden age and forward to the prospect of rediscovering Utopia. Its search takes many strange paths, and translated into positive day-to-day activity it has become a nebulous patchwork of disjointed interests. The Alternative Society as a revolutionary movement represents the furthest point of the spectrum, beyond Marxism, beyond syndicalism, beyond even formal anarchism. Its concepts and styles do however correspond with those of the anarchist whose movement is increasingly torn between industrial syndicalist models of traumatic upheaval and post-industrial non-violent cultural revolution. In either aspect libertarianism reflects and depends upon those broader social tensions and discontents to which all revolutionaries must attach themselves if they are to succeed. Libertarianism provides a means to turn the sources of unrest towards creating an alternative system, and to channel them into active opposition to the present order, but as yet it is in its infancy.

IX

Conclusion

Many of the ideas and activities associated with the emergent revolutionary movement in modern Britain have been identified as the expression of a 'New Left'. The concept is however less than satisfactory when linked to a movement lacking both cohesion and originality. The humanist intellectuals and disillusioned Communists of the late 1950s stand uneasily alongside the Third World guerrillas and student rebels to whom the label was applied a decade later. The term 'New Left' serves as a flag of convenience to describe the otherwise indescribable; it denotes a transmutable portmanteau, capable of changing its size and shape to accommodate all who fulfil basic qualifications of internationalism, anti-Stalinism and anti-capitalism. But in this open-ended process the original 'New Left' has failed to translate its wide-ranging aspirations into effective, lasting organisations, or to formulate and communicate any coherent body of original thought.

Instead the characteristic forms of the so-called 'New Left' in Britain have owed less to the well-publicised writings of particular sociologists and propagandists than to a revival of some older and nearly forgotten 'Lefts', such as Anarchism and Trotskyism. They have been modified in various degrees in the course of their renaissance and mixed together to meet historical situations their long-dead originators could not have foreseen. If anything, the 'New Left' amounts to a reawakening in radicalism after a generation of relative conformity; its newness lies not in the substance of its ideas but in the context and the agencies through which its often confused theories have been applied. The movement for revolutionary social and political change, which the term describes, contains three principal traditions of socialism. Each reflects its own distinctive beliefs, sources of inspiration, range of temperaments and visions of Utopia, and each has its own answers to the many practical difficulties that confront those who choose to tread the road to revolution.

The first of these main groupings in the revolutionary movement acknowledges the importance of continuity in British history. It concedes that constitutional monarchy and parliamentary government are more deeply entrenched in that history than popular revolt and institutional upheaval, but claims for radicals, from the Civil War to the General Strike, a parallel tradition which has yet to fulfil its potential. Allowing for these two strands in British society, this school propounds a scheme of gradual revolution. Its theoretical foundation is a Marxist analysis of the class structure of present society and of the inevitable transition from capitalism to socialism, and its social and political roots are in the historical, constantly evolving organisations of the working class. There is no contradiction in this approach: revolution denotes the degree of the change in the sweeping away of established institutions of government and in the transformation of economic and social relationships, while gradualism indicates the style and pace of the change.

The Gradualists claim that socialism can be reached peacefully without either bloodshed or a conspiratorial, militaristic seizure of power. They deplore what they see as neo-Bolshevik sectarianism and dismiss as unrealistic the escapism of much of the Alternative Society. Direct action has its role, however, in the industrial power of the trade unions, which complements parliamentary representation. The Gradualist school encompasses the Labour Party revolutionaries, including those connected with the Institute for Workers' Control, the Voice of the Unions group, Militant, and the 'Left-Unity'-oriented Communist Party. The latter apart, the Gradualists rarely appeal directly to their prospective supporters outside the accepted context of the 'Labour movement', the Labour Party, the Trade Unions and the Co-operative Societies, or attempt to establish independent rival organisations.

Consequently, the Gradualists' particular ideas, in so far as they have been clearly formed, have been subordinated to the tactical interest of their retaining Labour Party membership, and their impact upon public opinion reduced. Their influence has however contributed to the rise of the left at all levels of the party, in the constituencies, in the Young Socialists, and on the parliamentary backbenches as well as among the activists in the trade unions. Those union leaders who believe in gradual revolution owe their positions and continued rank-and-file support less to any unequivocal exposition of ultimate purpose than to their capacity to exact from capitalism the fruits of its produce. It is sometimes difficult therefore to measure the precise degree of support Gradualist ideas enjoy within the Labour Movement, except that it is a minority viewpoint, which, with Communist 'left-unity' support and by dedication and skilful political manoeuvres, has been able to summon sufficient support in some critical situations to carry through its policies.

The revolutionary aims of Gradualists are stated obliquely, and their caution contrasts sharply with the second main grouping, which embodies the revolutionary spirit in its most uncompromising aspect. Like the Gradualists, this school is firmly wedded to a class analysis of society, and to an image of a chained, enslaved proletariat awaiting liberation from the crisis of capitalism. Its supporters, however, take a more apocalyptic view of the course of that crisis and how socialists should meet it. They foresee cataclysmic collapse and furious conflict in which the capitalists will be moved to defend their interests by all available means and will strike down all attempts by the working class to resist oppression and exploitation. Violence is the inevitable consequence of this clash of interests and socialists must be prepared, so the Apocalyptic revolutionaries argue, to defend themselves by force if they are to win. To meet this eventuality, workers and socialists must create new organisations outside existing unions and parties which have become irredeemably locked into the present system. These new bodies will be the armies of the revolution and the roots of the new order, geared to constant struggle, direct action and to eliminating all remnants of the *ancien régime*, as they proceed to establish a system of rule by workers' councils.

The scheme of revolution is represented by the Leninist-based groups, the Trotskyists, International Socialists, Maoists, together with some of the syndicalist-inclined anarchists. Their ideas—of a turbulent, traumatic upheaval in the manner of Russia in 1917—are those most generally associated with revolution, and since the end of the 1960s they have been the most dynamic and prolific element of the revolutionary left. The Apocalyptic school has captured the idealism, urgency and iconoclasm of students, youth, and members of some social groups with real or imagined discontents. But it has failed to attract large numbers of trade unionists, to whom their propaganda and agitation is primarily directed. Because the ambitions of the Apocalyptics are so great—to build entirely new parties, to win over the proletariat and carry through a classic revolution—their shortcomings overshadow the significance of the recent unprecedented growth.

Their weakness derives from their total immersion in the darker corners of European history and in the experiences of modern revolutions in far away places of which the majority know little. Their obsession with violence as an inevitable part of revolution is similarly alien to British tradition. Most of their actual violence has been limited to street demonstrations and in colleges and universities but there is the promise of a greater violence to come, and considerable ferocity in their propaganda, in furious diatribes against all those who do not share their particular point of view and in hysterical forecasts of the crisis and collapse to come. Compared with many other western countries, Italy, Portugal since 1974, France, West Germany, or the United States, the actual level of violence involving Apocalyptic revolutionaries has been relatively low, and most of them have rejected individual acts of terrorism as a serious instrument in the revolutionary struggle. The horrors and the counter-productiveness of terrorism in Northern Ireland has further convinced them of the errors of such a strategy.

During the same period as the emergence of the Apocalyptic stream as a tangible force, a third current has begun to develop. The Libertarian movement is concerned not with ideology, the State and power, but with the individual, his life-style and his relationships with others. It combines some of the essential principles of anarchism with the newer phenomena of the alternative society, community politics and activity among minorities. The goals of Libertarianism are a decentralised post-industrial society which presents a radical alternative both to western capitalism and Marxist-based socialism. Its Utopianism also expresses itself in a mystical attachment to a pre-industrial society, which produces a romantic vision of mankind as far removed from the everyday experiences of the majority as the Apocalyptic continental or Asian ideologies.

The activist aspect of Libertarianism, to work to change society from below, is the political face of a much wider cultural revolution which is also spiritual, introspective and contemplative. Among the broad range of activities and experiences that comprise the Libertarian movement those that are consciously revolutionary and the extent of their influence are difficult to determine. Libertarianism is a fragmented, amorphous concept whose organised expression is small-scale, piecemeal and irregular. Activism begins in the experiences of individuals, mainly the educated young whose experiments to discover new alternative ways of life to the family or the work ethic bring them into conflict with authority or established values. This develops into an awareness that the individual's aspirations cannot be isolated from the society around him and so that must also be changed.

As a source of a politically committed, alienated group, however, the counter-culture of the Alternative Society is less developed in Britain than, for example, in the United States, although it is a basic component of Libertarianism. There is also a discernible streak of pacifism and radical Christianity in Libertarianism but at the same time—as if to demonstrate the danger of generalisations—there is also an undercurrent of violence, of which the most best-known examples have been the Angry Brigade bombings and the incidents during the Windsor Pop Festival of 1974.

The Libertarian revolution is a long-term scheme of cultural and social adjustment, to which the abandonment of political institutions is regarded as the final crowning act. It is a situation which cannot be reached unless substantial numbers reject their present acquisitive way of life in favour of this more simple and less materialistic alternative. At present there are no indications that this will occur, although the sudden awareness that the earth's energy resources are finite has given a new impetus to some Libertarian ideas of energy and material conservation. Nor can the Libertarian goal be reached through conventional political methods, nor even through conventional, that is Marxian, notions of revolution: Libertarian activism is the politics of anti-politics.

In certain respects the three wings of the revolutionary movement, the Gradualist, the Apocalyptic and the Libertarian, overlap. The former two rely to a great extent on Marxism and the historic mission of the working class. In some instances, where circumstances have been unfavourable to the development of an independent revolutionary movement, Apocalyptics have attempted to conceal themselves in Gradualism. The Apocalyptic vision of the style of change is also found among some non-pacifist Libertarians, and the two have grown together with the youth 'counter-culture'. Some generalisations about them all are therefore permissible.

For all the groups and organisations which conceive their activities in terms of masses rather than individuals, the idea of revolution is deeply entwined with the myth of the 'working-class'. The prime object of their attention is a monolithic proletariat organised in trade unions, and the failure of Gradualists and Apocalyptics to communicate their ideas to a wider audience begins with this basic misconception. Trade unions do not possess identical interests and are not equally and continuously engaged in a life-or-death struggle with capitalism. Large unions and small, skilled workers and unskilled, highly paid or low-paid, public sector employees and private sector, old crafts and new techniques, all give rise to conflicting interests which cut across the revolutionaries' most strongly held beliefs.

From among the range of unions the prime targets are the key groups in public service industries, such as mining, electricity supply, railways and the docks, and those in the larger unions, such as the Amalgamated Union of Engineering Workers and the Transport and General Workers' Union, where influence could lead to power through block-voting at Labour Party conferences. Although the influence of Gradualists, and to a lesser extent Apocalyptics, is discernible at all

211

levels from branches to national committees, no individual union is dominated or controlled by one revolutionary body, although the combined efforts of Communists, Labour Marxists and uncommitted socialists have in some instances been able to combine to secure the passing of commonly acceptable policies.

Rank and file support for revolutionaries in trade unions is however scattered, regionally and industrially. The west of Scotland, Lancashire, and South Yorkshire are the areas, traditionally militant, where they have met with the most favourable responses. The revolutionaries have otherwise attracted pockets of sympathy from workers in troubled or declining industries with records of poor economic performance and disharmonious industrial relations; from among groups of workers guarding privileges or better pay against claims of lesser skilled men or from rivals or new industries; those in smaller unorganised, low-paid industries, neglected by their unions and engaged in protracted unofficial disputes—the Apocalyptics have devoted much effort here, partly to show how treacherous are the ruling union 'bureaucrats'; and among skilled and semi-professional groups who seek to imitate more militant manual workers and are concerned to preserve their status or to improve it.

Many of these interests do not represent forces for change and progress, but denote resistance to technological and economic advances which would lead to the replacement of men by machinery or computers, or would diminish the status gained by particular jobs since the end of the last century. Revolution for the working class does not therefore necessarily mean progress, but can equally be a regressive, defensive response to unacceptable challenges and circumstances. This is true of the Gradualists, who see themselves as the inheritors of a guild socialist tradition, and, with Apocalyptics, oppose the centralisation and internationalisation of capitalism into impersonal, unaccountable corporations.

The influence that revolutionaries do possess in industry derives firstly from their dedication. They pursue, fiercely and rigorously, the economic interests of a rank and file who are prepared to let them continue with the task, irrespective of their political beliefs, provided they are able to deliver the goods, in the form of higher pay settlements and greater job security. One of the more frequently repeated myths surrounding this crucial but cloudy area of revolutionary activity is the extent to which the left is able to exploit disputes. Revolutionaries can very rarely 'cause' strikes by leading workers to withdraw their labour by virtue of revolutionary leadership alone. They try to influence the course of events once there is the raw material for conflict, through propaganda, factory gate meetings, fund raising, bringing in outside support, helping organise strike committees or picketing, and generally attempting to raise the temperature of disputes, to prolong them and to 'generalise' them, so bringing home to the workers the fundamental political significance of the ostensibly economic issues, and to bring about an irreconcilable clash of interests. The revolutionaries rely also on the unconscious revolutionism of workers who embark on long, bitter disputes or who occupy factories or farm workers' co-operatives; there may have been no political motive attached to such actions, but the revolutionaries seize upon them as evidence of capitalism's crisis and of the way in which workers can themselves bring about socialism.

None of this has happened, however, on a massive scale, and as a result of this relative lack of success, and in response to other social developments, revolutionaries have looked to other groups and situations for support.

Enough has been said in this book and elsewhere of the most prominent group, the students. Their involvement in direct action protests about the Vietnam war or about the structure or conditions in their colleges was crucial in providing the small existing revolutionary groups with a tangible base of support. But by the time the revolutionaries began to organise nationally, when sufficient numbers of students had become committed to some notions of revolutionary purpose, no matter how vague, the mood and novelty on which the broader protest movement depended had evaporated. The Revolutionary Socialists Students' Federation existed therefore for two troubled years from 1968, the year when the concept of the students as a new vanguard of change reached its height, only to be seen as yet another myth of frustrated revolutionaries. The events in France in that year at first demonstrated the potential power of the student activists, but on reflection after their eventual defeat they confirmed the impossibility of student-led revolt. The revolutionaries, particularly the Apocalyptic and Libertarian schools, have continued to draw many of their members from students, mainly those with a middle-class background who have something against which to rebel, but the turnover in the student population destroys any continuity and relatively few appear to retain their revolutionary zeal beyond the campus environment, although they may remain to lesser or greater extent socialist in belief.

The headstrong idealism and internationalism of the late sixties has developed along two separate paths, a Communist-influenced movement focusing on domestic and economic issues which is strongly felt in the National Union of Students, and a merging of student radicalism with the youth movement in general towards Libertarian activism on alternative projects at local level.

Those who have continued their active commitment beyond college or university have contributed to the radicalising of some professions, in the emergence of left-opposition lobbies in their unions and professional associations, and in the development of a radical critique of existing methods and assumptions. The teaching profession has experienced this, together with social work, local government and universities and colleges, particularly in the social sciences and psychiatry. There is thus developing a stratum of alienated revolutionary intelligentsia, the emergence of which is a basic precondition for a revolutionary movement; but this cannot advance without mass discontent and the utter incompetence of the old order to solve its problems.

Other minorities to which the revolutionaries have devoted much attention offer a much less secure foundation for a future movement. Partly in imitation of American example and partly in response to their difficulties in this country, the immigrant community was in the second half of the 1960s seen as a potential detonator for revolution in Britain, but the Black Power movement that emerged in that period, so much of which was expressed through a Maoist 'Third Worldist' ideology, lost its momentum.

As the black contribution has diminished other minority movements have arisen, the most valuable of which has been women's 'liberation'. Its course since 1970 has been unpredictable and much divided in approach and purpose: many local women's lib groups concentrate on practical assistance for single women, women with emotional or economic problems, and mothers, while others concentrate, with little reward, on ideologically-based campaigns to identify women as a minority oppressed by capitalism and in solidarity with other groups similarly afflicted. As a revolutionary instrument women's lib, and gay liberation, are basically part of a critique of the family as a social institution, which, its opponents allege, divides sexes and age groups into stereotyped roles for the purpose of securing conformity within 'bourgeois' morality and society. The family and the educational system, in which revolutionaries see a parallel process of social brainwashing, are the two non-economic, non-governmental institutions which draw most attention. The revolutionaries consider they are critical areas of struggle in which their task of totally transforming the mentality of acquisitive capitalism must begin by breaking down existing patterns of behaviour.

Above all, the modern British revolutionary is an urban creature. The city provides many of the problems around which the movement has grown and is the setting for most of its activities. Concern for the environment and the quality of life, problems of overcrowding, poor accommodation and criminality are all prominent in revolutionary propaganda. In the decaying centres of cities which mushroomed in the industrial revolution, the conflict between authority and those who for one reason or another find themselves resisting the will of councils, landlords, or police forces, has sharpened. The latter in particular have become vilified as the 'pigs', the number one enemy of the non-conformist, whether he is taking drugs or demonstrating. The Libertarians in particular focus on such targets and consider the urban community as a realistic alternative to the work place as the principal arena for revolutionary struggle, where social ties are stronger and more easily defended.

British revolutionaries seem little inclined at the present time to engage seriously in that most characteristic form of modern city-based revolutionism, urban guerrilla warfare. There is much discussion of terrorism in other parts of the world, mainly to learn from its mistakes as a part of revolutionary strategy; there has also been a reaction against the horrific campaigns of terror carried out by Irish extremists, in contrast to which the isolated incidents of terrorism by domestic revolutionary groups have been on a relatively small scale. They have occurred when groups of activists have seen the movements around which they first came together disintegrate: this was the case with the Scots Against War incidents in the twilight of the Ban-the-Bomb campaign, and the post-student movement, the Angry Brigade. Individual revolutionaries in Britain do have their contacts among overseas terrorist groups, and London offers a uniquely free centre for international gatherings, but British activists have not so far been involved in any major acts of international terror.

The British movement is however fervently internationalist in outlook; indeed obsessively so, to balance its otherwise parochial domestic roots and the introspective intensity of so many of its members. There is however very little evidence to support any notion of a centralised conspiracy organised by foreign powers to control the activities of any British revolutionary groups, or that revolutionaries are responsive to such wishes. Internationalism proclaims the essential optimism of the revolutionary, that he will triumph universally against all odds, and is expressed through the total, universal ideology that binds Japanese Zengakuren to German anarchists and British Young Liberals to Palestinian guerrillas. To non-believers this unity is spurious, even meaningless, and denotes the banding together of small groups who have to look outside their own borders for material support and encouragement. Many international links are established through personal contacts, exchanges of propaganda and ideas, and remotely through imitation of each other's methods and activities. These internationalist aspects of the modern revolutionary movement have not yet however reached the peak of their potential, nor is the direction of their development clear. The history of groupings such as the Fourth International illustrates the problems that can face even the most internationally-minded revolutionary.

It is indeed the shortcomings of the revolutionary movement as a political force that are first apparent. Its lack of electoral appeal, its failure to build alternative parties and organisations taken seriously in the mainstream of political life, and its lack of achievement through pressure within the system or from without, means that no revolutionary grouping or movement offers a serious imminent threat to the existence of the present system of parliamentary democracy.

The growth of the revolutionaries does however present some pressing problems for democracy. In the trade unions and Labour Party the steady advance of militant socialism over the last ten years has shifted the Labour movement well to the left and opened up new opportunities for revolutionaries. The Labour Party has proved particularly vulnerable to attacks on a number of fronts: from the militant unions, the 'Left-Unity' strategy of the Communist Party, its own neo-Marxist wing, and the alternating campaigns of vilification and infiltration by mainly Trotskyist groups. Striking as these efforts do at the heart of the democratic system, they pose one of the potentially most serious difficulties for the upholders of the present order.

For all its clamour, onslaughts on the system from without, as preached by the independent Apocalyptics, have not attained the same degree of success. Their use of direct action techniques has, however, a disruptive value that could threaten a degree of violence alien to British political life. This has occurred already in street demonstrations, on industrial picket lines and in numerous displays of student hooliganism. The rising tide of political violence, alongside an increase in criminal and social violence, poses a tangible threat to the manner in which differences between groups are settled and in which decisions are reached, inimical to the cause of stable representative government.

These problems represent fundamental long-term challenges to society. The concept of democracy for which Gradualists and Apocalyptics stand is utterly opposed to the interests and traditions of liberal empiricism and scepticism that have prevailed in Britain since the 17th century. Its morality is selective and arbitrary: freedom of expression and existence is permitted only for those of approved views and causes, to the absolute exclusion of all others who oppose the march of socialism. It also denies to the present system the right to defend itself against disruption and physical assault, and justifies violence and the elimination of opposition in the name of democracy. Oppression in one part of the world is vigorously condemned as a crime against humanity, but when the oppressors are socialists and the oppressed opposed to socialism, similar outrages of torture, prison without trial or the use of military force are ignored. Little original thought comes from the pens of revolutionaries and their propaganda is so often a superficial substitute for argument and theoretical development while their much-vaunted 'humanitarianism' is rarely more than a cloak for self-justification. The spread of this kind of philosophical absolutism and moral intransigence bodes ill for an open and tolerant society.

In the mid-1970s, however, the number of people advancing revolutionary ideas, and the force and energy with which they assert themselves, is greater than at any time during this century. It is indeed indicative of the most fundamental divisions of purpose and philosophy that have existed in this country since the Civil War period of the mid-17th century. The Diggers, Levellers, Ranters and Fifth Monarchy Men all have their parallels in the present-day Apocalyptic and Libertarians, with their unshakeable visions of a future Utopian society, while established institutions and rulers are imprisoned by problems of economic mismanagement, rapid social change, and uncertainty of how they are to escape.

In such respects, the contemporary revolutionary movement is symptomatic of a disjointed and disoriented age. The decline in traditional patterns of authority and the resultant iconoclasm are expressed in their most extreme form in the desire for revolutionary change. Revolution carries society's obsession with novelty and change to its ultimate conclusion, while at the same time is a reaction against the nature of progress in a material or technological sense. All revolutions seek to turn an existing world on its head: the revolution that so many seek today turns its own identity upside down by demanding total change to stop change, the revolution to end revolutions, and it represents the spirit of the age in other ways—in its spiritual exhaustion and its negation of creativity.

The revolutionaries are, however, the products of changes intended to remove political extremes and discontents, and which are accepted as such by the majority, rather than of a society which has become suddenly more unjust or oppressive. The attachment of disaffected elements to the revolutionaries' cause denotes a rejection of what materially and morally the present order has to offer, but does not necessarily indicate support for the particular plans for the reconstruction of society that the revolutionaries propose.

The further advance of the revolutionaries depends less on their ideological puritanism or even their relevance to the present political system or their own efforts.

The demoralisation of the old order, that manifests itself in apathy, ignorance and the lack of will to resist, is a gift to their cause, and such conditions have helped particularly revolutionaries working through the present system. But those who adopt this approach cannot always expect to have an open road; and although they may be in a position to contribute to the creation of an egalitarian, socialist society, the result would be tempered by the many other forces for change that exist in a complex, pluralistic society, and could be far removed from the revolutionaries' own plans. Their ultimate hopes would only become possible if they benefited from a mass rejection of the established parties, and failure in the efficiency and fairness of present institutions. This would only occur in a cataclysmic crisis with which the existing system and rulers were unable to cope and which left the ruins of economic collapse and a political vacuum. Such events would be beyond the control of any single revolutionary group or the whole movement combined, and they would throw up many nationalistic, revivalist and even military alternatives that could crush the socialist revolutionaries.

At the other extreme society may change in such a way that such support as does exist for the revolutionaries may evaporate and the purpose they now serve is no longer appropriate. Such considerations are however reserved for the future. Other factors are clearer: so long as there are elements of tension in society and so long as men pursue Utopias, however illusory, the revolutionary urge will not be satiated. The history of the movement I have attempted to describe has not yet run its course.

APPENDICES

A Communist Party Membership

1920	4,000	1960	26,052
1926	10,730	1961	27,541
1930	2,555	1962	32,492
1935	7,700	1963	33,008
1939	17,756	1964	34,281
1942	56,000	1965	33,539
1945	43,435	1966	32,708
1950	38,853	1967	32,562
1954	33,963	1968	32,048
1955	32,681	1969	30,607
1956	33,095	1970	29,300
1957	26,742	1971	28,803
1958	24,900	1973	29,943
1959	25,313	1974	28,756

Young Communist League
since 1956

1956	2,600	1967	5,642
1958	1,387	1969	3,850
1960	1,734	1970	3,452
1961	2,702	1971	3,200
1962	4,019	1972	3,000
1963	3,989	1973	2,890
1965	4,276	1974	2,355

SOURCES
L. J. Macfarlane: *The British Communist Party*
H. Pelling: *The British Communist Party*
K. Newton: *The Sociology of British Communism*
Comment, *Morning Star* and *Challenge*

B The Evolution of British Trotskyism

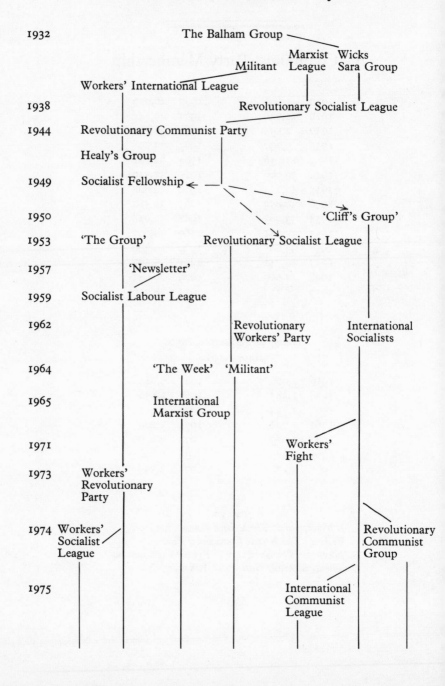

C   The Structure of the International Socialists

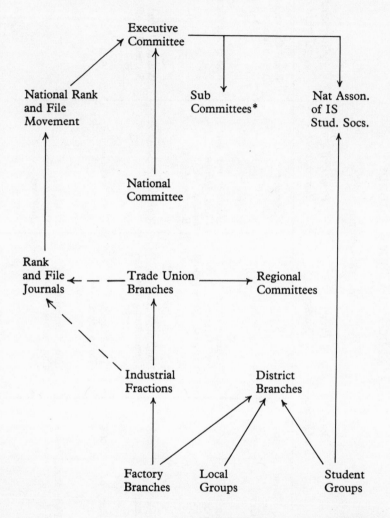

*Sub-committees include: Industry;
Students; Women; Black; Young Workers;
Education; International Ireland.

D The Pro-Chinese Groups

M-L = Marxist-Leninist

Title	Date Established	Previous Names	Principal Journals	Associated Groups
1 Committee to Defeat Revisionism for Communist Unity	1963		*Vanguard*	Local Communist Associations
2 Marxist-Leninist Organisation of Britain	1967	Action Centre for Marxist-Leninist Unity (1965)	*Hammer and Anvil; Class Against Class; Red Front.*	Red Front Movement
3 Working People's Party of England	1968	London Workers' Committee (1966)	*Workers' Broadsheet*	Workers' Party of Scotland (1966)
4 Communist Party of Britain (M-L)	1968	'The Marxist' Group (1966)	*The Worker*	
5 Communist Federation of Britain (M-L)	1969	Joint Committee of Communists (1966)	*Struggle; Marxist-Leninist Quarterly*	

6 Communist Party of England (M-L).	1972	Communist Federation of England (M-L) (1969); Internationalists (1967)	*Communist Daily England*	(i) Local Student Movements; (ii) Afro-Asian People's Solidarity Movement (iii) Black Workers Revolutionary Movement; (iv) Regional Study Groups
7 Communist Workers League of Britain (M-L)	1971	Irish National Liberation Solidarity Front; Irish Workers' Group	*Voice of the People*	
8 Association of Communist Workers'	1969			Revolutionary Women's Union
9 Communist Unity Association (M-L)	1973	Communist Unity Organisation (M-L); Marxist-Leninist Workers' Association		
10 London Alliance in Defence of Workers' Rights	1969			Schools Action Union; Progressive Student Movement.
11 Finsbury Communist Association	1965			
12 Black Unity and Freedom Party	1970		*Black Voice*	

E The Principal Anarchist and Syndicalist Groups

Title	Dates	Journals	Comments
1 Freedom Group	1886–	*Freedom*	Concerned only with production of the newspaper
2 Syndicalist Workers Federation	1946–	*Direct Action*	Its fortunes have fluctuated greatly and it has remained small.
3 Anarchist Federation of Britain	1964–1973		Grew to over 100 affiliated groups by 1969 but collapsed thereafter
4 Solidarity	1961–	*Solidarity*	Nationwide network of small, autonomous, but intensely active groups.
5 Anarchist Black Cross	1968–	*Black Flag*	Syndicalist-oriented but specialises in international work for anarchist prisoners.
6 Anarchist Syndicalist Alliance	1971–	*Red and Black Outlook*	Has tried to establish an Industrial Network
7 Anarchist Workers' Association	1971–	*Libertarian Struggle*	Known as the Organisation of Revolutionary Anarchists 1971–74

Notes

I

THE AWAKENING OF THE REVOLUTIONARIES

1. Sir Robert Mark, Commissioner of Police for the Metropolis, addressing students at the Police College, Bramshill (*The Times*, March 18, 1975).
2. John Berger: 'The Nature of Mass Demonstrations' in *New Society*, May 23, 1968.
3. Bernard Crick: Introduction to *Protest and Discontent* (edited by Bernard Crick and William A. Robson, Penguin Books 1970), p. xi.
4. Roger Rosewall: *The Struggle for Workers' Power* (International Socialist Pamphlet 1973).
5. General Election Manifesto of the International Marxist Group, February 1974.
6. Gay Liberation Front Manifesto (London 1971).
7. Quoted in David Childs: *Marx and the Marxists* (Benn 1973), pp. 301–2.
8. *New Left Review*, No. 1 January/February 1960.
9. *New Left Review*, No. 4 July/August 1960. Daly, who became an Independent Socialist member of Fife County Council in 1958, stood as an independent candidate in the general election of 1959 and was a founder member of the editorial board of the *New Left Review*.
10. Eric Heffer addressing a meeting of the Socialist Forum movement; quoted in *The Newsletter*, No. 12, July 27, 1957. The Socialist Forum was a Trotskyist-influenced body set up during 1957 for the purpose of 'discussing Marxist ideas'.
11. For the student movement in Britain see: R. Blackburn and A. Cockburn (eds): *Student Power* (Penguin 1968); C. Crouch: *The Student Revolt* (Bodley Head 1970); H. Kidd: *The Trouble at LSE* (Oxford University Press 1969); M. A. Rooke: *Anarchy and Apathy: Student Unrest 1968–70* (Hamish Hamilton 1971); T. Ali: *The Coming British Revolution* (Cape 1972); J. D. Halloran and Others: *Demonstrations and Communication* (Penguin 1970).

    For student revolt internationally: P. Buckman: *The Limits of Protest* (Gollancz 1970); B. Crick and W. A. Robson (eds), op. cit.; D. Cohn-Bendit: *Obsolete Communism: The Left-Wing Alternative* (Penguin 1969); I. Greig: *Today's Revolutionaries* (Foreign Affairs Publishing Company 1970); C. Posner (ed): *Reflections on the Revolution in France: 1968* (Penguin 1970); D. Childs: op. cit.; J. Gretton: *Students and Workers* (MacDonald 1969); G. Paloczi-Horvath: *Youth Up in Arms* (Weidenfeld 1971); P. Seale and M. McConville: *French Revolution 1968* (Penguin and Hamish Hamilton 1968); J.

Nagel (ed): *Student Power* (Merlin Press 1969); S. Spender: *The Year of the Young Rebels* (Weidenfeld 1969); G. Kennan: *Democracy and the Student Left* (Hutchinson 1968); G. F. McGuigan (ed): *Student Protest* (Methuen 1968).

12. The National Federation of Claimants' Unions was set up in April 1970, having grown from an original group founded by students at Birmingham University in 1968. Within two years there were approximately 100 branches throughout the country, many of which were closely allied to other local community action groups. Their aims are: the right to an adequate income without means test for all people; a free welfare state for all with services controlled by the people who use it; no secrets and the right to full information; no distinction between so-called deserving and undeserving cases; and their philosophy has been described as one of 'self-management' (Hilary Rose: 'Up Against the Welfare State' in *Socialist Register* (Merlin Press 1973, pp. 179–203)). CU's take a very strong line of resistance against authorities such as the Department of Health and Social Security: the slogan 'Play the SS Fruit Machine—if it doesn't pay, hit it hard' (*Claimants' Handbook for Strikers*) captures their attitude. The use of social security funds to help finance was particularly welcomed by revolutionaries of all sorts—Trotskyists, Maoists and Anarchists.

From the end of 1969 the women's lib movement began to take shape: *Shrew*, the magazine of the Women's 'Liberation Workshop' (an organisation of small autonomous groups closed to men) was followed by a conference at Ruskin College, Oxford, at the beginning of 1970 to launch the movement nationally, and by other journals such as *Socialist Women*, *Red Flag*, *Women's Voice*, in pursuit of the end of alleged economic and social exploitation, and free contraception and abortion.

The Gay Liberation Front was formed in 1970 and acquired 600 supporters in its first eight months existence, divided into a number of local workshops campaigning for 'gay' rights in industry, education and in the law, holding 'gay' dances, meetings and publishing a national newspaper *Come Together*.

II

A BRITISH ROAD TO SOCIALISM

1. Eric Heffer: 'Communists and the Labour Party', New Statesman, February 8, 1974.
2. *The Way Out* (Communist Party of Great Britain pamphlet, 1931).
3. L. J. Macfarlane: *The British Communist Party 1920–29* (Macgibbon and Kee 1966), p. 276.
4. *The British Road to Socialism* (Communist Party, October 1968, reprinted October 1972), p. 5.
5. ibid.
6. *The British Road to Socialism* (Communist Party, April 1952 edition).

7. ibid, (1972 edition) p. 19.
8. ibid, p. 21.
9. ibid, p. 29.
10. ibid, p. 49.
11. John Gollan: *The Case for Socialism in the Sixties* (November 1966), pp. 75–76.
12. Some Communists have always opposed this semantic dilution of the party's programme as indicative of the party's loss of revolutionary fervour. They would prefer to emphasise the factories and mass action as the predominant partners in the process with parliament taking second place. The Young Communists also, in their exuberance, are more inclined to urge the party to seize dying capitalism by the throat and not wait for the ideal situation to arise before going on to the offensive (see, for example, the editorial on 'Revolution' in *Challenge* the YCL journal of summer 1968, 2nd series No. 8, which speaks of smashing the system in action by the 'invincible' working class majority of the population).
13. Betty Matthews: *Changing Britain: the need for the Communist Party.*
14. *British Road to Socialism* (1972 edition), p. 51.
15. ibid, p. 54.
16. For detailed chart of membership figures see Appendix A.
17. A further 1350 who had been included in the previous year's total had not paid their fees (*Comment*, Vol. 12, No. 10, May 18, 1974). In the mid 1960s it had set itself a target of 50,000 members.
18. *The Role of the Communist Party* (1965) (Session IV of a syllabus for branch education classes).
19. Taken from: *Comment*, Vol. 5, No. 50, December 16, 1967; *Comment*, Vol. 7, No. 49, December 6, 1969; *Comment*, Vol. 9, No. 26, November 6, 1971; *Comment*, Vol. 11, Nos 24 and 25, December 1–15, 1973; *Comment*, Vol. 13, No. 26, December 27, 1975.
20. From a Resolution at the 33rd Party Congress: (*Comment*, Vol. 11, No. 24/25, December 1–15, 1973).
21. Henry Pelling: *The British Communist Party* (Black 1958).
22. K. Newton: *The Sociology of British Communism* (Allen Lane 1968), p. 23.
23. From a list in *The Role of the Communist Party;* a Party syllabus pamphlet (1965), p. 19.
24. See *The Role of Communist Party Branches* (1974).
25. *Handbook for Members of the Communist Party* (1962).
26. Gollan's speech was reprinted as a pamphlet, *Turn Left for Progress* (1965).
27. *Comment*, Vol. 4, No. 25, June 18, 1966.
28. *Report of the Committee on Party Organisation*, presented to the Executive Committee May 1965.
29. See Chapter VII.
30. *The Role of the Communist Party* (1965), p. 19.
31. ibid.

32. See the *Sunday Times*, March 10, 1974.
33. *Report of the Committee on Party Organisation* (1965).
34. *World Marxist Review*, Vol. 18, No. 2, February 1975.
35. For a critique of the 'New Left' from the Communist viewpoint see J. Woddis: *New Theories of Revolution* (Lawrence and Wishart 1972).
36. *The British Road to Socialism* (1968 edition), p. 24.
37. See Chapters VI and VIII for the consequénces of the rise and fall of CND for the revolutionary movement.
38. Its secretary, John Gabriel, writing in the *Morning Star*, March 21, 1974.
39. See *Comment*, Vol. 11, No. 4, February 24, 1973.
40. *Morning Star*, January 20, 1974.
41. Executive Committee Statement in *Comment*, Vol. 6, No. 36, September 7, 1968.
42. *Morning Star*, November 12, 1973.
43. Tariq Ali: *The Coming British Revolution* (Cape 1972), p. 84.
44. See Chapters IV, VI and VII respectively for the evolution of these rival concerns.
45. In *Solidarity*, Vol. 3, No. 11, 1964.
46. See Cmnd 3396, *Report of the Court of Inquiry into Trade Disputes at the Barbican and Horseferry Road Construction Sites in London* (1966).
47. *Morning Star*, December 18, 1973. The International Socialists also claimed credit for organising this operation (see Chapter VI).
48. *Comment*, Vol. 11, No. 24/25, December 1/15, 1973.
49. *Morning Star*, November 12, 1973.

III

THE PROPHECY UNFULFILLED

1. The standard work on Trotsky is Isaac Deutscher's three-volume biography: *The Prophet Armed*, *The Prophet Unarmed* and *The Prophet Outcast* (OUP, 1954, 1959 and 1963).
2. For the events of 1932 see Reg Groves's own account: *The Balham Group: How British Trotskyism Began* (Pluto Press 1974) and for subsequent years a brief account appears in G. Thayer: *The British Political Fringe* (Blond 1965).
3. I. Deutscher: *The Prophet Outcast* (OUP 1963), p. 58.
4. See *Documents of the Fourth International 1933–1940* (Pathfinder Press, New York 1973).
5. Deutscher, op. cit., p. 420.
6. *The Death Agony of Capitalism and the Tasks of the Fourth International* (in the 1972 Socialist Labour League pamphlet edition), p. 58.
7. ibid, p. 16.
8. T. Hayter: *Hayter of the Bourgeoisie* (Sidgwick and Jackson 1972), pp. 141–2.

9. *Death Agony of Capitalism*, pp. 27–8.
10. See Chapter IV for the foundation of the Revolutionary Communist Party.
11. Quoted in Ian H. Birchall: *Workers Against the Monolith* (Pluto Press 1974), p. 233.
12. Quoted in *Fourth International* No. 7, Autumn 1959, by M. Pablo.
13. From the minutes of its Foundation Congress, quoted in D. Hallas's Introduction to *The Origins of the International Socialists* (Pluto Press 1971), p. 3.
14. See Chapter VI for the International Socialist organisation.
15. In *Fourth International*, No. 1, Winter 1958.
16. ibid.
17. *Fourth International*, No. 12, Winter 1960–61.
18. See Chapter IV, part 2, for a discussion of the successor organisation to the R S L, the 'Militant' group.
19. *Fourth International*, No. 2, Spring 1958.
20. *Fourth International* (published by the International Committee), No. 2, Summer 1964.
21. The International Secretariat's commitment to colonial revolt was enhanced by the contribution of its general secretary, Michael Pablo. In 1960 he and a Dutch Trotskyist, Sal Santen, were gaoled in Holland for forging bank notes and documents for use by Algerian revolutionaries. On release the following year the Algerian leader, Muhammed Ben Bella, offered Pablo a ministerial post, which he accepted.
22. See A.J. Wilson, *Government and Society in Sri-Lanka 1947–73* (MacMillan 1974).
23. *The Newsletter*, No. 440, April 16, 1966.
24. P. Seale and M. McConville: *The French Revolution 1968* (Heinemann and Penguin 1968).
25. *Fourth International*, Vol. 7, No. 4, Summer 1972.
26. The S L L attacked the French for sabotaging the reconstruction of the International, disputing the validity of the Transitional Programme and querying the composition of the Committee itself. The S L L disapproved of the line of a Bolivian Workers' Revolutionary Party but conceded that the Bolivians, application for membership of the International had been received, for consideration at the next world congress. The O C I however claimed the Bolivians were plainly a Trotskyist party and their application had been immediately accepted. The S L L also claimed that the Greek section had remained on the Committee despite its division into two groups in 1966, while the French said the Greek section had been suspended pending the resolution of its differences when circumstances in Greece permitted.

Only four general congresses, constitutionally the highest authority of the International, had taken place in twenty years and the composition of the Committee over a period of six years was disputed. Even the smallest bodies had not been able to agree: the decisions of a

229

three-man committee set up to issue statements and to plan conferences were disputed by the French, who had one representative, against the British, who had two.

27. *Fourth International*, Vol. 7, No. 4, Summer 1972.
28. See Richard Gott: *Guerrilla Movements in Latin America* (Nelson 1970); Regis Debray: *Revolution in the Revolution* (Penguin 1968); Robert Moss: *Urban Guerrillas* (Temple Smith 1972).
29. For accounts of the revolt in France, see Seale and McConville, op. cit.; John Gretton: *Students and Workers* (MacDonald 1969); Charles Posner (ed): *Reflections on the Revolution in France: 1968* (Pelican 1970) and Daniel Cohn-Bendit: *Infantile Communism, the Left Wing Alternative* (Penguin 1969).
30. See Seale and McConville, op. cit.
31. See Chapter V for the origins and growth of the I M G.
32. *Fourth International*, Vol. 7, No. 4, Summer 1972.
33. *International*, Vol. 2, No. 1, Spring 1973, and for the subsequent quotations in this paragraph.
34. After the ban by the French government in June 1973 on the Ligue Communiste, the I M G petitioned for its lifting and acquired the signatures of Michael Foot, Eric Heffer, Frank Allaun, Ernie Roberts, John Gollan, Lord Gifford, Professors E. P. Thompson and Joan Robinson, Ken Coates, Kevin Halpin and Peter Doyle (Lab. Party Y S) among others.
35. *The Statutes of the Fourth International* (International Marxist Group 1972).
36. See Chapter VI, part two.
37. *Workers Fight and the Fourth International* (1973).
38. See Chapter IV, part two.
39. *The Fourth International and our attitude towards it* by Richard Stephenson (A Socialist Charter Publication) written in 1970 but not published until 1974.

IV

FACES OF TROTSKYISM

1. A 'Fusion Conference' held on March 11 and 12, 1944 was attended by 17 representatives of the Revolutionary Socialist League and 52 members of the Workers' International League. They formed the R C P with a total estimated membership of 335, of whom more than two-thirds had been in the W I L (see Jim Higgins's 'British Trotskyism 1938–48' in *International Socialism*, No. 13, Summer 1963).
2. *The Newsletter*, No. 92, March 7, 1959.
3. See G. Thayer: *The British Political Fringe* (Blond 1965), pp. 133–7.
4. *The Newsletter*, No. 376, January 2, 1965.
5. *The Newsletter*, No. 481, April 1, 1967.
6. *The Newsletter*, No. 437, March 26, 1966.
7. *The Newsletter*, No. 496, June 3, 1967.

8. Healy speaking at the 8th National Congress of the SLC. *The Newsletter*, No. 447, June 4, 1966.
9. *Workers' Press*, No. 297, November 9, 1970.
10. Report of the Central Committee of the SLL quoted in *The Newsletter*, No. 518, November 18, 1967.
11. *Workers' Press*, No. 1268, January 1, 1974.
12. E. H. Carr: *The Bolshevik Revolution*, Vol. 1 (Pelican 1966), p. 33.
13. *The Newsletter*, No. 138, February 13, 1960, reported the conclusions of an SLL National Committee meeting that 'new possibilities' had arisen in the youth field and in issue No. 157, June 25, 1960, announced the organisation's intention to become active in the Young Socialists. In 1965 the Labour Party National Executive Committee said in its annual report that the incursions had begun within a few weeks of the Young Socialists' foundation.
14. For a time Protz wrote for the *Militant* newspaper, and then moved on to the International Socialists for whom he edited *Socialist Worker* for a number of years until 1974 (see Chapter VI).
15. Figures are from the annual reports of the Labour Party National Executive Committee. Similarly those for NALSO, below.
16. Report of the National Executive Committee of the Labour Party 1964–65.
17. *Rebel*, No. 1, September 28, 1966.
18. See Chapter VI for the International Socialists.
19. *Militant*, No. 9, September 1965 and No. 29, September 1967.
20. *Militant*, No. 65, July 1970.
21. *Militant*, No. 170, August 31, 1973.
22. *Militant*, No. 99, April 7, 1972.
23. See George Thayer: *The British Political Fringe* (Blond 1965); Betty Reid: *Ultra Leftism in Britain* (Communist Party 1966); Ian Mitchell: *Introduction to the Left* (Solidarity Scotland No. 3); Anthony Sampson: *New Anatomy of Britain* (Hodder and Stoughton 1971); extracts from Reg Underhill's report appeared in *The Times*, December 12, 1975.
24. *Red Weekly*, No. 36, January 25, 1974.
25. See Ernie Roberts: *Workers' Control* (Allen and Unwin 1973), pp. 54–5.
26. *The Socialist Charter: A Programme for the Labour Party* (Chartist Publications 1973), p. 30.
27. ibid, p. 28.
28. See Chapter V, part three.
29. Report of the Labour Party NEC 1968–69: Report of the Committee of Enquiry into Party Organisation.
30. *Keep Left*, Vol. 15, No. 4, April 1966: National Secretary, Dave Ashby at its 6th Annual Conference.
31. *Keep Left*, Vol. 16, No. 11, November 1967.
32. *Workers' Press*, No. 678, February 7, 1972.

1. *The Week*, No. 1, January 1964.

2. See Thayer: *The British Political Fringe* (Blond 1965), p. 138, for the Trotskyist context.

3. *Voice of the Unions*, March 1965.

4. Tariq Ali: *The Coming British Revolution* (Cape 1972), p. 137.

5. Sponsors of the BRPF included the Duke of Bedford, Pablo Casals, President Ayub Khan, President Nkrumah, President Nyerere, Dr Max Born, Lord Boyd-Orr, Queen Elizabeth of the Belgians, Emperor Haile Selassie, Kenneth Kaunda, Vanessa Redgrave and Dr Albert Schweitzer (see *The Autobiography of Bertrand Russell*, Vol. 3 (Allen and Unwin 1969), p. 179.

6. John Saville in *The Week*, Vol. 5, No. 1, January 6, 1966.

7. *The Humberside Voice*, edited by Tony Topham, also published leaflets signed by the Strike Committee of the Hull Branch of the NUS (see *The Week*, Vol. 5, No. 20, May 19, 1966).

8. *The Week*, Vol. 5, No. 1, January 6, 1966.

9. *The Week*, Vol. 2, No. 16, November 5, 1964.

10. *Voice of the Unions*, November 1964.

11. See the story of this and a selection of Coates's writings in the period 1964–70: See Ken Coates: *The Crisis of British Socialism* (Spokesman Books 1971).

12. The full list of organisations sending delegates was: Arab Revolution; ASSET (London District Council); Bertrand Russell Peace Foundation; Bristol Sponsors for Peace in Vietnam; Cambridge Ad Hoc VSC: Committee for the Rights of Oman; Croydon South Young Socialists; Brighton YCND; Ealing No. 2 NUR Branch; East Walthamstow Young Socialists; Edinburgh Ad Hoc VSC; Edinburgh ASLEF No. 1 Branch; Exeter University Socialist Society; Ex-Servicemen's Movement for Peace; Haringey Committee for Peace in Vietnam; Hammersmith North CLP; Hampstead Young Socialists; Hackney Young Socialists; Hackney Central CLP; Hornchurch CLP; Horley Council for Peace in Vietnam; *Humberside Voice*; Hull Vietnam Solidarity Committee; International Socialism; Iraqui Students' Society; Lancaster University Socialist Union; Lewisham Trades Council; London Workers Committee; LSE Socialist Society; Merton BCPF; Mid-Beds CLP; National Awami Party (UK); NALSO; *New Left Review*; Nottingham VSC; *Nottingham Voice*; Oxford Vietnam Peace Movement; Putney CLP; St Mary's (Twickenham) College Socialist Society; St Pancras North Young Socialists; Southall Indian Workers' Association; Socialist Action (Bromley); Sussex University Vietnam Committee; *The Week*; Willesden Clerical and Administrative Workers' Union; Willesden East CLP.

The council comprised:

President: Bertrand Russell

Chairman: Ralph Schoenman

Ken Coates (Notts VSC)
Quintin Hoare (*New Left Review*)
Pat Jordan (*The Week*)
John La Rose
John Palmer (International Socialism)
Jim Scott (Young Socialists)
Tony Topham (*Humberside Voice,* Hull VSC)
Chris Farley (BRPF)

Dave Horowitz (*New Left Review*)
Ted Knight (Lewisham Trades Council)
Ian Millar (Edinburgh VSC)
Ralph Rosenbaum
Ernie Tate
Barbara Wilson

(*The Week*, Vol. 5, No. 23, June 9, 1966).

13. James D. Halloran, Philip Elliott and Graham Murdoch: *Demonstrations and Communication: A Case Study* (Penguin 1970), p. 71.

14. *The Week*, Vol. 9, No. 12, March 20, 1968.

15. *The Week*, Vol. 9, No. 9, February 28, 1968.

16 Tariq Ali: op. cit.; ibid.

17. *Red Mole*, No. 39, March 30, 1972.

18. *International*, Vol. 1, No. 2, June 1968.

19. *International*, Vol. 1, No. 8, December 1968.

20. *International*, Vol. 1, No. 3, July 1968.

21. *International*, Vol. 2, No. 1, January 1969.

22. Groups supporting the Palestine Solidarity Campaign were: the International Socialists, RSSF, *Black Dwarf*, *New Left Review*, Britain Vietnam Solidarity Front, General Union of Arab Students, General Union of Palestine Students, Arab Revolution, Free Palestine, and the Friends of Palestine (*Black Dwarf*, No. 16, May 2, 1969).

23. *Black Dwarf*, Vol. 13, No. 1, June 1968. The magazine's title and volume number continued those of an early 19th century radical journal.

24. See Ian Greig: *Today's Revolutionaries* (Foreign Affairs Publishing Company 1970), p. 80.

25. ibid, pp. 81–82; also *International*, Vol. 1, No. 8, December 1968, *New Left Review*, No. 53, January–February 1969.

26. *International*, Vol. 1, No. 8, December 1968.

27. See Chapter VII.

28. *Red Mole*, No. 39, March 30, 1972.

29. Between 1968 and 1973 Agit Prop produced a wide range of literature and information for use by revolutionaries, including a bulletin, the *Agit Prop Red Notes*. At the beginning of 1973 it closed down after one of the members of the Agit Prop collective was arrested on a charge concerning illegal possession of arms, and because the collective could no longer afford the £43 per week rent it was paying for its premises in Bethnal Green, which it handed over to a 'Gay' Commune and Bookshop called Bethnal Rouge.

30. *Red Mole*, No. 39, March 30, 1972.

31. See Chapter VI for the AIL. Saor Eire had broken away from the

Irish Workers' Group, one of whose members, Gerry Lawless, a republican of twenty years standing, is an active IMG member and has spoken on the continent on Fourth International platforms.

32. *Red Mole*, No. 51, December 11, 1972. The IMG's appeal for £10,000 to launch the weekly paper was supported by 19 trade unionists and Trotskyists in Europe.

33. *Red Weekly*, No. 35, January 18, 1974.

34. ibid.

35. Tariq Ali secured 424 votes in Sheffield Attercliffe, John Ross of the IMG National Committee 202 votes in Newham North East against Reg Prentice, and Bob Purdie gained only 90 votes in Queen's Park, Glasgow.

36. Caren Meyer in the *London Evening News*, July 18, 1974.

37. *Capitalist Crisis and the Struggle for Workers Power* (General Election Manifesto of the IMG, February 1974).

38. Lord Justice Scarman: *The Red Lion Square Disorder of June 15, 1974*. Comd. 5919 (HMSO 1975).

39. *Red Weekly*, No. 91, March 6, 1975.

40. *Capitalist Crisis and the Struggle for Workers Power* (General Election Manifesto of the IMG, February 1974).

41. *Red Weekly*, No. 52, May 16, 1974.

42. *Red Weekly*, No. 15, August 24, 1973.

43. *Red Weekly*, No. 85, January 25, 1975.

44. *Red Weekly*, No. 91, March 6, 1975.

45. *Red Weekly*, No. 105, June 12, 1975.

46. *Red Weekly*, No. 93, March 20, 1975.

47. *Red Weekly*, No. 106, June 19, 1975.

48. K. Coates: *What is the IWC?* (IWC Pamphlet No. 14).

49. Michael Barratt Brown in *New Society*, April 11, 1968.

50. *Workers' Control Bulletin*, No. 14, March 23, 1974.

51. See S. Holland: *The Socialist Challenge* (Quartet Books 1975). Holland has served on various committees of the Labour Party National Executive.

52. K. Coates: *Can we Kill that Bill?* (Spokesman Pamphlet No. 16, January 1971).

53. Pat Jordan: *The Fight for Control: Militants in the Trade Unions* (IMG publication 1971).

54. See K. Coates and A. Topham: *The New Unionism: the Case for Workers' Control* (Penguin 1974).

55. From offices in Bertrand Russell House, Gamble Street, Nottingham, the Institute for Workers' Control, Bertrand Russell Peace Foundation, Spokesman Books, and the Russell Press Ltd (formerly the Partisan Press) all operate. Writers such as Coates, Topham, Barratt-Brown and Ernie Roberts, have contributed to IWC and Russell Press publications, mainly on aspects of workers' control and socialist theory. Their work and the official positions held by leading activists within the organisations located at Bertrand Russell House overlap

234

to such an extent that for all practical purposes the divisions between the different sections have ceased to exist.

56. E. Roberts, *Workers' Control* (Allen and Unwin 1973), p. 225.
57. Walter Kendall, *Voice of the Unions*, November 1974. See also Kendall in *Tribune*, April 25, 1975.
58. Walter Kendall, *Voice of the Unions*, April 1974.
59. *Voice of the Unions*, November 1967.
60. *Voice of the Unions*, July/August 1970.
61. Roberts, op. cit., p. 223.
62. ibid, p. 263.

VI

'NEITHER WASHINGTON NOR MOSCOW...'

1. The *Daily Telegraph*, March 10, 1975.
2. See Ian H. Birchall: 'History of the International Socialists. Part I: from theory into practice' in *International Socialism*, No. 76, March 1975.
3. *International Socialism*, No. 4, Spring 1961.
4. *International Socialism*, No. 1, Spring 1960. It hoped that 'the initial untutored moral protest which brings new people on to the road will be used consciously to fire a political understanding and activity which might change the character of our labour movement if nothing else'.
5. *International Socialism*, No. 2, Autumn 1960.
6. See Chapter IV, part two, for the International Socialist contribution to the Labour Party Young Socialists.
7. *International Socialism*, No. 13, Summer 1963.
8. *International Socialism*, No. 16, Spring 1964.
9. See Chapter V, part one.
10. *International Socialism*, No. 24, Spring 1966. Yet only a few months earlier the IS had reiterated its adherence to Labour Party membership: 'to desert the party, to choose to contract out of the most significant arena for political struggle . . . is suicide for serious socialists'. *International Socialism*, No. 22, Autumn 1965.
11. *International Socialism*, No. 13, Summer 1963.
12. *International Socialism*, No. 27, Winter 1966–67.
13. See Chapter VIII, part three.
14. See Colin Crouch: *The Student Revolt* (Bodley Head 1970), p. 109, footnote.
15. Peter Sedgwick, of the International Socialists, wrote in *Black Dwarf* (No. 6, October 15, 1968) of Herbert Marcuse, supposedly one of the 'New Left's' most influential writers, that: 'Having read Marcuse's work attentively over a number of years, I find it hard to trace any very precise connections between his most characteristic ideas and anything that is being written, said or done on the international left nowadays'.
16. As early as 1966, John Palmer of the International Socialist Executive

Committee addressed Young Socialists in Belfast. (See Paul Arthur's *The People's Democracy 1968–73* (Blackstaff Press, Belfast 1974)).

17. Ginny West in *Socialist Worker*, No. 206, February 7, 1971.
18. *Socialist Worker*, No. 254, January 16, 1972.
19. *Socialist Worker*, No. 256, January 29, 1972.
20. *Socialist Worker*, No. 266, April 8, 1972.
21. *Socialist Worker*, No. 360, February 9, 1974.
22. *Times Educational Supplement*, March 10, 1973. See also John Izbicki in the *Daily Telegraph*, March 31, 1975, who reported that the International Socialists by that date had 230 members in the NUT, 100 other teachers and 150 lecturers in colleges of further education and polytechnics.
23. *Freedom*, Vol. 35, No. 41, October 12, 1974.
24. *Case-Con*, No. 9, October 1972.
25. See Steve Jeffreys: 'The Challenge of the Rank and File' in *International Socialism*, No. 76, March 1975.
26. Tony Cliff: *Factory Branches* (IS Pamphlet, undated).
27. ibid.
28. *Socialist Worker*, No. 360, February 9, 1974.
29. *Socialist Worker*, No. 315, March 24, 1973.
30. See Gerard Kemp: 'Left Wing Extremists Plot Take-Over of Industry' in the *Daily Telegraph*, March 7, 1975. This also gave a list of all the IS-supported Rank and File newspapers.
31. The largest were in the National Union of Teachers; National Association of Local Government Officers; National Union of Journalists; Association of Teachers in Technical Institutions; Amalgamated Union of Engineering Workers; Transport and General Workers' Union; National Union of Public Employees; Civil and Public Services Association; Association of Scientific Technical and Managerial Staffs.
32. Tony Cliff: op. cit.
33. Roger Rosewall: *The Struggle for Workers' Power* (IS Pamphlet 1973).
34. *International Socialism*, No. 72, October 1974.
35. The four members were John Palmer, who had been active in the Anti-Interment League; Frank Campbell, a building worker on the IS National Committee; Ben Galvin, a clothing worker, and Rachel Carroll of NALGO (see *Socialist Worker*, No. 264, March 25, 1972).
36. See Appendix C, 'The Structure of the International Socialists'.
37. *Socialist Worker*, No. 417, March 22, 1975. The Committee also decided to tighten up security following revelations in the *Daily Telegraph* about the organisation's activities.
38. In mid-June 1973, Tony Cliff reported that in the first eight weeks since the IS annual conference in the middle of March 211 people had joined with a further 281 in the following four weeks. Of these 56 had been TGWU members, 51 were in the AUEW and 29 in the NUT. (*Socialist Worker*, No. 328, June 23, 1973). In the middle of July he told the National Committee that a total of 950 members had

joined since the conference, 112 in the TGWU and 115 in the AUEW, and membership in Yorkshire had doubled (*Socialist Worker*, No. 332, July 21, 1973). In one week at the end of the month a further 113 people were reported to have joined (*Socialist Worker*, No. 334, August 4, 1973), and by the middle of August 1973, the total number of people who had supposedly joined the IS since mid-March of that year was 1,260, of whom 315 joined in July (*Socialist Worker*, No. 336, August 18, 1973).

39. See Andrew Rigby: *Communes in Britain* (Routledge 1974) for a description of an IS activist commune.
40. *Socialist Worker*, No. 409, January 25, 1975.
41. *Socialist Worker*, No. 423, May 3, 1975.
42. Roger Rosewall: op. cit.
43. ibid.

VII
THE EIGHT PARTIES OF ANTI-REVISIONISM

1. The pro-Chinese 'anti-revisionists' were defeated by 436 votes to 4 at the 28th Party Congress in 1963.
2. For the origins and early history of the CDRCU see G. Thayer: *The British Political Fringe* (Blond, 1965), pp. 119–26, and K. Newton: *The Sociology of British Communism* (Allen Lane 1969), pp. 19–20.
3. M. McCreery: *Destroy the Old to Build the New* (1964).
4. *Red Front*, Vol. 1, No. 1, October 1967.
5. *Red Front*, July/August 1971.
6. *Workers' Broadsheet*, Vol. 6, No. 1, January 1971. The five points were: working people's power; revolution; self-defence; liberation (National and sexual) and a Workers' National Plan to run the economy free of American capitalist domination.
7. *Workers' Broadsheet*, Vol. 1, No. 8, March 1967.
8. *The Times*, January 14, 1971.
9. See Hardial Bain's article 'Necessity for Change', reprinted in G.F. McGuigan (ed): *Student Protest* (Methuen 1968), pp. 133–60.
10. Joint Committee of Communists on 'The Question of Party Building' in *Documents of the CFB(M-L)* (June 1972).
11. Reg Birch: *Guerrilla Struggle and the Working Class* (1973).
12. Reg Birch in the preface to *The Working Class and its Party*. The programme of the Communist Party of Britain (Marxist-Leninist) adopted at its Second Congress, April 9–12, 1971.
13. The Programme of the Communist Workers' League of Britain (Marxist-Leninist) in its journal *Voice of the People*, Vol. 2, No. 2, March/April 1972.
14. *The Worker*—Newspaper of the Communist Party of Britain (Marxist-Leninist), May 1970.
15. *Students and the Class War* (CPB, 1973), p. 13.
16. *Workers' Broadsheet*, Vol. 4, No. 2, July 1968.

17. *The Worker*, December 15, 1972.
18. Mathew Lygate, the chairman, editor of the party newspaper and one-time parliamentary candidate, received a sentence of 24 years' imprisonment; William McPherson was sentenced to 26 years, Ian Doran to 25 years and Colin Lawson, the treasurer, to six years.
19. John Heather, Charles Holland and Anthony Osborne received 12 month sentences suspended for two years for possessing petrol bombs, and John Clarke received a six-month suspended sentence. They were each also fined for assaulting police.
20. *Communist England and Red Patriot*, January 30, 1973.
21. *Workers' Broadsheet*, Vol. 6, No. 7, May 1972.
22. Birch: *Guerrilla Struggle and the Working Class*.
23. ibid. For 'mass line' we may use one of Mao's own definitions in *Quotations from Chairman Mao Tse-tung* (Foreign Language Press, Peking 1972), p. 128. 'In all the practical work of our Party all correct leadership is necessarily "from the masses, to the masses". This means: take the ideas of the masses (scattered and unsystematic ideas) and concentrate them (through study turn them into concentrated and systematic ideas) then go to the masses and propagate and explain these ideas until the masses embrace them as their own . . .'
24. *Communist England and Red Patriot*, January 30, 1973.
25. From the address to the opening conference of the Marxist-Leninist Organisation of Britain by Maureen Scott. *Red Front*, Vol. 1, No. 1, October 1967.
26. Peter Sedgwick: 'Varieties of Socialist Thought' in *Protest and Discontent* (ed. by W. B. Crick and W. A. Robson) (Penguin 1970), pp. 63–64.
27. *The Worker*, October 1, 1972.
28. *London Student*, No. 1, May 1973.
29. *London Student*, No. 5, June 1973.
30. Benjamin W. Heineman Jr: *The Politics of the Powerless* (OUP 1972), p. 161.
31. ibid, p. 193.
32. *Workers' Broadsheet*, Vol. 5, No. 3, November 1969. The article suggested that the Royal Ulster Constabulary had been reformed for permitting similar attacks to take place on Catholics. No reform of the police in London had taken place because the people had not yet revolted. It appealed for support from Irishmen in London 'to fight our common enemy'.
33. *The Worker*, November 1971.
34. For an account of the BUFP see Alexander Kirby 'Black Consciousness' in *Direct Action and Democratic Politics* (ed. R. Benewick and T. Smith) (Allen and Unwin 1972), pp. 154–8.
35. *Liberation Struggle*, April 1972.
36. *Workers' Broadsheet*, Vol. 4, No. 1, June 1968. See Robert Moss: *Urban Guerrilla* (Temple Smith 1972), pp. 112–29, for an account of the FLQ.

37. For a detailed account of the European movement, see F.W. Schlomann and P. Friedlingstein: *Die Maoisten: Pekings Filialen in Westeuropa* (Stuttgart 1971).
38. Regis Debray: *Revolution in the Revolution* (Pelican 1968), pp. 122–3.
39. ibid, p. 124.
40. The Times News Team: *The Black Man in Search of Power* (Nelson 1968), p. 151.

VIII

THE LIBERTARIAN ALTERNATIVE

1. Bakunin to the editorial board of the newspaper *La Liberté* on October 5, 1872, contained in *Michael Bakunin: Selected Writings*, edited by Arthur Lehning (Cape 1973), pp. 235–63. The letter was never delivered.
2. G. Woodcock: *Anarchism* (Pelican 1963), p. 15.
3. ibid, p. 414.
4. Stuart Christie and Albert Meltzer: *The Floodgates of Anarchy* (Sphere Books 1972), p. 11.
5. N. Walter: *About Anarchism* (Freedom Press 1969).
6. *Anarchy*, No. 2, April 1961.
7. Christie and Meltzer, op. cit., p. 52.
8. See Woodcock, op. cit., and L.K. Krimermann and L. Perry (eds), *Patterns of Anarchy* (Anchor Press 1966), for description and discussion of many anarchist ideas both historical and modern.
9. Quoted in *Anarchy*, No. 11, February 1962. The survey also illustrated the point that anarchism is the last refuge of the politically restless for it located 34 former Communist Party members, 67 ex-Labour Party members, 19 formerly in the Independent Labour Party, 10 who were in the Socialist Party of Great Britain and former Trotskyists.
10. Peter Newell in *Freedom*, Vol. 29, No. 3, January 27, 1968.
11. Christie and Meltzer, op. cit., pp. 120–1.
12. *Black Flag* (Journal of the Anarchist Black Cross, edited by Stuart Christie), Vol. 2, No. 6, May 1971.
13. 'As We Don't See It' (*Solidarity* 1971).
14. *Freedom*, Vol. 32, No. 3, January 23, 1971.
15. See C. Driver: *The Disarmers* (Hodder and Stoughton 1964); F. Parkin: *Middle Class Radicalism* (Manchester University Press 1968); G. Thayer: *The British Political Fringe* (Blond 1966), and *The Autobiography of Bertrand Russell*, Vol. 3 (Allen and Unwin 1969).
16. Alan Lovell in *New Left Review*, No. 8, March/April 1961: see also Nicolas and Ruth Walter: 'The Committee of 100 and Anarchism', in *Anarchy*, No. 52, June 1965.
17. Quoted in *Anarchy*, No. 10, December 1961.
18. It changed the title of its magazine from *Agitator for Workers' Power* to *Solidarity for Workers' Power* in January 1962 and subsequently adopted 'Solidarity' as the name of its organisation.

19. *Solidarity*, Vol. 1, No. 9, June 1962.
20. See *The Way Ahead for a New Peace Movement* (Solidarity Scotland Pamphlet No. 1, June 1966).
21. See *Anarchy 85*, Vol. 8, No. 3, March 1968, which is a transcript of a BBC Third Programme radio broadcast of January 1968.
22. The pamphlet was reprinted as *Anarchy*, No. 29, July 1963.
23. 'The Spies who stayed out in the cold.' *Inside Story*, Nos. 8 and 9, March/April 1973, and May/June 1973.
24. See *Freedom*, Vol. 27, No. 37, November 26, 1966.
25. *Freedom*, Vol. 25, No. 14, May 9, 1964.
26. In 1968 Lawrence formed a short lived Workers' Mutual Aid Association and was secretary during that year of the London Workers' May Day Committee which organised marches and demonstrations supported by, among others, the Communist Party and the International Socialists.
27. *Ludd*, No. 1, May 15, 1966.
28. Adam Roberts: 'The Uncertain Anarchists' in *New Society*, May 27, 1965.
29. *Freedom*, Vol. 29, No. 33, October 26, 1968.
30. For the philosophy and history of Situationism, see *Leaving the Twentieth Century* (Free Fall Press 1974).
31. 'Portrait of Protest', *New Society*, October 31, 1968.
32. A conference that year set up a co-ordinating committee to organise activities and propaganda efforts while maintaining the principle of local independence. This was too loose an arrangement for one group which joined the IS, but it attracted some IS members who formed a Solidarity group in Lancashire.
33. *Socialism or Barbarism* (Solidarity Pamphlet No. 11).
34. 'As We See It' (*Solidarity* 1967) reprinted in *As We Don't See It* (*Solidarity* 1971).
35. The source of this notoriety was Mark Fore's pamphlet: *Strategy for Industrial Struggle* (*Solidarity* 1972) which referred to the 'long and honourable history of sabotage'.
36. *Black Flag*, Vol. 2, No. 14, October 1972.
37. *Black Flag*, Vol. 2, No. 15, January 1973.
38. *Black Flag*, Vol. 2, No. 6, June 1971.
39. *Black Flag*, Vol. 2, No. 10, February 1972.
40. 'If You Want Peace Prepare for War' published by the Stoke Newington 8 Defence Group.
41. ibid.
42. ibid.
43. Angry Brigade Communiqué No. 6 issued on March 6, 1971 and reprinted in Agitprop Red Notes (undated). Also quoted in Gordon Carr: *The Angry Brigade* (Gollancz 1975), pp. 99–100. This very informative account traces the emergence of the Angry Brigade, its place in revolutionary libertarianism and describes the trials of those accused of being its members. It also has some useful background

material on the influence of Situationism on the Brigade and its links with the First of May Group.

44. *Libertarian Struggle*, May 1975.

45. *Black and Red Outlook*, March 1973.

46. See *Solidarity*, Vol. 7, Nos. 5, 6, 7. Manchester Solidarity forced the issue by threatening to disband and join the London group; Clydeside however, one of the most active, disassociated itself from Solidarity as a result of the introduction of national membership, in a pamphlet entitled *Now We See It, Now We Don't See It*.

47. *Freedom*, Vol. 35, No. 11, March 16, 1974.

48. In a letter to *Freedom*, Vol. 32, No. 32, October 16, 1971.

49. Organisations originally supporting BWNIC included the Peace Pledge Union, *Peace News*, Fellowship of Reconciliation, War Resisters' International and Pax Christi, a Catholic pacifist group.

50. See for example: Theodore Roszack: *The Making of a Counter Culture* (Faber 1970); Charles Reich: *The Greening of America* (Penguin 1974); Michael Lerner: 'Anarchism and the American Counter-Culture' in Anarchism Today (edited by D.E. Apter and J. Joll) (Macmillan 1971).

51. Lewis Herber, in *Anarchy*, No. 69, November 1966, quoted in D.E. Stafford: 'Anarchists in Britain Today' in *Anarchism Today*, op. cit.

52. 'Anarchism and Ecology' in *The Ecologist*, Vol. 4, No. 3, March/April 1974.

53. *Libertarian Newsletter*, No. 2, October 1973.

54. In *White Trash* ('produced by five individuals living together', undated).

55. See Richard Boston's 'Anti-University' in *New Society*, May 16, 1968. The 'university' was lent £300 by the Institute of Phenomenological Studies, which was formed after a conference of 'New Left' theorists and activists in London. Its proceedings were reproduced under the title of *The Dialectics of Liberation*, edited by David Cooper (Penguin 1968). The Anti-University premises were rooms rented from the Bertrand Russell Peace Foundation, then in east London.

56. Ron Bailey: *The Squatters* (Penguin 1972), p. 34.

57. See W.H.S. Armitage: *Heavens Below: Utopian Experiments in England 1560–1960* (Routledge 1961), pp. 305–16.

58. See Andrew Rigby: *Alternative Realities* (Routledge 1974). This study deals from first-hand knowledge with many other aspects of the Alternative Society and draws attention to its anarchist content.

59. Its predecessor was the Vegan Communities Movement which had 22 members in August 1965. The Commune Movement began in October 1968 with 28 members, but by March 1971 had 354 with a circulation of 3,000 for its magazine (Rigby, op. cit., pp. 93 ff). By the winter of 1973/74, 21 separate communes were affiliated to it, of all types including an Anarchist Commune. The Movement itself is

affiliated to the National Council for Civil Liberties (*Commune*, journal of the Commune Movement, No. 44, Winter 1973/74.)

60. Rigby, op. cit., p. 68. BIT was founded in 1968 and received, in instalments, £15,000 grant from the Gulbenkian Foundation. It said in 1973 that it handled some 1,000 telephone calls for help a week, 300 visitors and 90 letters mostly concerned with accommodation, jobs, legal, political and medical subjects. (*BIT Newsletter*, January 1973).

61. *CLAP Catalogue*, March 1974. Published by Peace News.

62. *Dwarf News*, No. 8, January/February 1972.

63. *Resurgence*, Vol. 4, No. 2, 1972.

64. G. Woodcock in *The Ecologist*, op. cit.

65. See *Peace News*, No. 1880, July 21, 1972 and No. 1884, August 18, 1972.

Select Bibliography

I INTRODUCTORY AND GENERAL

(a) Books

H. Arendt: *On Revolution* (Faber 1963).

R. Benewick and T. Smith (eds): *Direct Action and Democratic Politics* (Allen and Unwin 1972).

R. Blackburn and A. Cockburn (eds): *The Incompatibles: Trade Union Militancy and the Consensus* (Penguin 1967).

R. Blackburn and A. Cockburn (eds): *Student Power* (Penguin 1969).

P. Buckman: *The Limits of Protest* (Gollancz 1970).

P. Calvert: *Revolution* (Pall Mall 1970).

A. Carter: *Direct Action and Democratic Politics* (Routledge 1973).

D. Childs: *Marx and the Marxists* (1973).

R. Clutterbuck: *Protest and the Urban Guerrilla* (Cassell 1973).

G.D.H. Cole: *A History of Socialist Thought*, Vols. 1–5 (Macmillan 1953–60).

D. Cooper (ed): *The Dialectics of Liberation* (Penguin 1968).

M. Cranston (ed): *The New Left* (Bodley Head 1970).

B. Crick and W.A. Robson (eds): *Protest and Discontent* (Pelican 1970).

B. Crozier (ed): *We Will Bury You* (Tom Stacey 1970).

C. Crouch: *The Student Revolt* (Bodley Head 1970).

P. Duff: *Left, Left, Left* (Allison and Busby 1971).

P. Ferris: *The New Militants: Crisis in the Trade Unions* (Penguin 1972).

A. Glyn and R. Sutcliffe: *British Capitalism, Workers and the Profits Squeeze* (Penguin 1972).

I. Greig: *Subversion* (Tom Stacey 1972).

P. Hain: *Don't Play With Apartheid* (Allen and Unwin 1971).

J.D. Halloran and others: *Demonstrations and Communication: A Case Study* (Penguin 1970).

E. Hobsbawm: *Revolutionaries* (Weidenfeld 1973).

R. Hyman: *Strikes* (Fontana/Collins 1972).

G. Kaufman (ed): *The Left* (Blond 1966).

A. Lane and K. Roberts: *Strike at Pilkingtons* (Fontana 1971).

L. Lapedz (ed): *Revisionism* (Allen and Unwin 1962).

K. Leech: *Youthquake* (Sheldon Press 1973).

R. Lewis: *Outlaws of America* (Penguin 1972).

A. MacIntyre: *Marcuse* (Fontana 1972).

H. Marcuse: *One Dimensional Man* (Sphere 1968).

R. Miliband and J. Saville (eds): *The Socialist Register* (Merlin Press) (annually).

R. Moss: *Urban Guerrillas* (Temple Smith 1972).

J. Nagel (ed): *Student Power* (Merlin Press 1969).

P. Rivers: *Politics by Pressure* (Harrap 1974).

G. K. Roberts: *Political Parties and Pressure Groups in Britain* (Weidenfeld 1970).

M. A. Rooke: *Anarchy and Apathy: Student Unrest 1968–70* (Hamish Hamilton 1971).

P. Seale and M. McConville: *French Revolution 1968* (Penguin and Heinemann 1968).

S. Spender: *The Year of the Young Rebels* (Weidenfeld 1969).

M. Stewart: *Protest or Power* (Allen and Unwin 1974).

G. Thayer: *The British Political Fringe* (Blond 1965).

M. Tomison: *The English Sickness* (Tom Stacey 1972).

P. Wilkinson: *Political Terrorism* (Macmillan 1974).

R. Williams (ed): *The May Day Manifesto 1968* (Penguin 1968).

B. Wilson: *The Youth Culture and the Universities* (Faber 1970).

D. Cohn Bendit: *Infantile Communism—The Left Wing Alternative* (Penguin 1970).

G. Paloczi-Horvath: *Youth up in Arms* (Weidenfeld 1971).

H. Kidd: *The Trouble at the LSE* (Oxford University Press 1969).

G. Kennan: *Democracy and the Student Left* (Hutchinson 1968).

G. F. McGuigan (ed): *Student Protest* (Methuen 1968).

N. McInnes: *The Western Marxists* (Alcove Press 1972).

C. Posner (ed): *Reflections on the Revolt in France: 1968* (Penguin 1970).

(*b*) Newspapers and Magazines

East-West Digest; Economist; The Guardian; New Left Review; New Society; New Statesman; People's News Service; Daily Telegraph; The Times; Time Out; Tribune.

II A BRITISH ROAD TO SOCIALISM?

(a) Newspapers and Magazines

Challenge; Comment; Marxism Today; Morning Star (formerly *Daily Worker*).

(b) Books and Pamphlets

A. Buchan: *The Right to Work* (Calder and Boyers 1972).

J. R. Campbell: *Hands off the Trade Unions* (1965).

J. Gollan: *Turn Left for Progress* (1965).

J. Gollan: *The Case for Socialism in the Sixties* (1966).

J. Gollan: *What is the Socialist Way Forward?* (1970).

J. Klugmann: *History of the Communist Party of Great Britain*, Vols. 1 and 2 (Lawrence and Wishart 1968 and 1969).

L. J. Macfarlane: *The British Communist Party* (Macgibbon and Kee 1966).

B. Matthews: *Changing Britain: the need for the Communist Party* (1965).

K. Newton: *The Sociology of British Communism* (Allen Lane 1969).

H. Pelling: *The British Communist Party* (Black 1958).

B. Ramelson: *Incomes Policy: the Great Wage Freeze Trick* (1966).
B. Ramelson: *Keep the Unions Free* (1968).
B. Ramelson: *Carr's Bill and How to Kill It* (1971).
B. Reid: *Ultra-Leftism in Britain* (1969).
J. Woddis: *New Theories of Revolution* (Lawrence and Wishart 1972).
British Road to Socialism (1951, 1958 and 1968 editions).
Communist Policy for Britain (1964).
Documents on the World Communist Congress (1968).
Handbook for Members of the Communist Party (1962).
New Britain, People's Britain (1966).
Report of the Committee on Party Organisation (1965).
The Role of the Communist Party (1965).
The Role of Communist Party Branches (1973).
(Where no publisher is given the item is a Communist Party publication).

III THE PROPHECY UNFULFILLED

(a) Newspapers and Magazines
European Marxist Review; Fourth International (International Secretariat 1958–62); *Fourth International* (International Committee 1964–75); *International; International Marxist Review; Intercontinental Press; Red Flag.*

(b) Books and Pamphlets
I.H. Birchall: *Workers Against the Monolith* (Pluto Press 1974).
I. Deutscher: *Trotsky* (3 vols) (Oxford University Press 1954–59).
R. Groves: *The Balham Group* (Pluto Press 1974).
R. Stephenson: *The Fourth International and Our Attitude towards It* (Socialist Charter Publications 1974).
G. Thayer: *The Further Shores of Politics* (Allen Lane 1968).
Statutes of the Fourth International (IMG Publications, undated).
The Death Agony of Capitalism and the Tasks of the Fourth International (Socialist Labour League edition 1972).
Workers' Fight and the Fourth International (Phoenix Pamphlet Number 5, 1973).
Documents of the Fourth International 1933–40 (Pathfinder Press, New York, 1973).
R. Gott: *Guerrilla Movements in Latin America* (Nelson 1970).

IV FACES OF TROTSKYISM

(a) Newspapers and Magazines
Chartist; Keep Left; Labour Review; Militant; Newsletter; Rebel; Workers' Press.
(b) Books and Pamphlets
M. Banda: *The Theory and Practice of Revisionism* (Workers' Press Pamphlet 1971).

Cliff Slaughter: *A Balance Sheet of Revisionism* (Newsletter Pamphlet 1969).
Cliff Slaughter: *Who Are the International Socialists?* (Workers' Press Pamphlet 1971).
The Socialist Charter: A Programme for the Labour Party (Chartist Publications 1973).

V NEW LEFTS AND OLD

(a) Newspapers and Magazines
Black Dwarf; Red Mole; Red Weekly; Socialist Woman; The Week; Voice of the Unions; Workers' Control Bulletin.

(b) Books and Pamphlets
T. Ali: *The Coming British Revolution* (Jonathan Cape 1972).
M. Barratt-Brown: *From Labourism to Socialism* (Spokesman Books 1972).
M. Barratt-Brown and K. Coates: *The 'Big Flame' and What is the IWC* (Institute for Workers' Control Pamphlet No. 14).
A. Benn, W. Greendale and others: *Workers' Control* (Institute for Workers' Control, Pamphlet No. 36).
K. Coates (ed): *A Future for British Socialism* (1967).
K. Coates: *Can We Kill that Bill?* (Spokesman Pamphlet No. 16).
K. Coates: *The Crisis of British Socialism* (Spokesman Books 1971).
K. Coates and A. Topham: *The New Unionism* (Penguin edition 1974).
T. Hayter: *Hayter of the Bourgeoisie* (Sidgwick and Jackson 1971).
S. Holland: *The Socialist Challenge* (Quartet Books 1975).
E. Roberts: *Workers' Control* (Allen and Unwin 1973).

VI 'NEITHER WASHINGTON NOR MOSCOW...'

(a) Newspapers and Magazines
Anti-Internment News; Case Con; International Socialism; Rank and File Teacher; Revolutionary Communist; Socialist Review; Socialist Worker; Workers' Fight.

(b) Books and Pamphlets
P. Arthur: *The People's Democracy 1968–73* (The Blackstaff Press, Belfast 1974).
S. Buddle, R. Moss and C. Sparks: *Students and the Struggle for Socialism* (IS Pamphlet 1972).
T. Cliff and C. Barker: *Incomes Policy, Legislation and Shop Stewards* (1966).
T. Cliff: *Factory Branches* (IS Pamphlet, undated).
The Origins of the International Socialists (Pluto Press 1971).
R. Kline: *Can Socialism Come through Parliament?* (IS Pamphlet, undated).
R. Rosewall: *The Struggle for Workers' Power* (IS Pamphlet, 1973).
Organise Against the National Front (Socialist Worker Pamphlet 1974).

(a) Newspapers and Magazines

Afro-Asian Solidarity; Class Against Class; Communist England; Grass Roots; Irish Liberation Press; Liberation Struggle; Marxist-Leninist Quarterly; Progressive Student; Red Front; Red Vanguard; Scottish Vanguard; Struggle; The Marxist; The Worker; Tri-Continental Outpost; Vanguard; Voice of the People; Women's Voice; Workers' Broadsheet; Worker's England Daily News Release.

(b) Books and Pamphlets

R. Birch: *Guerrilla Struggle and the Working Class* (1971).

I. Greig: *Today's Revolutionaries* (Foreign Affairs Publishing Company 1970).

B.W. Heinemann Jnr: *The Politics of the Powerless* (Oxford University Press 1972).

D. Hiro: *Black British, White British* (Eyre and Spottiswood 1971).

M. McCreery: *The Way Forward* (1963).

M. McCreery: *Destroy The Old to Build the New* (1964).

M. McCreery: *Organise at the Place of Work* (1964).

F.W. Schloman and P. Friedlingstein: *Die Maoisten* (Stuttgart 1971).

S.R. Schram: *The Political Thought of Mao-tse Tung* (Penguin 1971).

Broad Fronts and United Fronts: An Analysis (Communist Unity Association (M-L) (1972).

Documents of the Communist Federation of Britain (M-L) (1972).

Students and the Class War (Communist Party of Britain (M-L) (undated)

The British Working Class and its Party (Communist Party of Britain (M-L) (1971).

The Times News Team: *The Black Man in Search of Power* (Nelson 1968).

VIII THE LIBERTARIAN ALTERNATIVE

(a) Newspapers and Magazines

Advice Manual; Anarchy; Black Flag; Black and Red Outlook; BIT Newsletter; Community Action; Communes; Catonville Roadrunner; Direct Action; Dwarf News: Fapto; Freedom; Freedom News; Frendz; Inside Story; Ink; IT; Minus One; Muther Grumble; Ned Gate; OZ; Peace News; Resurgence; Seven Days; South East London Suburban Press; Solidarity; Street Farmer; Undercurrents; Up Against the Law; White Trash.

(b) Books and Pamphlets

D.E. Apter and J. Joll (eds): *Anarchism Today* (Macmillan 1971).

R. Bailey: *The Squatters* (Penguin 1973).

A. Carter: *The Political Theory of Anarchism* (Routledge 1971).

P. Cardan: *The Meaning of Socialism* (Solidarity Pamphlet No. 6).

M. Fore: *Strategy for Industrial Struggle* (Solidarity Pamphlet No. 37).

K.I. Krimerman and L. Perry (eds): *Patterns of Anarchy* (Anchor 1966).

I.R. Mitchell: *Introduction to the Left* (Solidarity Scotland Pamphlet No. 3).

F. Parkin: *Middle Class Radicalism* (Manchester University Press 1968).

A. Rigby: *Alternative Realities* (Routledge 1974).

A. Rigby: *Communes in Britain* (Routledge 1974).

The Autobiography of Bertrand Russell, Vol. 3 (Allen and Unwin 1969).

N. Walter: *About Anarchism* (Freedom Press 1969).

C. Ward: *Anarchy in Action* (Allen and Unwin 1973).

G. Woodcock: *Anarchism* (Penguin 1963).

Socialism or Barbarism (Solidarity Pamphlet No. 11).

The Death of CND (Solidarity Pamphlet No. 28).

As We Don't See It (Solidarity London 1971).

The Way Ahead for a New Peace Movement (Solidarity Scotland Pamphlet No. 1, 1966).

If You Want Peace Prepare for War (Stoke Newington Eight Defence Group).

The Voice of Syndicalism (Syndicalist Workers' Federation 1973).

(It should be remembered that anarchist and libertarian groups are often careless about such matters as precise dates and publishers for their journals and pamphlets).

Index